# The Day the Dancers Stayed

*Performing in the Filipino/American Diaspora*

Theodore S. Gonzalves



TEMPLE UNIVERSITY PRESS
Philadelphia

Temple University Press
1601 North Broad Street
Philadelphia PA 19122
www.temple.edu/tempress


Published 2010
Printed in the United States of America

♾ The paper used in this publication meets the requirements of the American National Standard for Information Sciences—Permanence of Paper for Printed Library Materials, ANSI Z39.48-1992

Library of Congress Cataloging-in-Publication Data

Gonzalves, Theodore S.
The day the dancers stayed : performing in the Filipino-American diaspora / Theodore S. Gonzalves.
p. cm.
Includes bibliographical references and index.
ISBN 978-1-59213-728-2 (cloth : alk. paper)
ISBN 978-1-59213-729-9 (pbk. : alk. paper)
1. Folklore—Philippines—Performance. 2. Folk dancing, Philippine. 3. Folk music—Philippines. 4. National characteristics, Philippine. 5. Filipino Americans—History. 6. Filipino Americans—Social life and customs. I. Title.

GR325.G66 2009
793.3'19599—dc22 2009016342

2 4 6 8 9 7 5 3 1

# The Day the Dancers Stayed

*"Not bad, not bad at all," Diotallevi said. "To arrive at the truth through the painstaking reconstruction of a false text."*

—Umberto Eco, *Foucault's Pendulum*

# Contents

# Acknowledgments

**MY DEEPEST THANKS** go to my first and greatest teachers, Teodoro Magallion Gonzalves (1926–2001) and Salvación Francisco Gonzalves. This book is dedicated to them. The love and support of Rudy Gonzalves has sustained me throughout our journeys. Annabelle G. Cortez and the Cortez family have always made me feel welcome. The future of the funk is in the hands of Diego, Rosalí, and Julián. Over the years, I probably should have listened more to the advice of the following advisers: Olivia Fojas, Daniel Phil Gonzales, Linda Gonzales, Dean Grafilo, Marisa Viloria, Debra Belale, Allan Manalo, Joyce Juan Manalo, Edgar Dormitorio, Julpha Maniquis, Chris Ferreria, Carlos Villa, Karin Aguilar–San Juan, Dwight Hopkins, August Espiritu, and Anna Gonzalez.

Special thanks go to my neighbors—Trisha Lagaso Goldberg, David A. M. Golberg, and Primo Salim Lagaso Goldberg—who have kept me afloat at one time or another with wonderful acts of friendship out here in the middle of the Pacific. *Mahalo nui loa* for your kindness and friendship: Jacquie Brown, John Castro, Melisa Casumbal, Kim Chanbonpin, Jennifer Chandler, Clark Cuadro, Mike Cueva, Rhodora Derpo, Jon-Jon Domingo, Cindy Franklin, Sonny Ganaden, Lesa Griffith, Emil Guillermo, Patricia Espiritu Halagao, A. J. Halagao, Gelareh Khoie, Rod Labrador, Charles Lawrence, Hung Le, Mari Matsuda, David Mayeda, Mandy Morris, Konrad Ng, Pati Poblete, Christine Quemuel, Joey Salazar, Scott Sato, Michelle Cruz Skinner, Maya Soetoro-Ng, Ben Tirnauer, Haunani Trask, and Paul Zarate.

My colleagues at the University of Hawai'i, Mānoa, have been generous with their encouragement and time. *Maraming salamat po* to my comrades in the Department of American Studies, especially Robert Perkinson, David Stannard, and Mari Yoshihara (whose recitals I look forward to each year). The administrative support of Gerry Uyeunten and the staff of Moore 324 has been a blessing. Sandy Enoki deserves my deepest gratitude for guiding me through the surprisingly dense thicket of paperwork in an office that aspires to become paperless. Her laughter heard on our wing of the floor is as instantly recognizable as it is infectious. It has been an honor to teach the following students: Constancio Arnaldo, Cheryl Beredo, Margaret Hay, Alicia Hultin, Maria Mehr, Lorenzo Perillo, Janeen Power, Vince Raboteau, Danny Simon, and Emilia Wiggins.

My line of work has allowed me to learn from and collaborate with a wonderful network of scholars and writers. George Lipsitz deserves special thanks for reading several drafts of this manuscript. I have stolen some of my best lines from him. R. Bin Wong provided excellent support and asked all the right questions. Biting from Run-DMC, Gary Okihiro inspired a bunch of kids in Northern California's South Bay to think about ethnic studies as our house. Robert A. Hill deepened my appreciation for the vocation of vindication. Lisa Lowe and Yen Le Espiritu welcomed me to La Jolla and gave me another intellectual home outside of the real O.C. Dorinne Kondo encouraged me to speak up when the going got rough. Scott Wong agreed to disagree, and we have been friends ever since. Raúl Fernandez turned me on to the music of Joe Bataan, whose tunes have never left heavy rotation in my house and car. Eugene van Erven kindly read an earlier version of this manuscript and offered helpful advice and encouragement.

My partners in the field of Filipino/American and Asian American/ethnic studies continue to inspire me. My warm thanks to Amy Agbayani, Dean Alegado, Ibrahim Aoude, Kim Alidio, Anna Alves, Christine Balance, Rick Baldoz, Nerissa Balce, Kiko Benitez, John David Blanco, Marivi Soliven Blanco, Rick Bonus (Barique Obonus), Eloisa Borah, Lucy Mae San Pablo Burns, Jeff Chang, Juliana Chang, Catherine Choy, Denise Cruz, Sharon Delmendo, Kale Fajardo, Candace Fujikane, Dorothy Fujita Rony, Vernadette Gonzalez, Vina Lanzona, Dawn Mabalon, Ruth Mabanglo, Martin Manalansan, Linda Maram, Franklin Odo, Jon Okamura, Rhacel Parreñas, Oscar Peñaranda, Liz Pisares, JoAnna Poblete-Cross, Barbara Posadas, Vicente Rafael, Eric Reyes, Lulu Reyes, Rowena Robles, Darlene Rodrigues, Dylan Rodriguez, Evelyn Rodriguez, Robyn Rodriguez, John Rosa, Sarita See, Celine Parreñas Shimizu, James Sobredo, Neferti Tadiar, Dana Takagi, Mary Talusan, Allyson Tintiangco-Cubales, Tony Tiongson,

Rowena Tomaneng, Ricardo Trimillos, Charlene Tung, Sunny Vergara, Oliver Wang, and Eric Wat.

The research for this book was made possible by a U.S. Fulbright Senior Scholar Award, a Meet the Composer Award, grants from the University Research Council of the University of Hawai'i, and a Florence T. Moeson Fellowship at the Library of Congress. Tim Tayag kept me busy as a camera operator; I thank him for the opportunity to see the Philippines on foot. My deep gratitude goes to Richie Quirino for the honor of jamming with him at his home studio and on our occasional gigs around town. It has always been an honor to play with Joey Ayala; I treasure my memories of the Dumaguete and Kauai performances. The spirit and talent of Bob Aves and Grace Nono are unmatched. I thank Boni Juan and Mae Paner for their generosity during my first junket to Manila. I had the great pleasure of learning from and traveling with Joel Jacinto as he led his Los Angeles–based troupe on an educational tour of the Philippines. What a sight it was to watch Kayamanan ng Lahi perform with Ramon Obusan's Folkloric Group at the master's compound. Many thanks go to Esmeralda Cunanan, the staff of the Philippine American Educational Foundation, and the cohort of scholars I shared my time with in Manila. My dearest thanks to Aileen Beltran, Isabel Kenny, and R. Zamora Linmark.

The following individuals have my sincere appreciation for facilitating my access to documents, materials, and other resources: Remé Grefalda (Asian Division, Library of Congress); Clem Bautista, Gina Vergara-Bautista, Deanna Espinas, and Patricia Brown (Filipino American Historical Society of Hawai'i); Dorothy and Fred Cordova (Filipino American National Historical Society, Seattle); Reynaldo Alejandro (New York Public Library Performing Arts Collection), Anna Alves (Samahang Pilipino Archives, UCLA); Samuel Parnes (for help with photocopying PCN programs); Chris Millado (Cultural Center of the Philippines); Helene Whitson (San Francisco State University); Christina Woo (Langson Library, University of California, Irvine); Dan Tsang (Langson Library, University of California, Irvine); and Salvacion Arlante (University of the Philippines, Diliman, University Archives and Records Depository Section). A number of organizers, performers, and artists shared their production notes and other materials for this project, including Cyndi Abundabar, Sharlene Aquiler, Ninah Asuncion, Debra Belale, Ruth Constantino, Catherine M. Cruz, Edgar Dormitorio, Matt Esparrago, Patricio Ginelsa, Jr., Joel Jacinto, Boni Juan, Emily Lawsin, Frank Lozier, Edward Manongdo, Warren Manuntag, Jose M. Montano, Jr., Iris Pacis, R. J. Payomo, Oscar Peñaranda, and Helen Toribio.

Janet Francendese never disappointed me as an editor. Her production team kept my eyes on the prize. The anonymous readers offered detailed and substantive suggestions.

Finally, special thanks go to Charita L. Castro for her hospitality during the final stages of the manuscript's preparation. On occasion, she would hear me sing at one end of the dining table: Are we almost there, are we getting close? Are we getting near, that's not far to go. I need to know, are we almost there? Otherwise, I would sing: It feels like home to me.

# Prologue

## The Mock Battle, 1898

The U.S.–Philippine war began with a fantastic performance: the American hero, a veteran commander taking control of a crew of fresh-faced sailors in a corner of the Pacific few back home had heard about; the nemesis, a Spaniard at the helm of his empire's last stand in a far-flung colony. Both were aided by an efficient Belgian consul who brokered a plan to save Spanish honor, guarantee a bloodless victory, and, most important, keep the revolutionary native general in the dark about the entire operation. But before we get to the main attraction, the fanfare.

By the time U.S. Navy Admiral George Dewey sailed into Manila Bay on May 1, 1898, to capture or destroy the Spanish fleet, a letter written by Spanish Ambassador Enrique Dupuy de Lome insulting President William McKinley had been published in William Randolph Hearst's New York *Journal,* an explosion aboard the *U.S.S. Maine,* harbored in Havana, had killed 246 sailors, and the U.S. Congress had passed the Teller Amendment, which "[disclaimed] any disposition of intention to exercise sovereignty, jurisdiction, or control over [Cuba] except for pacification thereof, and asserts its determination, when that is accomplished, to leave the government and control of the island to its people."[1] In late April, Congress declared war against Spain, and the U.S. Navy secretary cabled Admiral Dewey with orders to engage the enemy, not in the Caribbean but across the globe in the Philippines, where military commanders knew the empire was weakest, with a flotilla described as antiquated and decrepit. The Americans were not alone in Manila Bay. Bismarck's unification of Germany in 1871 had created a powerful state with a per capita income that rivaled that in the United States. Coming late to the nineteenth-century land grab, the kaiser sent ships to both the Caribbean and the Pacific.[2] While Britain had more at stake financially in the Philippines than other European powers, the Germans sent five warships to Manila, and London sent two. German Naval Commander Otto von Diederichs angered Dewey by refusing to honor the blockade, prompting the U.S. commander to say, "If Germany wants war, all right, we are ready."[3]

In an interview after the May 1 battle, captains involved in the action claimed that "it was the hand of God that turned aside the Spanish shells on that morning and left our ships and men scatheless." Dewey agreed: "Oh, yes, I believe it. God knows where all the shells went. . . . If I were the good Presbyterian some persons have said I am, I should certainly say that the Lord meant to punish Spain for her years of wickedness and misrule in these islands. We have taken an empire and have lost scarcely a man."[4] Not quite. While Dewey controlled the bay with a blockade, it was Filipino General Emilio Aguinaldo and his army that had success against the Spanish on land. By late May, the rebel leader's troops had captured five thousand Spaniards and surrounded the walled city section of Intramuros in an attempt to starve the colonizing army. On June 12, Aguinaldo declared the Philippines free from Spain, the first such declaration of independence in Asia in the twentieth century. Washington refused recognition. The result was a standstill: a bay blockaded by the U.S. fleet; the outlying areas of Manila's *arrabales* (suburbs) controlled by Filipino troops; and an increasingly frustrated Spanish administration cut off from support. Over the next two months, thousands of reinforcements for Dewey arrived from the United States. With the help of Belgian Consul Edouard André, Dewey began secret negotiations with his Spanish opposite, Governor-General Basilio Augustín. The Spanish commander, whose family had been taken prisoner by Filipino troops, sent a telegram to his superiors describing the harsh conditions the Spaniards faced in the city—starvation, sickness, weak and swollen legs from exposure while defending trenches, and low morale among the troops. For telling the truth and proposing surrender, Augustín was dismissed and ordered to transfer command to General Fermin Jaudenes, whose job it was to hold the city for Spain ("*conservar las Filipinas a la soberania de la España*").[5] Maintaining sovereignty over the islands would prove to be difficult, especially when military and administrative opinion began to turn against the powerful Catholic church in the colony. For example, Captain Don Juan de la Concha, in command of a cruiser, said he was "unwilling to lose Spanish lives in fighting for the monks," claiming that the Philippine colony was "priest-ridden." Jaudenes agreed.[6] The Spanish problem was not simply about losing face through military defeat; more specifically, it was about to whom they should lose. Both U.S. and Spanish commanders did not think much of their Filipino counterparts. During negotiations between Dewey's camp and Jaudenes, U.S. Army General Wesley Merritt, commander of the San Francisco–based VIII Corps, shared his views of Filipinos, that he had come "with orders not to treat with the Indians; not to recognize them, and not to promise anything," adding, "Aguinaldo is just the same to me as a boy in the street."[7] Jaudenes said he was "willing to surrender to white people, but never to niggers."[8]

The players had agreed on the terms for the mock battle for Manila. Only André, Dewey, Merritt, and Jaudenes knew of the complete plans. The success of the performance hinged on keeping Filipino troops out of the city while U.S. and Spanish troops exchanged places. The event would reinforce the Filipinos' debt to their new American masters for their gift of regime change. On August 12, Madrid agreed to a truce, but the news did not arrive. Dewey had cut the underwater cable. On the morning of August 13, the mock battle for Manila began. As the squadron mobilized, the band on board the British cruiser the *Immortalité* serenaded the Americans with "patriotic airs."[9] At 9 A.M., the "attack" commenced with the flagship *Olympia* lobbing a few shells into the old fort at Malate while the Spanish guns on the coast provided no response. Land-based U.S. forces held back Filipinos outside the central city. The historian Teodoro Agoncillo understood the theatrical nature of the event when he wrote: "The few casualties on both sides in the phony attack were due to some 'actors' bungling their 'lines,' or possibly to the fact that very few officers were let in on the charade."[10] According to plan, Dewey's staff transmitted the code for surrender to Jaudenes; the Spanish obliged by raising the white flag at 11:20 A.M., just in time for lunch. Later that afternoon, the German cruiser *Kaiserin Augusta,* which had on board a special guest—the recently dismissed Spanish Commander Augustín—made its way back to Madrid via Hong Kong.[11] To bring the morning's shock and awe to a close, the crew of the *Immortalité* fired a twenty-one-gun salute in honor of the U.S. flag that was hoisted atop Manila's Fort Santiago, prompting Dewey to say, "I hope it floats there forever."[12] Embittered by the tussle with von Diederichs, Dewey could not have been more prophetic in speaking to a New York *Herald* reporter when he said, "Our next war will be with Germany."[13]

## Seditious Plays, 1902–1906

By year's end, U.S. President McKinley had proclaimed a policy of "benevolent assimilation" for the Philippines. The ground forces were not quick to return home. In a matter of weeks, on February 4, 1899, the U.S.–Philippine War broke out. Although McKinley's successor, Theodore Roosevelt, officially ended the war on July 4, 1902, a protracted struggle continued for years in the hills and throughout villages. According to Doreen G. Fernandez, this was when the playwrights' work began. For the next five years, "seditious plays" became a form of guerrilla warfare, in direct violation of Act 292, the Sedition Act, which made utterances and other actions supporting Philippine independence a crime.[14] Government publications cited the "smoldering embers" of the "insurrection" that burned throughout the archipelago. Michael Cullinane cites the seditious plays as "the most controversial acts of the overall confrontation between oppositionists and the colonial government."[15] Vicente Rafael poses the repertoire of the seditious plays against the archive generated by U.S. census takers.[16] For Fernandez and other observers, the plays were as "vital and immediate as a call to arms."[17] Playwrights, actors, stagehands, and audience members risked arrest, imprisonment, and fines by working on and attending the plays. U.S. colonial officials often sat clueless through several productions as plays that seemed to be about innocuous romances or featured characters with curious names conveyed alternative meanings to local audiences. The plays, written and performed in Tagalog, were a hit among the masses throughout Manila and outlying suburbs partly because the authors, often of modest means themselves, used popular theatrical conventions and forms, as well as their knowledge of popular culture, to create set and costume design, deep cultural references in the text and lyrics, and other devices that conveyed subversive meaning. Some Americans eventually penetrated the less clever disguises and became better informed about what was taking place on stage. For example, on the evening of May 8, 1903, Juan Matapang Cruz's *Hindi Aco Patay* (I Am Not Dead) played to a large audience at the Teatro Nueva Luna in Mabalon. Toward the play's conclusion, the image of a red sun on a revolutionary nationalist flag of the Katipunan (the leading anti-imperialist group first organized against the Spanish, then the Americans) rose in the background. On seeing this, a drunken U.S. soldier "threw an empty beer bottle at it, then climbed the stage with some others and tore the scenery apart."[18] The play would later be banned; the props from the stage confiscated; and the playwright arrested and sentenced for two years. Several other playwrights, actors, and stagehands would be jailed or fined.

The inaugural moment of Filipino American history occurred when war and performance were one—not on the occasion of a storied landing by intrepid seafarers, or with the settlement of an obscure outpost at the edge of a "new world," or with the signing of a landmark peace accord, or with the election or elevation of a person of Filipino descent to the rank or governor, beauty queen, or pop star of the month. The inaugural moment of Filipino American history took place at the intersection of combat and cultural production, when a mock battle was answered by a seditious play at the beginning of the twentieth century, two decades before Henry Luce claimed an American Century for his *Time* magazine readers. This inaugural moment, a curious and dynamic time when authors of an Asian republic mined the U.S. Declaration of Independence to enunciate that republic's own arrival and break from Madrid, went unrecognized amid a contest between two powers in very different times in their imperial careers: Spain, grappling its own humiliating decline with the loss of possessions in the Caribbean and the Pacific, and the ascendant United States trying gracefully to walk softly while carrying its big stick across the "American lake" west of California. With the mock battle of Manila Bay, Filipino revolutionaries were consigned to the role of spectators in a sorry play between masters of imperial theater. Taking the conflict simultaneously underground yet in full view of a public, seditious playwrights eschewed escapist entertainment, regional tastes, and religious plays that celebrated Christian conversion. Rather, they created the first national performance repertoire to signal that the struggle was not over, to imagine an audience gathered for an evening as members of a fully sovereign nation.

## Mock Battle Redux, 1997

More than a century after Admiral Dewey roared into Manila Bay to claim victory over what observers described as a "decrepit" Spanish fleet on May 1, 1898, the staged combat that opened the U.S.–Philippine War continued to reverberate across the Pacific, in a shopping plaza. Activists and community leaders based in the port city that served as the launching point for thousands of infantrymen from the U.S. heartland remember that overlooked war in a way that differs from the textbook version. They do not cheer for the decisive naval operation that resulted in the colonization of the Philippines, much less think about the commander of the Asiatic Squadron as a hero. They trouble the nation's official account of the past and insist on a reckoning with the present that reexamines what is meant by the "special relationship."

But first, they will need to change the text at the base of the commemorative statue. Shortly after the war, the sculptor Robert Aitken, an instructor at the San Francisco Art Institute, abandoned his plan to honor President William McKinley and shifted his attention to Dewey's adventure. He created a ninety-foot monument in the form of a bronze statue of a lithe woman atop a granite shaft. Rather than depicting either McKinley or Dewey figuratively, he opted for another representation altogether.[19] Aitken's model was the voluptuous twenty-two-year-old Alma de Bretteville. Wearing a diaphanous gown, "Big Alma" (who stood six feet tall) was depicted by the sculptor in a leap, carrying a circular palm in one hand (as if to signal the "peace" at war's end) and a trident in the other (hailing the Dewey as Poseidon, God of the Sea). Completed in 1901, the monument was dedicated by President Theodore Roosevelt on May 14, 1903, at Union Square, a busy retail area just north of Market Street and the site of pro-union rallies. By the 1980s, locals and officials were complaining about trash, pigeons, and homeless people converging in the square. Jim Chappell, president of San Francisco's Planning and Urban Research Association, said, "The key here is to keep the square active. Homeless people only move in when middle-class people abandon a place." It was time to give park a facelift, and Mayor Willie Brown tagged it as a pet project: "[Union Square] is the center of our urban landscape . . . a place where kings, queens and presidents always come."[20]

In 1997, the city sent out a call for proposals to turn the "space into a place," according to the city planner and project manager Evan Rose.[21] Competitors submitted plans along with a twenty dollar entry fee, hoping to land bragging rights and the one hundred thousand dollar prize. Design parameters were open, but all submissions needed to heed one requirement: the inclusion of the Dewey monument. Now part of the city's patrimony, Aitken's sculpture had survived the 1906 earthquake and the addition in 1942 of a one thousand stall parking garage under the park. The review committee pored over three hundred entries from ten countries to re-make the 2.6 acre square. The winning design was submitted by landscape architects from Sausalito and featured a piazza with wide stairways, generously sized terraces, and open-air performance spaces. In all, the total cost of the overhaul was twenty-five million dollars.

For most of the local coverage of the remodel and refit of the plaza, reporters referred to Aitken's creation as both a *monument* and a *memorial.* The definitions of the two terms overlap, pointing to common origins: *monere* ("to remind") and *memoriale* ("record," "memory"). We can take a cue here from Marita Sturken, who delves into the politics of remembering when studying the Vietnam Veterans Memorial in Washington, D.C. Building on Arthur Danto's comments, she differentiates between the two terms: "Monuments are not generally built to commemorate defeats; the defeated dead are remembered in memorials. Whereas a monument most often signifies victory, a memorial refers to the life or lives sacrificed for a particular set of values. Whatever triumph a memorial may refer to, its depiction of victory is always tempered by a foregrounding of the lives lost. . . . Memorials tend to emphasize specific texts or lists of the dead, whereas monuments offer less explanation; a memorial seems to demand the naming of those lost, whereas monuments are usually anonymous."[22] Some explanation for the events in Manila Bay were chiseled into the monument's base—for example, Navy Secretary John Long's orders to Dewey to capture or destroy the Spanish fleet; a list of the seven ships in the Asiatic Squadron; and a recounting of the events of May 1, 1898, in which Dewey's fleet "attacked and destroyed the Spanish fleet of ten war ships. Reduced the forts and held the city in subjection until the arrival of troops from America."

At the moment city leaders planned to renew their commitments to such a history, voices from the Filipino community called the entire story into question. Members of the San Francisco Arts Commission, working with community activists, drafted text for a "corrective plaque" that would serve an educational purpose. One version starts by contextualizing the erection of the monument as an act of patriotism following the U.S. defeat of Spain in the Spanish–American War but then goes on to recount events that took place afterward: the signing of the Treaty of Paris; the start of the U.S.–Philippine War; the half-million Filipino civilians (compared with ten thousand U.S. soldiers) killed; the creation of a direct colony; and the eventual independence of the Philippines in 1946—a fifty-year history lesson condensed into just over one hundred words.[23] The Dewey monument currently has 155 words on its four-sided base. Agreeing with the sentiment to alter the text, Rene Ciria-Cruz, editor in chief of *Filipinas,* a monthly magazine based in San Francisco, said: "I just wish people would clarify the description of what's being remembered. Otherwise, it becomes a monument to the 'white man's burden.'"[24] While some voiced the idea of taking down the monument altogether, Dennis Normandy, who chaired the San Francisco–Manila Sister City Committee and a member of the city's Public Utilities Commission, noted that "the preponderance of opinion is to have a plaque added that can discuss the relationship."[25] Hoping that members of the community would submit their own suggestions for the corrective plaque's wording,

Bay Area activists solicited opinions and hoped to install the panel in May 2006. That effort has been ground down in the city's arts and parks and recreation bureaucracies.[26]

That last word, "relationship," gives us an indication that what activists seek at the base of a granite column are not simply alternative accounts of a distant past but, rather, ways to engage an *ongoing* legacy or perhaps to challenge possible endings for a performance that has not yet concluded.

# Introduction

THIS BOOK TRACES a genealogy of the Pilipino Cultural Night (PCN), a cultural form made popular by Filipino students in the United States in the late 1970s and early 1980s. Every performance of the PCN is ultimately about one evening—as if no others will follow or, at least, no one else will bring it off in quite the same way. You hit your mark, recite the lines, and execute the action as directed; now you make your way to the exit. In pulling back from the cellular experience of playing one's part well, there are, in fact, more than a thousand nights to explore and wonder about. In *The Day the Dancers Stayed,* I consider the relationship between the invention of performance repertoire and the development of diasporic identification.

The PCN has become the most popular expressive form of culture developed by Filipino American college students since the 1980s. Tracing how the show came to be involves understanding something about how the past and present inform each other. This project is not a production or documentary history of the PCN, although more than a few college courses and the occasional article have been devoted to that topic. Neither does it participate in a celebratory mode of chronicling Filipino American dance and performance for its own sake. A scheme of that order could involve a survey of expressive forms of culture in their most so-called primitive state, spied in the hinterlands and provinces, followed by an accounting of exogenous influences from Spain or Muslim-dominated southern regions. Next, Americans would bring their brand of popular culture to the Philippines in the beginning of the twentieth century, anchoring a cultural logic to the reality of formal colonization. The triumph would be fully realized with post–World War II sovereignty for the Philippines, along with critical acclaim for dance companies going abroad. Finally, generations of youth in the United States, at the diasporic edge of the Philippines, would take up the sturdy forms, beaming with ethnic pride and steadied by nostalgic reflection.

But this is not that kind of book. Rather than dismiss the PCN as an anodyne exercise for divas to revel in adoring applause, I see the show as an opportunity by legions of students to address their bodies to what has been perceived as the irreversibility of linear time, the inevitability of national formations, and the incommensurability of Filipino experiences throughout the diaspora. This genealogy tracks how invented traditions provide oblique challenges to understanding the arc and tumble of U.S.–Philippine relations. When Svetlana Boym, an artist and careful analyst of nostalgia, writes, "The stronger the loss, the more it is overcompensated with commemorations, the starker the distance from the past, and the more it is prone to idealizations," she might as well be referring to any one of the Pilipino Cultural Nights that have been produced or are in the planning stages.[1] With the show as my primary object of analysis, I will make use of Boym's notion that when one looks back, one is often looking *sideways* or *laterally* rather than literally: For Filipino American students in the United States to perform aspects of Philippine history and culture on stage is not merely to pine for another location but to desire a different accounting of time, versions of the past that counter official Philippine and U.S. state narratives, which are themselves attempts to order people in and through time. Whether performers of Filipino descent in the United States know it or not, the staging and presentation of national identities has had a long, and often twisted or hidden, history that should allow us to explore what might have been lost, overcompensated, and idealized.

The Pilipino Cultural Night is a performance staged annually by thousands of students on dozens of college and university campuses throughout the United States and Canada. The show consists of two elements: the performance of Philippine folkloric forms through music, costume, and dance and a theatrical narrative, or "skit," that is interspersed between the folkloric dances. PCNs share many features with other ethnically themed presentations in the United States—for example, Vietnamese American pageants, interpretations of Mexican ballet *folklorico,* and religiously themed parades and festivals organized by Italian American communities.[2]

I examine the meaning of the PCN's elements against the politics of the day. I demonstrate that the folk forms on which the students have relied as anchors to a timeless past are, in fact, modern techniques and repertoires that can be traced to the 1930s. The romantic nationalists of that period believed that Philippine sovereignty not only promised a juridical separation of the colonizer from the colonized, but also necessitated the creation of a cultural repertoire that was both *specific* to the Philippines and *comparable* to the cultural repertoire of other nation-states. I track how the international reception of Filipino dance theater in the late 1950s served as the backdrop of essentialist assertions of Philippine culture by savvy post–World War II elites in Manila. Such claims to cultural authority merged with political moves within the capital to anchor the country within the U.S. Asia–Pacific sphere of influence. From the 1980s through the present, the PCN has become a self-perpetuating activity for thousands of participants throughout the United States. Not merely the show itself but the matrix of activity surrounding its production, according to one of my informants, serves as a rite of passage for acting in concert and refashioning the terms of what it means to be "Filipino American."

There is no such thing as a "small" PCN. Nearly all productions are planned months in advance, are elaborately staged, and enlist hundreds of cast and crew members. Traditionally, the PCN is the largest event mounted by a campus's Filipino student organization. Organizers, choreographers, consultants, actors, writers, and musicians volunteer thousands of hours in rehearsal and planning. The shows have created friendly rivalries between campuses over the staging of the dances and the complexity of the theatrical narrative. This has also necessitated the creation of a master calendar for the "PCN season"—generally, February through May—to allow students, relatives, and friends the opportunity to attend multiple shows or to avoid scheduling shows against each other. One campus student organization in Southern California founded a retention group when it was discovered that performers were being placed on academic probation for missing classes and devoting so much time to the PCN. Faculty have occasionally encouraged the activity by agreeing to offer course credit for students' rehearsal time.

Elements of the PCN emerged in the late 1970s, and the shows were fully realized as a genre in the early 1980s as the number of Filipino students attending colleges and universities grew to its largest up to that point. The shows' popularity mirrors the growth of the broader Filipino community in the United States, which jumped 126 percent between 1970 and 1980. At the University of California, the number of undergraduate degrees conferred to students self-identifying as Filipinos more than quadrupled between 1982 and 1992.[3]

The outsider will most likely recognize in the PCN the dance-theater presentations that became popular internationally in the late 1950s. Some specialists who are knowledgeable about Philippine dance history will be able to reach even further back to note that the national repertoire was created in the 1930s as elites in Manila anticipated Philippine independence and the need to create a unique cultural repertoire. While most parents beam at their children's performances, some wonder aloud what all the fuss is about. The performers, however, know why the shows are important. They take to the stage primarily for each other, as if the experience of the PCN were itself a kind of sacrament or an ethnically specific graduation ceremony that invents a community against the larger backdrop of a culture that expects nation, ethnicity, and identity to be languages of the past.[4] For PCN performers, "Filipino culture," rendered through the show's dances, seems to be a timeless thing—as if it has always existed; as if performing the movements, donning the costumes, and playing the native instruments in the present gives the performer a simultaneity with an unchanged past. Nothing could be further from the truth.

The title of this book is a play on the Filipino American writer Bienvenido Santos's "The Day the Dancers Came," a short story that was first published by the *Philippines Free Press* in 1960. The protagonist, the elderly Fil Acayan, anticipates the performance in Chicago of a dance troupe from his native Philippines. Fil is terribly excited by the troupe's arrival. He prepares a meal for the young dancers, tries to convince his recalcitrant buddy and roommate to attend the show, and brings along a "magic sound mirror" to record audio from his seat in the audience. The performance represents much more than an evening's entertainment. In Fil, the dancers activate a powerful investment in the graceful and familiar movements he might have once known, perhaps even participated in, in his younger days. Those movements that are animated, stylized, and lifted with song and costume are actually elements of a national repertoire. At a personal and individuated level, folk dances offer a visceral connection to the overseas viewer to home, youth, idyllic simplicity, and reliably gendered roles. At a collective level, the choreography reminds viewers of how a nation may be expressed as a community in motion—directed, purposeful, disciplined, commensurable with the stagecraft of other nations, and, ultimately, answerable to the invented body politic. We can imagine that Fil arrived in the United States sometime in the early 1920s, along with thousands of *kababayan* (fellow Filipinos), well before the Philippines would become a commonwealth and a generation before the granting of sovereignty in 1946. Like many romantic nationalists, Fil feminizes the nation by linking women's dancing bodies with a dimmed sense of the home he has left behind, rhapsodizing about their "talking eyes." At the very center of the story are those crucial elements: Fil's anticipation of a performance in which one can fulfill the promise of reuniting wayward son with mother nation and his investment in repertoire—that the rehearsed, collective action are tokens for his membership in a community unavailable to him in the United States.

In Santos's story, the dancers eventually leave. Their youthful and jet-setting lives are a stark contrast to the slowed and sedentary tempo of Fil's advanced years. In *The Day the Dancers Stayed,* however, anticipation and investment are played out over several generations of students' performing bodies and between the Philippines and the United States. In this book, the dancers are not only members of a fabled troupe from far away; they are also active players along one of the forward edges of both the Philippine diaspora and the U.S. multiculture. They are interpreters and inventors of their own histories—Philippine *and* American. The dancers and their show are here to stay.

## Repertoire and the Surrogate

Two works that anchor my thinking regarding history, memory, and performance are Diana Taylor's *The Archive and the Repertoire* and Joseph Roach's *Cities of the Dead.* I appreciate how Taylor pushes us to consider that *los Estados Unidos* is not simply a synonym for "America" and that our writing as students of expressive forms of culture benefits from widened perspectives that track cultural work across national borders, languages and dialects, and communities. By taking in the uneven development of the Americas as something much larger and more complex than the "mainland," her work also foregrounds trauma and terror as processes that do not belong to one time period, regime, or era.[5] Rather, we have to confront how multiple "presents" are summoned in various expressive forms of culture.

Taylor also offers a useful distinction between archives and repertoires. The former is associated with the stuff of institutions and the things that are often taken for granted inside them—texts, artifacts, documents, and so on—making them more precious. The archivist aims to preserve and make permanent, recording information into various magnetic, photographic, digital, and other media. The repertoire hews closer to the live, the visceral, the embodied, the temporary and fleeting. We can associate it with that which is informal, experimental, unstable, unreliable, gestural, and spoken. We should be careful to note from Taylor's distinction that archives and repertoires act not independently of but, rather, dialectically on each other. Without privileging one over the other, students of expressive forms of culture understand that performances are "vital acts of transfer," that the things we do with our bodies to learn and share repertoires are also ways to communicate histories, lessons, identities, affinities, and commitments of all sorts.[6]

Joseph Roach's circum-Atlantic genealogy of performance resonates with Taylor's global approach to writing about repertoire as a site for producing alternative historical accounts of the world as enacted by the ordinary and the self-empowered. I import from Roach his three-sided relationship of memory, performance, and substitution. For the organizers and performers of a PCN, it is the act of substitution—for Roach, *surrogation*—that is at the heart of the show.[7] As student performers don period costumes; recite lines to evoke the timbre of ancestors, prophets, or heroines; or contort their bodies to mime seemingly timeless sacraments, they undertake the kind of work that Roach describes: "In the life of a community, *the process of surrogation does not begin or end* but continues as actual or perceived vacancies occur in the network of relations that constitutes the social fabric. Into the cavities created by loss through death or other forms of *departure* . . . survivors attempt to fit satisfactory *alternates.*"[8]

The PCN is less about the construction of a finished *product* each year than about a *process* without end—never an end, never the past giving way to the present, never the hurts of history allayed, smoothed over, explained away, justified, or excused. The performative work of the Pilipino Cultural Night strikes a deep, resonant chord with participants (performers, crew, and audiences) because the substitutions are never complete, never completely satisfying, and are therefore in need of endless staging and restaging. The show's space permits only a temporary fix of one night (albeit a year in the offing). Like Rabelais's carnivalesque, or Derek Walcott's witness of the *ramleela,* the social order to which the participants aspire is restored *after* the event while the show reinvents hierarchies in the evening.[9] In addition, the participants hold far too many expectations for any show to be able to satisfy a student body's desire *to complete,* or *to carry out thoroughly,* which is one way to think about the history of the term "performance," which I will discuss later.

Could not the history of the Philippines as a Western colony—substituting Americans for Spaniards in 1898, for starters—be the driving force that accounts for those scores of cavities created by loss or other forms of departure? The shows are cavities without enclosures in which the irreversibility of modern time is arrested and into which the student bodies insert themselves. Add to the array of survivors the seditious playwrights of old, the soldiers such as the Filipino rebel Andres Bonifacio, who paid his own dues on stage as a vernacular actor. Move forward through the century to the Philippine diaspora's Californian coasts and valleys, where students assume the stance of other *katipuneros* and *ilustrados* (anticolonial revolutionaries and elite activists). They play the parts year after year, filling vacancies left open long ago. The PCN is not a singular show but a process of surrogation without end.

What could those *other forms of departure* mean? Such removal could also refer to the purposeful erasure of empire from U.S. historiography, the active refusal to take account of actual agents—the fully engaged and sovereign actors (who are instead reduced to *insurrectos,* bandits or insurgents). PCNs have repeatedly attempted to perform such characters back onto the stage of history. And yet Roach notes that this "process of trying out various candidates in different situations" often results in the "doomed search for originals by continuously auditioning stand-ins."[10] What we have are performances like the PCN that stand in "for an elusive entity that it is not but that it must vainly aspire both to embody and to replace."[11] Pilipino Cultural Nights are not literal but lateral truths, acts of performative surrogation, the sideways substitution of a student body into time's breach.

In this book, I point to very specific examples of how repertoires imported from the Philippines by Filipino American student performers are actively joined with scenarios and narratives borne out of their U.S.-based lives. Of course, more is going on than facile *re*citation and remembrance. In addition to the idea of articulation in the declarative or enunciative sense, performances demonstrate the potential to join disparate elements. Taking a cue from Stuart Hall, "An articulation is thus the form of the connection that can make a unity of two different elements, under certain conditions."[12] But let us not confuse performance's ability to allow generations to speak to each other as evidence of agreement or consensus. A closer look at these repertoires reveals oblique critiques and disagreements registered between child and parent, mentee and mentor, student and teacher. Cultural productions like PCNs echo the critically imaginative work of other U.S. immigrants and allow us to look more deeply into Filipino American lives. In his powerfully evocative analysis of Clifford Odets's play *Awake and Sing* (1935), Robert Warshow listened closely to the kind of intergenerational dialogue taking place in New York's working-class Jewish communities in the early twentieth century. In Odets's work, Warshow deftly teased out the experience of an audience's recognition of ethnicity on stage—a recognition of themselves—that could easily have been used to describe those attending Pilipino Cultural Night productions, where one could see "a continuous series of familiar signposts, each suggesting with the immediate communication of poetry the whole complex of life of the characters: what they are, what they want, how they stand with the world."[13] Warshow's take on Odets can help us understand how the children of Filipino immigrants saw and continue to see their parents—sometimes heroically while at other times relegated to nostalgia, "coming off a boat, having to find a job the next day" and "for the rest of his life, likely to be taken up by the numberless techniques of getting by."[14] Pilipino Cultural Nights are also shot through with latent anger, bitterness, and resentment toward prior generations, obliquely critiquing them for not communicating enough of the culture and for pursuing economic security and social prestige, because "without a dollar you don't look the world in the eye."[15] The narrators and performers of PCNs are like the immigrant children that Warshow writes about, a U.S. generation born or raised that possesses "a kind of edge, as if they were a day older in history than everyone else."[16]

Asian American literary scholarship helps to drive home the point of these intergenerational antagonisms. For example, Erin Ninh's detailed analyses of tension expressed through different generations helps us understand that the "subject's relation to the nation must come to terms with the immigrant family as that nation's intermediary and agent."[17] We can turn to those narratives that, in her terms, express "a pervading anger and bitterness at conditions of their upbringing which they cannot name with finality or certitude."[18] Filipino and Filipino American authors such as Bienvenido Santos and R. Zamora Linmark have given us characters that fit Warshow's bill of having an edge. The young Kalihi protagonists in Linmark's first novel, *Rolling the R's*, speak boldly and at every opportunity, without prompting by parents and against the advice and teaching of their elders. Zamora has noted that the characters in the novel should not be understood as taking part in the colloquial process of coming of age but are fully realized as they are—brash, playful, smart-alecky, and contemptuous as they resist with a full-throated pidgin the standardized English required for their book reports.[19] In Santos's short story "The Day the Dancers Came," the elderly, working-class Filipino protagonist looks forward to the visit of a troupe of young dancers from his native Philippines, only to be disappointed by the gulfs that exist between them. The old-timer, trapped by low wages and even lower self-esteem, has internalized the dominant codes of his day: He sees himself as *basura* (trash) compared with the lithe bodies of the dancers he thinks he knows.[20] Even though these two examples are works of fiction, they speak powerful truths about how cultural producers can, on occasion, refuse the romance of the immigrant's journey to the "new world." Those harsh lessons of disappointment, shame, and anger are voiced by actual people such as Valerie Corpus, who came to the United States in 1979 at sixteen. "I hated everything," she said. She even began directing her anger toward her mother, pointing to her everyday annoyances—having to do without maids (to whom the family had access in the Philippines), witnessing public displays of affection, or suffering a white woman's scowl on a subway after being told that "I had no right to be here."[21]

Cultural performances often take us directly into our most difficult and painful experiences—between "home" and "homeland," across (and *against*) generations, and even within ethnic and national groups that we occasionally assume to be welcoming. In contemporary scholarly discussions, Victor Turner's idea of subjects living "betwixt and between" has become ubiquitous when describing all of those liminal states from which we go, to which we aspire, and of which we dream. As a backbone to the world's labor flows, Filipinos in the diaspora know all too well about the costs of living one's life "in between."

I also take from Turner's work the notion of performance as that which attempts to deliver on a promise, traced to the old French term *parfournir,* "to complete" or "to carry out thoroughly." A performance, then, is the "*proper finale* of an experience."[22] Lawyers rely on a definition of performance that highlights "the fulfillment or accomplishment of a promise, contract, or other obligation according to its terms, relieving such person of all further obligation or liability thereunder."[23] From the fourteenth century, we can find references to performance as the execution of an agreement, the fulfillment of one's obligation to another. How may we understand performance when there is not, in legal parlance, a "meeting of the minds"? Can we envision performance as the carrying out of other kinds of obligations or the execution of agreement (or, at least, its attempt) across generations and geographic locales? I believe we can if we adopt a genealogical approach to history writing and history telling and cultural criticism that Roach, Taylor, and Turner suggest in their work. Tracing the histories of a performing-arts genre like the PCN is precisely the kind of task that is well suited to genealogical inquiry, for "it operates on a field of entangled and confused parchments, on documents that have been scratched over and recopied many times."[24]

Trying to make sense out of those tangled and confused parchments means being open to what Reynaldo Ileto refers to as nonlinear emplotments. He reminds us of the challenge that is no doubt shared throughout the Philippine diaspora: "From the moment typical Filipino students begin to learn about themselves, their society, history, and culture through books, the mass media, and the classroom, they become immersed in ideas of development, emergence, linear time, scientific reason, humane pragmatism, governmental ordering, and nation building."[25] From my years of teaching on ten college and university campuses in California and Hawai'i, it sounds like those "typical Filipino students" share a lot with their U.S. counterparts. Are not most of us socialized into the schema that Ileto draws out, which underscores the marking of histories into "arbitrary historical periods," the selective highlighting and suppression of events, and the "evolutionary ordering of phenomena" from primitive to advanced? Indeed, it would be difficult—if not impossible—to argue that most of the students working and living at this forward edge of the Philippine diaspora in the United States have not internalized such linear emplotments, and for good reason. The history of the Philippines that has been communicated with churchly fervor posits that familiar narrative arc beginning with the Fall (Spanish colonization), followed by baroque Darkness (sixteenth- and seventeenth-century European sensibilities), and emerging into the Recovery (with nineteenth-century native elites speaking for the masses). Regime change brought about by the Americans only confirms the inevitability of Progress in the twentieth century.[26] Those of us who want to contribute to a more dynamic and critical account of Philippine and Filipino American histories and cultures take these familiar arcs with a grain of salt. Too much is hidden beneath the chronicles that advance subjects from darkness to light and from chaos to consensus.

Rather than attempt to capture the "exact and pure essence of things" (Foucault's phrasing), students of the performative open themselves to a line of work where we can prize the accidents that make up our repertoires, not the origins of things but "an unstable assemblage of faults, fissures and heterogeneous layers that threaten the fragile inheritor from within and from underneath."[27] We could, as the most careful of us entreat, to think about the cultural work we produce that emphasizes the "lowly, complex and contingent." How can we give equal status to all of those "interruptions, repetitions, and reversals, uncovering the subjugations, confrontations, power struggles, and resistances that linear history tends to conceal"?[28] Whether as scholars or as performers, we are often fragile inheritors and clumsy inventors of the "past."

## Changing the Subjects: Performance and Filipino American Studies

For the thousands of young Filipino Americans who have taken to the stage, participating in performing-arts genres such as the PCN has offered some of the only history lessons available about the Philippine Revolution of 1896, the literary politics of Carlos Bulosan, the struggle of the *sakadas* in Hawai'i, or the back-breaking labor in Salinas, Delano, Spokane, or Chicago. Performing a play or choreographing dances offers not only the possibility of entertainment, but also the chance to encounter the past in a corporeal fashion, to sustain an oblique critique of American assimilation, or to call a community into being.[29]

This book can be read as a study of youth cultures, especially since students in the United States and the Philippines are at the center of the productions discussed. But while this is not strictly a social history of youth activities, since we examine the ambitions and anxieties of educators, sponsors, and administrators, students' bodies have been crucial in the expression of the "nation," both in the Philippines and throughout the diaspora.[30] Many other works highlight a particular geographic locale in which a scene or subculture has taken hold. My attention builds on existing studies in the field by widening the focus beyond discrete ethnogeographic communities (for example, New York City, Los Angeles, Honolulu, or Seattle) while tracing a genealogy of trans-Pacific cultural production between the United States and the Philippines. My aim is not to demonstrate how the cultural forms are developed in the Philippines and are then inherited and deployed effortlessly in the United States but, instead, to argue that the PCN represents the invention, and occasionally also the misinterpretation, of cultural repertoire. I also highlight macrostructural dimensions to cultural work—from the anticipation of independence with the passage of the Tidings–McDuffie Act of 1934, the post–World War II reassertion of U.S. hegemony in Asia to contain nationalist movements throughout the region, and the postindustrial and martial-law-era politicization of Filipino youth on college campuses in the United States to the present moment that hails the Philippines as the "second front" in the endless war on terror. Also, my work highlights the interplay between youth cultures as imagined by the participants and organizers (student leaders, choreographers, writers, actors, and dancers) and the work of state and institutional agents (university administrators, educators, state-sponsored artistic directors). That interplay between state agents and student bodies demonstrates that popular cultural forms are never exclusively acts of resistance or tools of discipline and repression. Stuart Hall recognized that symbols, performances, and repertoires belong neither to the elite nor to the aggrieved when he wrote, "There is no guarantee that, because at one time it was linked with a pertinent struggle, that it will always be the living expression of a class. . . . Culture is not already permanently inscribed with the conditions of a class before that struggle begins."[31] We should be concerned with popular culture not because it guarantees or is synonymous with resistance, but because it has been and continues to be a place of possibility, one of the grounds on which struggle may be waged.[32]

The conversations that have been taking place in the field broadly conceived as performance studies have been invaluable for my work. Scholars have resisted labeling performance studies as a stand-alone discipline, embracing instead an eclectic approach that has made use of methodologies from both the social sciences and the humanities.[33] I have already mentioned the importance of work by Taylor and Roach on this project. An additional inspiration for considering performative aspects of Filipino American cultures has been the field of dance theory and ethnography, often associated with scholars such as Susan Leigh Foster, Marta Savigliano, and Barbara Browning, each providing complex testimony about choreographed bodies as metaphors and evidence for social movements, but also as conduits for a variety of information that is not always accessible in "traditional" modes of producing knowledge.[34] Scholars such as David Román, Daphne Brooks, Ann Cvetkovich, and Jose Muñoz offer powerful examples of how crisis is at the very center of contemporary American life and how the relative "health" of individual bodies is not simply a metaphor for the body politic but can also be the source of trenchant critiques. A crisis-centered stance insists on paying close attention to the contradictory, experimental, and contingent aspects of academic work. I think it attracts a kind of scholar who draws inspiration from what Jan Cohen-Cruz refers to as "local acts"—those community-based approaches to understanding performance as much as undertaking scholarship.[35] Such approaches are at the very foundation of Asian American studies, and the number of scholars working at the intersection of that field with performing arts and popular culture is growing. A hallmark of Asian American studies has been the notion that race is both irreducible as a category of analysis (in that race is not merely a function of another analytic) and a constantly shifting project in determining social relations.[36]

Filipino American studies asks questions that are at the center of contemporary scholarship in the humanities and social sciences. Research in three areas deserves particular notice: first, in the fields of security studies and international relations, where the projection of U.S. military power continues unabated throughout the world; second, how the global economy continues to unfold with drastic consequences for the world's transnational labor flows; and third, how Filipino American studies can also shed light on the curious, contradictory, and dynamic ways in which modern identities and communities are configured. Over the course of the twentieth century, the United States has exercised an unparalleled military presence in the Philippines, a condition that accounts for a significant part of the lives of soldiers, retirees, dependents, and other community members. The United States benefited from ninety-nine-year, rent-free leases to operate its largest overseas bases, as well as indirect control of Philippine military forces through the establishment of the Joint U.S. Military Advisory Group. Even though the Philippines attained sovereignty in 1946, the post–September 11, 2001, era has witnessed the restoration of that military presence with the re-tasking of the *Balikatan* (shoulder-to-shoulder) exercises to prepare troops for the "second front" on the war on terror. And just as Ferdinand Marcos leveraged U.S. materiel and funding to fend off what he claimed to be armed communist threats while growing his personal assets, President Gloria Macapagal Arroyo reenlisted Philippine forces in the affirmation of bilateral mutual defense treaties between the two countries.[37] In the United States, the dominant and often romanticized narratives of agricultural and service-sector labor for which Filipinos have been recruited have overshadowed generations of service in the U.S. Armed Forces that began in World War I. Overlapping with plantation and fieldwork done by thousands of Filipinos are complex histories of migration and settlement facilitated by military careers. Such service has accounted for the establishment of second-, third-, and fourth-generation Filipino American communities throughout the United States, from Hawaiian Army and Navy enclaves in Pearlridge to marine families in Bremerton, Washington; naval families in Alameda and San Pedro, California; and second- and third-generation families in Virginia Beach, Virginia.[38]

Those tracking the global flows of contemporarily distributed labor would do well to study the fate of the Filipino diaspora. Current conversations in the United States that implore politicians to "save our jobs" are anchored in an economic paradigm that does not always adequately acknowledge how transnational capital has dispersed the forces of production. As a result of government-led drives to export local labor, Filipinos have witnessed and participated in patterns of work of which most people in the United States simply have no sense. Eleven percent of the Filipino population (more than eight hundred thousand workers) lives overseas, traveling to more than one hundred eighty countries as domestic helpers, engineers, nurses, bricklayers, teachers, farmers, seafarers, stenographers, hairdressers, crane operators, cooks, and entertainers. Their remittances account for one-tenth of their home country's gross national product. Transnational capital looks to the Philippines as a model for how to manage one of the most globally dispersed workforces in modern times.[39]

Finally, in theorizing complex subjectivities, Filipino Americans have long confounded the fixity of racial categorizations in U.S. law, the premium placed on a linear narrative of assimilation, and the insistence on identity as an individuated articulation of difference. Foundational research emphasized narratives in Asian American studies that constituted the recovery or reconstitution of cultural memory or the telling of local histories. Of course, these continue to be important, challenging, and needed at all levels of education, perhaps even more so at the primary and secondary levels. But studies about Filipino American lives have as much to say about crisis as they do about continuity and confrontation, as well as consensus.[40]

The field has been primarily anchored in history and the social sciences—namely, sociology and anthropology. Barbara Posadas's *Filipino Americans* offers a general and well-structured overview of Filipinos as a U.S. ethnic minority. Works by Catherine Choy, Dorothy Fujita-Rony, Augusto Espiritu, and Linda Maram pay close attention to developing historical research of Filipinos from the early twentieth century to the present while demonstrating the gendered and trans-Pacific focuses for their work on nurses, agricultural workers, and writers. Deserving special attention are Espiritu's and Maram's texts, both offering novel approaches to the intellectual and performative lives of specific authors and communities, with special attention to the midcentury contexts of Philippine independence and working-class Filipino American youth cultures in the United States.[41]

Social scientists such as Jonathan Okamura, Rhacel Parreñas, Yen Le Espiritu, Rick Bonus, Emily Ignacio, and Martin Manalansan problematize the notion of diaspora as simply an extension of national subjectivities "beyond" the Philippine nation. Their grounded analyses allow us to focus on new kinds of communities being built, contextualized, and imagined in locales that reflect rooting and routing throughout the world: in Hawai'i, Europe, near the Canadian and Mexican borders, in New York, or on the Internet. Their work raises a critique within contemporary U.S.-based social-science work—namely, that the premium placed on assimilation to "American culture" no longer holds. They allow us to get beyond facile statements about the persistence of ethnic identity and how overseas communities imagine "homelands" from safe, suburban spaces.[42] Three more works ably demonstrate what is going on in the field. Sharon Delmendo's *Star-Entangled Banner,* the ambitious volume edited by Angel Shaw and Luis Francia titled *Vestiges of War,* and Allan Isaac's analyses of literary works point to the need to demystify U.S.–Philippine relations by turning to that inaugural moment of imperialism at the beginning of the twentieth century. Their works continue to be inspired partly by developments announced within the landmark American studies collection edited by Amy Kaplan and Donald Pease, *The Cultures of United States Imperialism.* As scholars and practitioners of the arts, Delmendo, Shaw, Francia, and

Isaac bear witness to the role that the imagination and cultural work continue to play in the unfolding of the field.[43]

This cohort of scholars and writers partake in scholarship described by Renato Constantino as partisan and by Howard Zinn as partial—that no "subject" of academic writing merely waits to be spoken for or represented, and that any description of the world "must be a partial description, so a choice is made about what part of reality to describe, and behind that choice is often a definite *interest,* in the sense of something useful for a particular individual or group."[44] In that regard, Filipino American studies can be understood as a field of inquiry that has grown out of the mass-based social struggles of the late 1960s and early 1970s. That work would have modest beginnings in the training of a handful of scholars in Philippine studies by Boone Schirmer at Goddard College; in the dozens of initiatives launched through campus and conference proceedings; in the home-grown courses on art, language, history, and culture anchored in churches, self-help organizations, and unions; and in the dozens of independent publications, pamphlets, monographs, and self-financed studies only occasionally backed by large publishers. Some contexts need to be kept in mind: not only the critique of the domestic nature of the Civil Rights Movement, but also the politicization of communities throughout the United States after Ferdinand Marcos's declaration of martial law in 1972. Activists organizing around San Francisco's International Hotel throughout the 1970s would issue a clarion call for social justice around the issue of affordable housing in the wake of city planners' razing of the city to create the "Wall Street of the West."

Each of these events, and dozens more concerning language use, access to higher education, the indignities suffered under anti-miscegenation laws, struggles over community policing, and campaigns for equitable health care and employee protection, would help to drive the field's initial questions. Some works that adopted a crisis-centered and engaged approach are Royal Morales's *Makibaka* ("struggle"; published in the same year that the Marcos regime declared martial law); the introduction to Filipino American literature written by Oscar Peñaranda, Sam Tagatac, and Serafin Syquia in the first edition of *Aiiieeeee!*; E. San Juan Jr.'s book-length analysis of Carlos Bulosan's extant writings; and a groundbreaking anthology edited by students at the University of California, Los Angeles, entitled *Letters in Exile.* A lot of this critical writing would find its artistic and aesthetic sensibility worked out in the pages of anthologies devoted to graphic arts and literature such as *Aion, Gidra, Bridge,* and *East–West.*[45]

Artists such as the self-described "Flip poets" of San Francisco in the 1970s have been central to the invention and assertion of a critical Filipino

American subjectivity. The writers and performers Al Robles, Serafin Syquia, Luis Syquia, Oscar Peñaranda, Emily Cachapero, and Virginia Cerenio (to name a few) linked the work of literature with community service. Robles and others created the Manilatown Senior Services Center, while Serafin Syquia developed creative-writing workshops for youth who lacked access to arts education. Subsequent groups of students and activists contributed their own talents by returning to the tradition of publishing work by younger writers: *Maganda* (University of California, Berkeley) and the second volume of *Liwanag* (San Francisco State University) are two examples of a generation that took cues while making their own way with student-driven literary cultures in the 1990s. The literary scene for Filipino Americans has been active. Spoken-word collectives, fusing hip hop's energy with the politicized consciousness of young writers and performers, have flourished in Los Angeles, San Francisco, Seattle, Chicago, and New York. A cohort of poets and writers continue to teach in youth-based programs; organize readings and fundraisers; and publish chapbooks, edited volumes, novels, short stories, and children's books. In the 1990s, another cohort of artists experimenting with film signaled an exciting development among Filipino American artists. Centered for the most part in Los Angeles, a group of designers, filmmakers, writers, and directors worked on each other's projects and demonstrated the vitality of new forms of cultural production that had not been widely used by Filipino Americans to that point. Functioning as a loose network, they would include Celine Salazar Parreñas, John Castro, Ernesto Foronda, Marlon Fuentes, and Pancho Gonzalez. Their strategies involved transparent realism, surreal parody, avant-gardist lyricism, and documentary fiction. Each demonstrated a profoundly keen awareness of Filipino history against the larger visual and filmic record dominated by one-sided treatments of wartime documentarians, ethnologists, and thousands of Hollywood feature-film directors that have used the Philippines as a backdrop for every war fought by the United States.

The work that has been forged by scholars such as Sunaina Maira and Martin Manalansan in the larger area known as Asian American diasporic cultural studies also serves as an important touchstone for my work and provides a solid link between performance studies and ethnic studies. This area is notable not only for continually pushing scholarly boundaries beyond the ideation of Asian America tethered exclusively to the North American West Coast, but also for another important reason: It focuses on practices and processes and not solely on the ruminative and beleaguered nature of individuated *identity*. When well-grounded and detailed social-science work such as Maira's and Manalansan's pays close attention to the multilayered and multisited signification of terms such as *biyuti*, or to the collaborative dissonance and tension heard in the club scene on a Friday or Saturday night in Manhattan, all of us benefit from being able to refuse outdated and useless paradigms that have been used by all manner of power to target young, colored, and queer bodies. Maira keenly observes that the young, brown, and hip are no dupes. Rather than simply internalizing the dominant codes of parent or homeland, they "attempt to make sense of, or at least to accommodate to, discourses of multiculturalism and racialization, and to respond to family narratives of class mobility and cultural displacement." She finds in their reflexivity and re-mixed cultural work the stirrings of a "critical nostalgia."[46] Filipino American and South Asian American communities who share overlapping demographic and socioeconomic locations in contemporary U.S. society serve as a reminder to me and, I hope, to other scholars who want to mine these scenes for future comparative cultural analysis. This rather amorphous field of Asian American diasporic cultural studies, as I see it, is not simply a place to trumpet everything done *in the name of* one's championed tribe. It is, rather, the analytical framework to asses how empirically grounded analyses of practices, processes, and repertoire continue to demystify the rule of empire between Asia and the Americas and to provide a meaningful accounting of the life chances and choices made *here* and *there,* at home and abroad.

## Researching the Project and the Organization of the Text

I analyzed material drawn from archival sources in the United States and the Philippines, as well as that gathered from qualitative methods. The latter involved the use of long interviews and participant observation techniques developed along with my work as a musician, composer, and theater performer. I began my research for this book casually, first as an audience member, then as a musician and stage performer. Many times during the course of researching material for this book I felt that I was not engaged in research at all. I wrote and circulated publicity copy; auditioned singers and actors; rehearsed in concert halls, living rooms, and parking garages; wrote and improvised scripts, musical scores, and memorized lines; played a lead character; managed to avoid getting my ankle crushed between eight-foot clapping bamboo poles; and transported musical equipment, public-address systems, cast members, paint, costumes, PVC pipes, and lumber for sets. I participated in PCNs in California from 1989 to 2001.

One of my goals in this book is to look across generations and geographic locations without resorting to easy generalizations or uncritical essentialisms. The nature of colonialism's trauma—whether in the Philippines or throughout its diaspora—requires that we learn how to interpret the echoes and traces of one period in others. Those invested in the building and maintaining the status quo have always insisted that the rest of us live in their categories, especially ones that neatly mark off the past (as timeless, completed, and never recurring) from the present. This book recognizes how each generation offers its own vision and version of the past, present, and future. We can and should wander beyond where our professions often warn against and wonder about what those communities have to say about each other.

The first two chapters provide detailed background material for the creation of the Pilipino Cultural Night. These chapters focus on two key moments: the creation of a national folkloric repertoire and the touristic popularization of dance-theater presentations. Chapter 1 focuses on the foundational work undertaken by Manila-based educators of the 1930s as they anticipated the colony's transition to commonwealth and eventually to sovereign nation. Here we learn of the anxiety of patrons and educators such as Jorge Bocobo, president of the University of the Philippines, and the physical educator and folklorist Francisca Reyes Aquino over what the *bodabil* (vaudeville) musician Lou Borromeo represented: the inevitability of American popular culture's "corruption" of the lives of young Filipinos when both the United States and the Philippines were formally bound by colonialism. Aquino invented a national folkloric repertoire that became a crucial tool for inculcating a kinetic nationalism disciplined into the bodies of young folks.

In Chapter 2, I focus attention on the emergence of the Bayanihan Philippine Dance Company (hereafter, the Bayanihan) in defining for PCN organizers, tourists, and others the performative vocabulary of Filipino culture through its popular dance-theater performances. As the Philippines formalized its neocolonial embrace with United States, the career of the Bayanihan demonstrated the corresponding cultural logic of how national subjects are portrayed on the international stage. As folk dance was adapted into dance theater, from the schools to the concert hall, this celebrated dance company claimed representational authority in its work. Those claims and the response from several critics in the Philippines and the United States remind us that questions of national identity are also at play when performers take the stage.

Chapter 3 focuses on an early cultural-night show that helped to define what has become known as the "PCN genre." I select three contexts to highlight these changes: the postindustrialization of the U.S. economy; the reaction to race, taxes, and education in the *Bakke v. University of California*

*Board of Regents* decision; and the political realignment of the Reagan Democrats. We see the continued immigration of underemployed professionals to the United States whose children seek senses of themselves amid attacks on ethnic-studies curricula and affirmative-action policies. In Chapter 4, I analyze versions of the PCN that have emerged since the creation of the genre in the 1980s. While several other presentations predated the 1983 show—shows that used variety-style formats such as revues, declamations, dances, short plays, and other mixed-media installations—the PCNs produced since then have served as the true proving grounds for the strengthening of the form. How was this achieved? How did the diffuse cultural productions of a seemingly heterogeneous group of Philippine- and U.S.-born Filipinos become standardized and replicated? I identify what has become the basic structure of the PCN and describe constitutive relationships that have demonstrated that the form has become frustratingly predictable. Finally, in Chapter 5 I analyze the San Francisco comedy troupe Tongue in a Mood's parody of the PCN genre, *PCN Salute,* which boils a show that can take hours down to a twenty-minute sketch. The parody functioned as a critique of the now familiar essentialized cultural repertoire and demonstrated how popular forms continue to be sites for engaging contemporary discussions about representation and power. The jester reminds us how cultural work can continue to knock us off center and refuse predictable endings.

CULTURAL PERFORMERS who take to the stage as folkloric dancers or historical figures often appear to have the veneer of authenticity—or, at the least, they are able to convey a sense of comfort to the viewer and participant that what is being presented collapses historical time, that what is presented to the viewer is some transcendent and ahistorical figure conjured out of primordial pasts. In contrast to the immediacy and plasticity of our common and everyday entertainment, the cultural performer represents the embodied equivalent of the romanticized oral history—the true voice of the people. That process of embodiment is not natural, even though at times Filipino cultural productions seem so effortless, even *soulful,* as if analysis were not necessary. Whether as a performer, audience member, or critic of the PCN, I am grateful to have shared the company of artists, academics, and activists who believed there was something valuable to learn from the PCN and from Filipino American cultural production. I am thinking here of how Sarita See uses the phrase "excessive embodiment" to meditate on the notion of absences and presences when referring to the work of the Filipino visual artist Paul Pfeiffer. While some of Pfeiffer's work digitally removes the figure from the frame, critics like

See can take from artists a reminder that bodies are also burdened with surplus value and information.[47] In this case, the native body is set free from modernity itself: unbridled and self-possessed, free of colonial mastery and industrial discipline. Consider how this notion is challenged by the dramaturg and performance-studies scholar Lucy Mae San Pablo Burns, who accounts for the "multiple functions" of the Filipino dancing body: "It is a corporeal metaphor for the ambivalent status of Filipinos as U.S. colonial subjects; it provides an archival embodiment of the anti-Filipino movement through dance; and finally, it serves as material evidence of the 'success' of the American imperial project."[48] Again, as with See's "excessive embodiment," Burns's account of multiple functions of performance helps us realize that repertoires can be at the center of analyzing the relationship between political choices and aesthetic chances.

These choices and chances can at times seem dizzying, given the tempo and scope of globalization. Undisciplined performers can wreak havoc on any well-planned show, and by extension unruly bodies pose threats to the body politic. As Arjun Appadurai points out in *Fear of Small Numbers*, the supposedly organized majority is increasingly threatened by the irrepressible few.[49] The immigrant, rabble-rouser, heckler, dissident, even the desegregated teenage partygoer—all can threaten a polity's sense of order. Such dangerous figures have been subject to bodily censure by various means—from humiliation and ridicule to deportation, physical violence, even disappearance.[50] Against the backdrop of Filipino bodies scattering throughout the globe as a truly dispersed workforce (Robyn Rodriguez refers to this ensnared situation as a liminal condition of "migrant citizenship"),[51] the repertoires I analyze in this book isolate and attempt to lock down some of those bodies into durable and predictable repertoires, while the performances attempt those lateral substitutions across several periods and places.

# 1 The Art of the State

## *Inventing Philippine Folkloric Forms (Manila, 1934)*

*The nation state sees the entire territory as its performance area; it organizes the space as a huge enclosure, with definite places of entrances and exits. These exits and entrances are manned by companies of workers they call immigration officials. The borders are manned by armed guards to keep away invaders; but it is also to confine the population within a certain territory. The nation state performs its own being hourly, through its daily exercise of power over the exits and entrances, by means of passports and visas and flags. . . . The state performs its rituals of power not only by being able to control exits and entrances into the territorial space, its entire performance space, but also by being also to move people between the various enclosures within the national territorial space.*

—Ngũgĩ wa Thiong'o

## Vaudeville, *Vod-a-vil,* and *Bodabil*

Luis Borromeo began his musical training at an early age in the central Philippine region of Leyte. He caught the performing bug and traveled to San Francisco to see the 1915 Panama-Pacific International Exposition. Recognized by fellow Filipinos, he was later asked to perform at the Dutch Pavilion, where he was discovered. He signed a three-year contract to perform on the Orpheum Circuit, a large chain of vaudeville and motion-picture theaters.[1] Borromeo saw the United States from the inside of those venues, while scores of other musical acts from the Philippines with names like the Filipino Collegians, the Varsity Four, the Manila Filipino Orchestral Quartette, and the Royal Philippino (*sic*) String Band entertained millions at the Circuit Chautauqua.[2] Fans urged Borromeo to write about his home; he gave them "My Beautiful Philippines." After Borromeo returned from a large overseas tour, his revue became legendary at ballrooms, cabarets, and dance halls. The company featured an eclectic mix of performers:

the "Muslim Queen" Miss Mundi, the Sulu island saxophonist Dudu; the Chinese tenor Chong Ying, and the Malayan baritone Zaelea, as well as dancers, other song stylists, and instrumentalists. Their repertoire featured jazz, the blues, ballads, Latin tunes, and native folk melodies arranged as art songs. Musicians were only part of a larger act that also involved contortionists, comedians, animal trainers, and tap dancers.[3]

Borromeo's experiences might seem anomalous when compared with the thousands of labor migrants shipped to the United States and Hawai'i during the early twentieth century as neither alien nor citizen. But Borromeo and musicians like him parlayed careers in commercial entertainment that would anticipate the global reach of the Filipino entertainer in the second half of the century.[4] The first vaudeville troupes came to the archipelago just a few years after the formal conclusion of the U.S.–Philippine War. Minstrel troupes performed their buck-and-wing, clog, and tap routines for white American audiences. Other performers came to town, including the Japanese Infantile Company, the Baroufski Imperial Russian Circus, the Denishawn Company, Helen and Lucy Martin, and Richard and Raymond Williams. Soon, troupes from around the world would market directly to Filipinos, and all-native ensembles, largely based in Manila, would spring up throughout the islands. Luis Borromeo called these performances *vod-a-vil,* while his audiences re-dubbed it *bodabil.* Some of the earliest advertisements promised peerless variety: "Good American Orchestra, New Acts, New Songs, the Most Brilliant and Stupendous Minstrel First Part Extant, Beautiful Lights and Scenic Effects, Gorgeous Costuming, Ragtime Talks, Ragtime Songs, Ragtime Walks, Every Feature Bright and Up to Date PLUS—A Grand Walk of All Nations!"[5]

Some commentators in the Philippines had prematurely written jazz's obituary, assuming that the only worthwhile forms of entertainment were those patronized by the upper crust. "While it is true that the modern, snappy, syncopated music (jazz) is popular in the ballrooms of America, what we call the 'best people' frown upon it and continue their communion with the great masters of the art," wrote Ernesto Vallejo. "Jazz will never displace real music in the United States. In fact in recent years, it has had a tendency to become less popular."[6] Published in a Philippine newspaper in the late 1920s, Vallejo's observation could not have been more wrong. Jazz became "more real" as the years passed, aided by sophisticated marketing techniques, improved recording technology, and, most important, the uprooting and mixing of rural and urban populations that pushed music across the continent by rail car and steamship: from New Orleans to Greensboro, Kansas City, Chicago, New York, Detroit, San Francisco, and Stockton and, eventually, to Manila.[7] In the Philippines, jazz music and dancing were based primarily in the capital, coming by way of African American soldiers who had deserted their posts during the war. A soldier in General Emilio Aguinaldo's army, Artemio Agnes, recalled how African American soldiers "[sang and exposed] their Filipino counterparts to the blues and early gospel music that was still taking shape in their motherland."[8]

This chapter traces the beginning of a Philippine national performance repertoire to the early 1930s. The history of some of the twentieth century's more enduring expressive forms of culture emerged out of a generation's anxiety over their children's collective identity. This apprehension over identity was also about how Philippine nationalists, working as native stewards under U.S. colonial rule, prepared their young for the transition to polities they had been promised. Performers like Borromeo and others, such as Mike Velarde and his Jazztocrats, alarmed the cultural conservatives of the day. Their work represented part of what seemed wrong to a new generation of Filipino educators trained at American universities. With the importation of music, dance, fashion, consumer goods, movies, and other American staples, elders wondered aloud about what was "Filipino" about any of it. This older, patrician culture, one that came of age a few years after anti-Spanish and anti-U.S. revolts, witnessed transitions of stark contrast. On the one hand, they identified with the anticlerical legacy of the *ilustrados*—in fact, many saw themselves as the inheritors of that legacy and station. Religion, while embedded in and retranslated within native cultures for centuries, was criticized for its backwardness, mystifying ritual, and reliance on superstition. On the other hand, the modern antidote was found in the American/Western privileging of science, ordering the technology of a new social order—from penal systems to census taking, hospital care, schooling, business practices, and even physical education.[9] But the logic of American rationality could not fully contain or explain the popularity of the cabaret or *bodabil* among young Filipinos. The conservatives could stomach how the new speed of urban industry had revolutionized cigar making or craft work in Manila. But in the dance and song imported from America, the elders saw only a challenge.

This chapter focuses on the mechanics of surrogation in the work of two individuals who created new parameters for cultural production during the Philippines' transition from a colony to a commonwealth and eventually to a sovereign nation: Jorge G. Bocobo, president of the University of the Philippines, and the folk-dance scholar Francisca Reyes Aquino. Both substituted not only white/imported performers with native ones but also replaced a matrix of expressive forms that they created. I trace a genealogy of Filipino folk forms through extant writing, much of it in the form unpublished speeches, essays, and other transcripts, to the history of nationalist ambitions and anxieties during the 1930s. Filipino national folk forms have their origin in the modern educational and technical discipline of physical education. Rather than re-creating the dances of a remote tribe or idyllic rural setting that conjures a timeless and unchanged past, educators and their political sponsors instead invented a national repertoire that was originally rooted in anxieties about the future of polity.

## Patrician Manila

Whether revisionist or apologist, those engaged in Filipino historiography have described this early-twentieth-century cohort of native elites as "collaborators" who raced to reconsolidate their political, social, and economic hegemony over the nation's resources (natural, human-made, and labor). Bocobo represented a widespread tendency among native elites who, while not rejecting the material benefits of their colonial access, vigorously cautioned many about the cultural dominance of the United States. Figures like Bocobo help to tell a more nuanced story about how the zeal for profit among the elite was tempered by the cultural conservatism of a waning patrician generation.[10] By focusing on Aquino, we may demystify and historicize cultural practices such as Filipino folk dance, wrestling it away from discourses that claim its authenticity, timelessness, and refusal to change. Nearly all of the major historical accounts of Aquino's role in the nationalization of discrete ethnolinguistic, regional, and religious dance and song forms fail to mention the "laboring" of culture—specifically, that a university-sponsored research program generated the repertoire we now take for granted as "national Philippine dance." Aquino did more than research Philippine folkloric forms; she *invented* them.[11]

In the next section, I briefly review some turn-of-the-century events that shaped the reconsolidation of native elites' station and the emergence of a corresponding "national" temper directed from Manila. This account foregrounds the administrative world that Bocobo and Aquino would inherit and shape. Economically, the imposition of tariffs and free-trade agreements favored the United States and its elite clients. Politically, enfranchisement directly benefited the rich and few in the Philippine Assembly; voting restrictions held in all elections. On the educational front, a government-sponsored training program that focused on young Filipino boys advanced the notion that American instruction would be required to "modernize" and "uplift" the Filipino. Bocobo joined the first one hundred students selected for schooling in the United States in 1903.[12]

Few social historians have paid attention to the changes that occurred in and around Manila during the first half of the twentieth century. While more scholarship continues to unravel the distinct regional differences and convergences among its heterogeneous populations, such heterogeneity continues to be a function largely defined against or in relation to the urban crossroads of the capital. At the beginning of the twentieth century, Manila consisted of a handful of small neighborhoods, including San Nicolas, Binondo, Quiapo, Ermita, and Intramuros. By 1941, the city would encompass outlying neighborhoods, more than doubling its size by World War II. The city's population also would swell from rural migration. At the base of the changes was a city economy serving as the site where Filipino capital attempted to meet international demands for raw materials while the native population sought out finished imported goods. International and native interests centered their financial, transportation, and communications systems in the city.[13] The fate of the colonial economy early on was pinned to the fortunes of the U.S. economy. In 1909, the Payne–Aldrich Act brought "free trade" to the Philippines. Soon thereafter, the gulf between the haves and the have-nots would grow until such distances seemed natural and criticism of such relations were muted. The duty-free entry of Philippine agricultural raw materials into the United States and of U.S. manufactured goods into the Philippines increased the colony's dependence on the American market. By 1932, seven-eighths of Philippine exports were going to the United States. As the *burgis* accumulated wealth, their appetite for Western/American culture drove higher levels of importation. Haciendas grew larger, displacing tenant farmers and increasing the exploitation of lower classes. When the U.S. economy crashed in 1929, the dependent Philippine economy felt the sting. Farmers in Central Luzon protested the maldistribution of wealth, and their uprising would spur the development of the socialist and communist challenges to establishment politics.[14]

Public dissatisfaction with U.S. imperial policy in the Philippines waned, due in large part to the promise by American politicians that education would be a progressive tool for change. Educating the natives became not only an attractive goal for both governments; it also became a means for hundreds of men and women in the United States to take up adventurous and somewhat lucrative teaching careers in this "exotic colony."[15] While the program of Filipinization attempted to yield control of key posts in the colonial government to native functionaries, Article 23 of the Jones Act maintained an exclusive U.S. hold on the Department of Public Instruction. The use of English as the medium of instruction became the centerpiece of U.S. educational reform in the Philippines. "With American textbooks, Filipinos started learning not only a new language but also a new way of life, alien to their traditions and yet a caricature of their model," wrote Arthur MacArthur Jr., U.S. military governor of the Philippines. "This was the beginning of their miseducation, for they learned no longer as Filipinos but as colonials. . . . [T]hey were starting to become a new type of American." The general placed the work of the occupying army alongside that of the school system: "This appropriation is recommended primarily and exclusively as an adjunct to military operations calculated to pacify the people and to procure and expedite the restoration of tranquility throughout the archipelago."[16]

As military force worked in tandem with schools to "pacify the people," Filipino historians commented on how quickly politicians and elites internalized the lessons of a new empire. "Men of property and education switched their allegiance from one colonial power to another, with a short 'revolutionary' career in between." Nationalist historians such as Renato Constantino painted a picture of several leading elite politicians who, even though they were members of the Spanish consultative government, quickly favored U.S. annexation in exchange for political posts at the Supreme Court or other administrative posts. Typical of this example was Felipe Buencamino, a secretary of foreign affairs. Before the U.S. Committee on Insular Affairs in 1902 he declared that *he* was "an American and all the money in the Philippines, the air, the light and the sun [he] consider[ed] American."[17]

Washington benefited from this arrangement. With the help of the native elite, U.S. politicians could reassure their stateside constituents that annexation was welcomed universally by the Filipinos. Just as they claimed friends, government and military leaders also claimed foes. Delegitimizing the resistance included a range of legal strategies, including the passage of the 1902 Brigandage Act. Guerrilla fighters such as Macario Sakay, Julian Montalan, Cornelio Felizardo, and Lucio de Vega—all leaders of anti-U.S. armed militias—were labeled *ladrones* (bandits), their subversion punishable by death. Just the year before, the Sedition Law had made the articulation of Philippine nationalism by its masses a crime, punishable by death, imprisonment, or fine.[18] Benito Legarda, a leading member of the revolutionary government who later deserted it, spoke before a U.S. commission and claimed to have "never heard this word 'independence' spoken, nor do I think they [the revolutionary movement] are capable of understanding it, even up to this time." Other high-ranking officials such as Pedro Paterno and Felipe Buencamino gathered together some of the country's wealthiest and most influential men; their purpose in late December 1900 was to reorganize local governments and to call for the formal annexation of the

Philippines by the United States. Their *Asociacion de Paz* was the forerunner of the *Partido Federal* (Federal Party, or the Federalists). Word of this political maneuvering would reach some guerrilla forces. For example, the National Army of Iloilo castigated the native elite and targeted "'prominent persons who filled important office under the revolution' for changing their ideals and nationality as if they were just changing their clothing."[19]

U.S. military commanders, while fighting off a persistent guerrilla force dispersed throughout villages, gave way to civilian control. The imperative of the market—namely, pressures from U.S. industrial and agricultural interests such as the Sugar Trust—ensured that a civilian administration was not only inevitable but also desirable, for a number of reasons. First, civilian control could quell fears in the United States that the military was engaged in a brutal war of suppression. Severe censorship of wartime atrocities was the norm, effectively shielding stateside public opinion from mounting significant dissent. Couching the administration's policies in terms of "benevolent assimilation," as McKinley had done, provided latitude in shaping public opinion. More important, though, a civilian administration allowed McKinley to accomplish what MacArthur could not: legally execute contracts over private business, the sale of public lands, and the commencement of extractive labor and production in sugar, hemp, and coconut crops. The landed elite would be disciplined into dependence during this period, while U.S. troops attempted to corral the guerrilla forces throughout the countryside. The economic arrangements among the U.S. civilian government, industrial and agricultural interests, and the landed elite reestablished the hegemony of oligarchic capitalism, this time under the Americans—"same dog, different collar."[20]

The sloganeering for "independence" also worked within the relationship between the political constituencies and the native elite leaders. Pressing for independence would be part of the rhetorical flourish needed for one's political survival. Careful U.S. administrators wielded ultimate political control over the proceedings. Nationalists still had the hard job of selling fellow assembly members on U.S.-backed free trade. Many assembly members opposed the 1909 Payne–Aldrich bill, which, they argued, would drive the Philippines toward economic dependence on the United States. At the time, Manuel Quezon was the majority floor leader of the assembly and an opponent of the bill. However, meetings between the leader of the assembly with Governor General James Francis Smith and Vice-Governor William Cameron Forbes convinced the members to save their careers and support the bill. The U.S. administrators allowed for Quezon and his cohort to publicly call for protectionism while having made concessions to Washington that certain limits would be placed on the acquisition of some public lands for foreign use.[21] In 1912, the election of the Democrat Woodrow Wilson and a Democratic-led Congress renewed hopes that independence would not be a sham. The Jones Act, passed in 1916, established a bicameral legislature, with appointments made by the governor-general subject to confirmation by the Philippine Senate. Veto powers were granted to the governor-general and the U.S. president over any acts of the Philippine legislature.[22]

Popular sentiment had been growing against the presence of U.S. control and its association with a native leadership riddled with corruption, excess, and waste. Quezon focused that anti-imperial mood to his advantage, raising the memorable banner: "I prefer a government run like hell by Filipinos to a government run like heaven by Americans." Yet for all the platitudes about political independence, the direction of Philippine tastes or, more accurately, the manufacturing of consumption patterns among Filipino "consumers" was at work during the years of colonial rule. In the period between 1904 and 1934, Philippine imports from the United States increased 91 percent, and Philippine exports to the United States increased by a factor of 32. By 1934, 80 percent of Philippine exports went to the United States, while 65 percent of what Filipinos imported was from the United States.[23]

In the United States, sugar and tobacco interests stinging from the presence of cheap imports from the Philippines pressed for measures like the Cooper bill, calling for the eventual independence of the colony. Philippine "independence" was just as much an American movement as it was a Philippine one. Unions and farmers continued to fear the dampening of wages through the continued importation of labor and the competition resulting from the presence of tobacco, rice, and sugar. Paul A. Kramer's analysis of the debates surrounding Philippine independence is excellent, especially concerning the Jones and Welch bills and the Tydings–McDuffie Act. The work is particularly detailed in describing the gamesmanship of an array of economic and political interests—U.S. labor continuing to fear a flood of cheap labor and goods, working-class white men threatened by the alleged sexual "aggressiveness" of Filipino men toward local white women, rabid retentionists eager to further evangelicalize the Philippines, and liberals and anti-imperialists who found the idea of colonial administration of a non-white people to be antithetical to a republican creed. Kramer understands that "Imperial indigenism," as shown by retentionists and paternalists in the United States such as Dean Worcester, was bent on continually representing Filipinos as savages in need of Western/Christian (American/Protestant) salvation. The counter to this was framed in the form of "nationalist colonialism," argued by Filipino elites based in Manila and Washington. Power accrued to the latter by virtue of demonstrating their "capacity" for administering a nation. Also, to counter the notion that the Philippines had always been of great strategic interest, U.S. analysts and policy-makers understood that, given Japan's decisive and unexpected victory over Russia in 1904–1905, a win that caused all Western (i.e., "white") powers to soberly reassess the balance of power in the East Asian theater, their new southeast Asian colony might actually be a liability. Philippine independence, long sought after by Filipino nationalists, some U.S. Democrats, and anti-imperialists, was in large part due to pressure exerted by U.S. agricultural lobbies—namely, sugar and dairy—whose clients saw prices for their goods fall as more goods streamed in from the colony. What protectionists and nativists, especially white working-class men anxious about job security and sexual prowess, could not secure through economic and exclusion laws they found in immigration policy. On November 15, 1935, the Philippines attained commonwealth status.[24] This is the context out of which "culture" was mobilized: the anticipation of nervous stewards over the "kinetic accents" that Filipino students would take with them to face and perform in a "new" period of Philippine history.[25]

## The Gloomy Dean's "Native Virtue"

Bocobo was part of the first generation of U.S.-trained Filipino administrators, a child of late-nineteenth-century *ilustrado* elitism, but he also represented an ambivalent investment by Americans for their tutelage. He subscribed to a theory of culture that was not uncommon during this period of early-twentieth-century nationalisms, patterning himself after the anticolonial heroic model José Rizal—patrician, cultured, masculine, Christian (not necessarily Catholic), reform-minded, and romantically nationalistic. Bocobo located the university—especially the publicly funded, secular University of the Philippines—as the locus for the dissemination of "national culture."

Bocobo was born in 1886 in the Ilokano-dominated rice-producing province of Pangasinan, on the northern Philippine island of Luzon. He grew up hearing at least four dialects spoken in his hometown of Gerona, Tarlac. His facility with languages included Spanish (the language of instruction) and Latin. His biographer also recalls his ability to sing revolutionary songs against both Spain and the United States during his teenage years. Bocobo's first education about the Spanish–American War came from a U.S. sergeant and, later, from teachers sent by the U.S. government in 1901 to the Philippines.[26] A major turning point in his young life, as for many other young men at the time, was the move from the province to the big city. At seventeen, Bocobo joined one hundred other young men in the first batch of sixteen- to twenty-three-year-olds sent to the United States for training as a government-sponsored scholar, a *pensionado.* The group produced an archibishop, a law-school dean, physicians, Supreme Court justices, and politicians—a starter kit for the U.S. policy of "Filipinization." The boys' departure was organized with great fanfare. In late October 1903, Governor-General William Howard Taft sent the class off with the perfunctory counsel to study hard and remember that they would be representatives of their people's best and brightest. He also reminded the lads to "use more soap."[27] The young scholars were treated to a performance of *Los Martires de la Patria* at the Teatro Zorilla while the music of brass bands accompanied them onto the *Rohilla Maru* for the voyage to San Francisco. From Manila, they traveled to Southern California for precollege training at Southland high schools in Ventura, Compton, Claremont, Riverside, Pomona, and San Diego, where they were housed in various private homes.[28]

One curious set of events throughout the rest of the country that took place before their college placement involved the students' participation in the St. Louis World's Fair (formally known as the Louisiana Purchase Exposition) in 1904. The historian Kimberly Alidio notes how the foreign students acted not only as guides for the thousands of white patrons, many of whom were seeing Filipinos for the first time in person, but also as performers in their own oblique manner, countering the fair's depictions of "natives" as scantily clad and ritualistic, by "put[ting] themselves on display." The *pensionados* published pamphlets, wrote songs, and, in certain instances, interrupted the fair organizers' presentations of what constituted Filipino "natives." Bocobo wrote the following song about the experience: "In St. Louis we enjoyed the Pike / With spectacles we did like / As guides in the Philippine Exhibits / Where we were thought to be Igorots / We had fits."[29] Did the young men have "fits" because fellow Filipinos were depicted by the organizers as part of a "savage-to-civilized" narrative that justified U.S. colonization? Or did the boys object to being associated with a "tribal" identity when they saw themselves as something quite different? Perhaps "colonial" or "cosmopolitan." But "tribal"?[30]

In the fall of 1904, Bocobo enrolled at Indiana University's law school in Bloomington. He and three other visiting students from the Philippines were described in the city's daily paper as "our local boys."[31] After graduating three years later, Bocobo returned to Manila, required to perform public service for the same length of his sponsored education in the United States. Friends and family noticed a change. Depending on the situation, their English was accented with Tagalog, and vice versa. By 1924, Filipino migration to Hawai'i from his native Ilokos was in its second decade; the ranks of laborers heading to the United States grew with the passage of yet another border-policing exclusion law. In that year, Bocobo became dean of the University of the Philippines College of Law. For his persona as both moralist and disciplinarian, Bocobo earned the nickname, the "Gloomy Dean."[32]

A central concern for Bocobo was the preparation of urban college youth in Manila. He lamented the soul-thinning aspects of America's imported and popular expressive forms: dance, song, cinema, literature, and so on. To guard against this, Bocobo launched a number of reforms, programs, and campus-based initiatives aimed at inculcating a love for the nation by developing a uniquely Filipino grammar of nationalism. If the Philippines was to join the international "family of nations," then young Filipinos—his students at the university especially—needed to be able to perform their specific repertoire without hesitation. They needed not merely to recite it, but also to demonstrate it—a nationalism internalized viscerally but exhibited kinetically. Bemoaning the campus's developing reputation as a "Whoopee University," Bocobo limited students' attendance at dances to two per year. Violators of the policy were suspended.[33]

Bocobo's speeches, essays, and other unpublished writings shed much light on his thinking. These writings revealed a sense of urgency—an anxious parent, a civic "father." In 1934, the same year in which the Tydings–McDuffie Act established the Philippines as a commonwealth of the United States, Bocobo took office as president of the University of the Philippines.[34] In early August of that year, Bocobo sat down at the KZRM radio station to deliver his essay "Our National Assets," which was broadcast on the eve of the selection of delegates for the new Constitutional Convention. Just a few months before, on March 24, 1934, Theodore Roosevelt had signed the law that altered the Philippines' international status. "This is no time for bewailing and lamentation," Bocobo said. "Just over the hills our eyes behold the ineffable beauty of dawn gloriously breaking out into a new day." Speaking directly to his students, Bocobo asked, "What are some of these advantages with which our country is blessed, as we are about to shoulder the burdens of national freedom?"[35]

He identified five national assets: self-restraint; religious tolerance ("Catholics and Protestants in the islands are fully aware that the fight should not be between them, but it should be against their common foe, which is the spirit of evil that debases and corrupts human life"); "racial and cultural unity" ("Today, there is no real and discernible line of cleavage between Tagalogs, Visayans, Ilocanos, Bicols, and so forth. *All feel and act as Filipinos.* To invoke any regional sentiment is rightly considered improper and unpatriotic. In point of language and culture, it must be recognized that English provides a common medium of expression"); an absence of intra-class animosity in Philippine society ("As a whole our masses are steady and conservative. They are not moved to frenzy by communistic ideas. . . . Social justice is achieved gradually without violence and without radical innovation"); and a "deeply religious character."[36] Regarding the third asset, Bocobo joined a chorus that equated the articulation of ethnic or regional specificity with the unraveling of the national project, deeming such acts "improper" and "unpatriotic."

During his acceptance speech as president of the University of the Philippines, Bocobo extolled the Malayan heritage and the "new civilization" that would draw from the "character of the Far East." He held out for the role of such institutions as "sanctuaries of truth which [are] untinged and unswayed by race or opinion."[37] Such places, he claimed, also "assert their ancient duty and privilege to transform the darkness of prejudice and error and passion into the sunlight of science, which knows no national barrier and owes fealty to the greater strides in human thought and learning had their first impulse mostly in the universities."[38]

Bocobo's initial reforms for the University of the Philippines campus included instructing students to greet professors as they met on school grounds and in the classrooms; sponsoring fine arts and literature lecture series; disseminating magazines and other books on "culture" of "the better kind"; and the requirement of church attendance. While the university was officially chartered as a public and therefore secular institution, Bocobo's Christian chauvinism was on display with the "go-to-your-church" movement. Encouraging religious diversity meant supporting two committees—one for Catholics, the other for Protestants—to regularly attend services.[39] Some of his other reforms included the clamping down on the excess of social activities such as "expensive receptions and dances." It was not dance per se that bothered Bocobo but, rather, what the activities represented: a favoring of American culture—its style, clothing, music and movement—over what he promoted, "the preservation of Filipino folk songs and dances."[40] He was quite serious. For those who violated the dance quotas, Bocobo handed out suspensions.[41] It was during this period that Bocobo turned his interest in the revival of cultural heritage from underneath the accumulation of "Stateside disposables."[42]

Bocobo was interested not in Filipino imitation of the West but in the inevitability of a distinct national contribution to "world culture"—a system built on a premise of self-sufficient sovereign states: "The University of the Philippines, then, has a mission to do its share in the *rise of a new civilization* that shall draw the breath of life from the character of the Far

East. . . . *I dare harbor the hope that the generations yet unborn will witness in the Far East, where more than one half of mankind live, a new order and a new culture.*"[43] That he located Philippine culture within the orbit of the "Far East" should come as no surprise. He was raised in the privileged traffic of the town of Gerona—a microcosm of cultural activity, commerce, and information—a place where residents claimed complex regional affinities. His conservatism rooted him in deep traditions of late-nineteenth-century Filipino life—for example, his fluency and use of Spanish and his family's access to landholdings. When Bocobo pondered culture as a deep well of knowledge and practice, he turned to Asia's cultures in China and Japan, not exclusively to the United States.

The radical changes Bocobo spoke of set in motion other "shifting surfaces." The response to American culture demanded a level of "solemnity"—an ability "to dig down beneath this loam, this delicate, shifting surface, in order to expose the rough and elemental granite of our native traits to the storms of trial and distress." The archaeological model proposed here by Bocobo was also developmental. What lay beneath the "shifting surface" were not "national" treasures but merely "native traits." The laboring of culture still had to be set in motion, and Bocobo would turn to Aquino for that work.

Bocobo located the push for Philippine independence in the intellectual trend of romantic nationalisms à la Ernest Renan ("a nation is a spiritual principle") and Johann Herder (*Volksgeist*). He saw the primary justification for political independence in a nation's ability to "express its individuality and thus contribute its genius to the culture of the world. The new Philippines must therefore dig down deep into the soul of the nation in order to bring out its beauty in music and folk dances, in literature and other forms of culture."[44] In this statement, Bocobo's nation has as its deepest resource a soul—a particular contribution, a humanistic and, therefore, thoroughly modern impulse and enterprise of will. Note Bocobo's emphasis on "expression," "individuality," and "genius." Laced in Bocobo's aspirations was the temper of his time—one no longer cued by dynasty, mysticism, or divinity. Notice as well how the "modern" is crafted using "old" materials—recovered folk dances, epic chants, and craft-making styles.

Bocobo advocated for most of the tenets of late-nineteenth-century patrician chauvinism—that women should submit to patriarchy and capital to purchase the security of "femininity." He invoked the fable of Spartan mothers of antiquity committing their sons to battle. If the son was killed on the battlefield, then the mother took comfort in a solemn repose, confident that her son had escaped ignominy. However, if he returned alive after having lost the battle, she would turn away from him and mourn in shame. Bocobo reinvigorated the role of "woman" as "mother of the nation" charged with raising patriots.[45]

As a university administrator, Bocobo also began to rethink the larger implications of the recent history of the Philippines' contact with the United States. In an unpublished essay, Bocobo drafted a balance sheet assessing this "special relationship." Here began his more pronounced critique of American culture, thundering against the secularizing influence from the West. "How little understood is the all-comprehensive and the far-flung significance of the phrase—'benevolent assimilation.'" Bocobo often identified what he considered to be deep pre-Hispanic and Spanish-era "traits" or aspects of what one might consider "character." In one of Bocobo's unpublished addresses, he wrote: "Woe unto that race which, by inadaptability, or by weakness, or by sheer fatality, cannot preserve its *native virtues,* and is dazzled by the glitter and the tinsel of new customs and ideas beyond its ken."[46]

In the rest of the address from which this quote was taken, Bocobo conflated "race" and "civilization." Both were subject to attack from "new thoughts and practices" or threatened by the possibility of being "dazzled by the glitter and the tinsel of the new customs" that could lead to destruction. Some of the "benefits" of American contact included the improvement of infrastructure in the form of sanitation systems, roads, bridges, and educational reform. But the "disadvantages" seemed to outweigh the benefits: "The moral stamina of the Filipino seems to give way under the impact of American influence." Other tendencies included Filipinos' swaying to the "frivolous," the "superficial," and the "material." Bocobo earned his informal title as the "gloomy dean" with comments such as, "It is thus that we can explain the craze and mania for dancing that has taken the young people off their feet. . . . [The] cabarets, those hotbeds of corruption and dissipation! They have become the social centers of many communities in the Philippines. All classes of society, the rich and the poor, the mighty and the humble, meet there."[47] He criticized other youthful indulgences, such as participating in beauty pageants, rooting for fighters at boxing matches, and pledging salaries to an automobile (he thought cars were a fad). But song and dance of a certain type provided much irritation.

Bocobo railed against the music of the American moderns when he wrote, "There is that intensely barbaric and primitive conglomeration of jarring and nerve-shattering sounds known as jazz, which America has brought here as something brand-new and up-to-date, and which has, therefore, created in the islands a kind of hallucination."[48] For Bocobo, "benevolent assimilation" was not simply the "practical" policies of statecraft: educational, medical, governmental, and infrastructural reform.

Bocobo lamented in the speech that "an elevating sense of the beautiful is disappearing."[49]

In an address titled "Filipino Contact with America," Bocobo had the following to say about colonial rule: "The result is that American education is turning out men and women who are worshipper[s] of Mammon who cannot guide the future citizens toward life at its best and fullest."[50] To combat the effects of "American education," Bocobo emphasized the need for a curriculum that possessed the force of religiosity and the explanatory currency of modern social science. His academic preparation courtesy of U.S. institutions exposed him to the leading models of sociological thinking. He referred often to conversations he had with Charles T. Loram, known for his work on developing educational systems in South Africa, on what should be the "best offering of the Filipino people to world culture." Bocobo wrote of culture as a gift that had yet to be delivered. What does it mean to establish the patrimony of a people who are not yet sovereign? "What distinct and permanent contribution can our country offer to the culture of the world? Every civilized nation must give of its best to human advancement in order not only to enrich the universal heritage of culture but also to deserve a worthy place in the history of mankind."[51] He encouraged the staging of musical concerts and the need to educate the public about Philippine music in order to "contribute their genius and spirit to international culture."[52]

With the formation of his Committee on Philippine Folk Songs and Dances in the fall of 1934 Bocobo's sponsorship would put in motion the ethnographic fieldwork necessary for this laboring of culture. The committee's efforts garnered media attention, and in the eyes of one reporter, Bocobo could find someone to share in his denunciation of American popular culture: "We have too long permitted the bright, artificial incandescence of jazz to bedim the homely but honest luster of our own native *kundiman* (love song). To use another metaphor: we have permitted the flotsam and jetsam of the current of events to bury or to push back into the quiet waters the golden nuggets of our spiritual heritage. There, far from the vital stream of our national existence, these are in danger of being lost and forgotten forever."[53] Again we see the familiar elements of the romantic nationalist: the lament of something being "lost," the external threat to guard against, and the spiritual principle that one must recover or to which one must return. The members of the committee included Francisco Santiago, chairman of the music conservatory at the University of the Philippines; Dr. Cecilio Lopez; the anthropologist Otley Beyer; and Francisca Reyes Tolentino (later Aquino), director of women's physical education. The field research team consisted of Aquino, the photographer

Ramon Tolentino, and the musician Antonino Buenaventura. During the summer months, the team traveled as far south as Sulu and throughout the Ilokos region. Along the way, they visited penal colonies, convent schools, and markets and "stayed in remote barrios while waiting for the extremely shy natives to make up their minds and sing or dance."[54] Many other older dancers and performers would perform only if the researchers bribed them with food or money.[55] On their return from the field, the committee members staged a special "U.P. Night" at the Carnival Auditorium. The evening's program emphasized ethnographic accuracy with the presentation of dances without a unifying storyline or narrative. Instead, here was an opportunity for some sectors of Manila's university, military, and political elite to engage the "folk" through the command of its research. Manila was the "center" to which the disparate ethnolinguistic groups would "return"—performatively, if not physically. Here was where performance *really* happened: under the hot lights of the stage in the context of the "national command."[56]

## *O Kikay!* On Inventing Culture

Francisca Reyes Aquino was trained not in dance but in physical education in the Philippines and at Boston's Sargent College. Founded in 1881 in Cambridge, Massachusetts, by the physician Dudley Allen Sargent, the school became a key institution in the promotion of physical education as a multidiscipline during the early part of the twentieth century. In 1929, the college joined Boston University. Along with her predecessors at Springfield College, founded in 1885 to train Young Men's Christian Association (YMCA) administrators and professionals in the application of the Humanics philosophy, Aquino introduced physical education to the Philippine public-school system and was charged with researching folk song and dance over a number of years. Aquino's work was characterized by her insistence on conducting fieldwork in the recovery of expressive forms. Extant writings by Aquino (few survived the Japanese occupation), along with oral histories of some of her contemporaries and students, support her famous insistence: "Let no one distort it under the guise of modernization. Leave the folk dances as they are."[57]

At the base of Aquino's work, though, is a melancholy strain. In the midst of concrete foundations being poured into the ground for Beaux Arts-inspired government buildings in Manila, screens erected for the city's movie houses, and shiny household appliances gleaned from the latest Sears Roebuck catalogue installed in the homes of the well-heeled, educators such as Bocobo and Aquino spoke to not only their ambitions but their anxieties. What was the price to pay for faces made up with Max Factor and Revlon, for bodies fitted for tuxedoes in tropical weather or patent-leather uppers, for minds that were thoroughly convinced of the authority of William Faulkner and Herman Melville to the exclusion of Philippine vernacular literary traditions and communities? Dance, music, and other forms of folk culture were researched not merely for entertainment but for a polity's rooting.

While most scholars of Philippine dance are correct to point out that Aquino was a founding scholar of folk dance, few link her contributions to the many curricular changes taking place in Philippine education during the U.S. colonial administration of the islands. The introduction of physical-education training constituted another aspect of a particular kind of disciplining of subjects. Scholars have pointed to specific technology deployed during the colonial administration—practices that involved prison systems, sanitation protocols, photographic techniques, and so on. To this we may add the discourses and material practices of physical education. The movement consisted of an approach to an integrated and emerging social science. The YMCA and its attendant philosophy of fusing attention paid to mind, body, and spirit would be crucial in signaling a change in colonial orders in the Philippines—from the Spanish, who paid little attention to physical education, to U.S. educators, who wrestled with the disciplining of subjects, especially after the Civil War. An investigation into physical education offers another dimension with which an "American culture" was challenging its notion of Victorian ideals, embracing newer forms of social relations and physical regimentation.[58] Aquino's work helped not only to cull a usable catalogue of movement, costume, song, and dance, but also to anthologize the first repertoire for the anticipated nation. Her several works have become the standard for folk-form research in the Philippines. In this section, I discern Aquino's nationalist ambitions from some of her works. I pay special attention to how anxieties over the health of women figured into the development of this discipline.

Aquino began collecting folk songs, dances, and games in 1924; this material resulted in her master's thesis, later published as *Philippine Folk Dances and Games* (1926). For several years after that, she worked with a team that included Antonino Buenaventura and Ramon P. Tolentino. This research team was sponsored by the President's Committee on Folk Songs and Dances at the University of the Philippines. As they traveled from village to village, they "collected [dances] directly from the old people in out-of-the-way regions who had performed them in their younger days, and from the students or trainees who came from remote places where such dances are still kept alive and practiced."[59]

In the introduction to the 1946 edition of Aquino's *Philippine National Dances*, Bienvenido M. Gonzalez, president of the University of the Philippines, wrote: "It has been truly said that the Philippines offers a unique field for the study of civilizations from the most primitive, as represented by the Negrito, through the various stages, to the present culture which bears the clear stamp of the West. One may observe evidence of these various stages in the dances that are characteristic of the different levels of culture found in the Philippines. Realizing that with the further impact of Western culture, *many of these indigenous dances would be lost or extensively modified,* [Aquino's research team] undertook the study of folk dances as she found them in the less developed regions of the Philippines."[60] Aquino's catalogue is far from being a guide to dance repertoire. Gonzalez points to its narrative function: Cultural heterogeneity is represented in a social hierarchy, from the "primitive" Negrito to the unnamed "present culture" displayed by "Western" Filipinos. And there it is again—this doubling of the "West." On the one hand, the West that may be associated with "advancement," "progress," or the "modern." On the other hand, the West threatens to erase or distort the performative figure of the "indigenous." By the conclusion of World War II, this narrative took hold—trained professionals rescued the "indigenous" through conscientious fieldwork. *Philippine National Dances* was a manual and not merely a catalogue. Its function was to engage teachers and for students to perform its contents. The volume contained annotations of fifty-four folk dances, including accompanying musical scores. Movements were carefully catalogued, and the work was illustrated in a studio setting as well as against outdoor scenery. Costumes were also described and illustrated in detail. Serafin Aquino, also a graduate of Springfield and the author of another early work on Filipino physical education, located the civic function of folk dance: "The work being done to collect Filipino folk dances and to preserve their authenticity for future generations deserves the support of every patriotic citizen."[61] For physical educators of the prewar era, the folk forms that Aquino and others recovered provided tangible evidence for the expression of a distinctly Philippine nationalism. Aquino understood the dances to be much more than entertainment; they were physical expressions of patriotism. The "Objectives of Teaching Philippine Folk Dances," according to Aquino, were "to foster patriotism and nationalism through the study of our dances. To arouse better appreciation of Philippine music and folk dances. To provide, through dancing, a healthful form of relaxation and recreation. To develop a graceful and rhythmic coordination of body movements that improve posture. To arouse further and keep the interest of our children in taking part in and enjoying our own dances. To preserve for posterity folk dances and music indigenous to the different regions of the Philippines. To demonstrate the growth of Filipino culture through the evolution of Philippine dances."[62]

Aquino's history with folk-dance research began with a rather simple request. In 1921, she was a student assistant at the University of the Philippines and was given the task of presenting a program of folk dance during the Manila Fiesta Carnival. Her initial research at the National Library yielded little material. Some apocryphal accounts tell of Aquino taking an aimless stroll in her Manila neighborhood of Tondo. She struck up a conversation with a group of women doing laundry and asked whether they knew any dances that their elders might have taught them. The laundrywomen called men nearby to serve as their partners. They gathered up props such as fans and handkerchiefs. Several days later, Aquino had recorded the first of hundreds of dances, the *cariñosa*.[63]

Her system of recording dances involved drawing arrows and stick diagrams for arm positions, writing descriptive text, and creating other movement cues. She also asked the men and women to hum the accompanying tunes.[64] In the summer of 1927, Bocobo directed Aquino to "go to the *barrios* and record our dances before they become extinct."[65] Her fieldwork involved interviews with the performers and townsfolk, as well as "coaxing the most uncooperative" villagers. By 1934, Bocobo's advisory committee on folk dances and songs included Aquino (responsible for transcribing and notating the dances), Ramon Tolentino (who photographed the dances and locations), and Antonino Buenaventura (musical arranger and composer). Their research concluded in 1938.[66] The year before, with the formation of the University of the Philippines Folk Song and Dance Society, composed largely of Aquino's students, Bocobo had arranged for a recital and lectures for interested teachers and students. Many saw this period as the "beginning of renewed interest in folk dancing," while others "were indifferent and antagonistic toward folk dancing."[67] Most likely, this was so because of the increasing generational divide between students and teachers in Manila. The folk-dance research was one generation's answer to the importation of American jazz, music, cinema, literature, vaudeville, comedy, and other expressive forms of culture.[68]

The late 1930s also marked the intensification of folk dance as part of the physical-education program developed by U.S. educators. Filipino folk dances became part of playground demonstrations, athletic meets, and other schoolwide events. In 1945, with the conclusion of World War II, Aquino reconstituted her group as the Filipiniana Dance Troupe, supported in large part by the U.S. military. In 1947, Francisca Reyes Tolentino married Serafin Aquino, who was then the secretary-treasurer of the

Philippine Amateur Athletic Federation. Her postwar work included the resumption of her role as a dance educator with the founding the Philippine Folk Dance Society. With this latest incarnation of the troupe, Aquino mounted a defense not only against the encroachment of U.S. popular cultural forms, but increasingly against the stylization of native folk forms from a younger cohort of Filipino choreographers and musicians. Aquino's concern marked the next set of debates for the new post–World War II generation of dancers. Her Sunday clinics became clearinghouses for teachers and others interested in supporting an interpretation of an "authentic" expression of Filipino dance. One went to her to stay close to the grassroots, it was claimed. Many of Aquino's students would also say that you went to the Bayanihan if you wanted a "show." After having been granted a series of national awards for her work on folk dance, Aquino commented: "What matters now is for every Filipino to protect our tradition and let no one distort it under the guise of modernization. Leave the folk dances as they are. Heritage must not be sacrificed for progress."[69] In the 1930s, Aquino prepared her students with choreography that could act as a bulwark against American popular culture. Thirty years later, she defended that work against those who had stylized the national repertoire beyond her ability to recognize it.

## Physical Education

Aquino's training at the Sargent School in Boston from 1929 to 1931 exposed her to the field of physical education. Part of the story also involves a more general concern for the bodies of the young in a time of demographic shifts, the movement from rural homesteads to urban areas, the effects of hours of sitting in classrooms, and the anxieties over women's bodies throughout this period. From the late nineteenth century to the early 1930s, one million Asians and more than thirty-five million Eastern and Southern Europeans migrated to the United States.[70] The impact that this kind of settlement would have on cities such as New York, Philadelphia, and Chicago would be felt in everything from the mushrooming of multiethnic, multilingual, and multireligious trade-union campaigns to race riots and increased demand on cities' scarce resources. Bodies were in motion across the world, seeking jobs, education, and settlement—usually without the benefit of translators. But the worry that arose about the bodies of women and children during this time also reflected general concern about what effects industrialism—the increasingly difficult work environments—would have on ordinary folks.[71]

Physical training and the cultivation of the human body can be traced to a longer institutional history that goes back at least two generations. Sargent College and the International YMCA Training College in Springfield, Massachusetts, were only two of the leading centers of their kind. The American Association for the Advancement of Physical Education was organized in 1885. Its aim was both to theorize the cultivation of the human body and to establish physical education as a professional domain. This new profession began its analysis of physical training systems suitable for use in public schools.[72] A leading figure in the field, Luther Halsey Gulick, director of physical training in New York City schools in 1903, was also editor of the *American Physical Education Review.* He streamlined various physical education training systems and expanded course offerings with after-school activities. Girls' dance was a key feature of his program. In 1905, Gulick recruited Elizabeth Burchenal from Teachers College to assist him in developing the Girls' Branch of the Public Schools Athletic League. As the dance scholar and historian Linda Tomko notes, Gulick's and Burchenal's efforts demonstrated that "folk-dancing provided a flexible practice for struggling with, for contesting, issues of gender, ethnicity, and social order." Burchenal's Girls' Branch introduced folk dancing to redress the squalor of urban living spaces and public schools. Without play and dance, young bodies were subjected to muscular and respiratory ailments. The reforms offered by Burchenal and Gulick could be read as part of the more formal Progressive-era criticism of urban life: "The inadequate, unequal distribution of fundamental resources of sunlight, air, and square footage for safe play motivated several contemporary reform efforts in New York City."[73]

U.S. physical education, when compared with other nation's systems, expressed some unique dimensions. It was less authoritarian than Swedish calisthenics and less costly than German training programs, which required expensive equipment. But most, if not all, "national systems" shared an attitude regarding the relationship of bodily discipline to the health of the "body politic." Tomko's work can be used to push a related point: that an ideological function is being served in the subjectification of dance. "The conduct of a folk-dance, once learned, could remain in the hands and feet of the girls dancing it, with memory of sequence and musical cues from the accompanying score supplying the 'directives.'"[74]

While several writers championed the involvement of women in sports and other physical activities at the start of the twentieth century, their primary motivation stemmed from the notion that such activity would make women better fit as wives and mothers. Historians focused on these institutions could see the link between a well-managed gymnasium and the biological future of the nation. By the beginning of the twentieth century, physical education had developed from the addition of gymnastic exercises to a more formal profession whose structure was increasingly defined in a credentialized hierarchy: graduate training, the construction of facilities devoted exclusively to physical education, and the establishment of journals, organizations, and research. The American Physical Education Association announced the publication of the *American Physical Education Review* in 1895, with the journal's contributors arguing that the focus of physical education needed widening and that trained professionals were necessary.[75]

Sports and games also became more popular on college campuses. However, the specialized training required for physical education developed without professional mentorship. Women at Vassar swam, engaged in crewing, and played baseball, tennis, and basketball with only tacit support for these sports from the college. However, the professionals found it difficult to keep the attention of their students on the repetitive discipline of physical training. While interest in these and other sports grew, the demand for gymnastic drills dropped. Professionals reassessed the situation and began to pay greater attention to organizing the physical education curriculum more effectively. The question was not how to compete with the more popular activities but how to incorporate them into the college's regimen of physical education. Mary Mullet wrote in the *Ladies' Home Journal* that the benefits of physical education translated into a stronger and healthier housewife who would be "perfectly able to toy with a broom and amply able to knead the daily bread."[76]

Physical education in the Philippines was a twentieth-century reform, one of the many that marks the breach between Spanish colonial rule and U.S. colonial "tutelage." There were at least two anchors for Filipino physical education. The first involved the revisionist histories purported by Filipino nationalists; the second came from white male YMCA educators based in Manila immediately after the U.S.–Philippine War. The nationalist historians imagined a romantic link between educational reform and a patriotic historiography, with Rizal understood as an exemplary figure of the "new Filipino body." They also understood the Spanish as being hardly interested in physical movement. Filipino bodies, crudely put, were God's property, and the colonized, whose souls were targeted for conversion, labored for the crown and the cross but never for themselves—as in self-gratification or pleasure. Rizal's work, written during his study and leisure time in European cultural centers such as Paris, Barcelona, Madrid, Berlin, and Geneva, displays a youthful, elite colonial male's penchant for bourgeois recreation. This included the muscular play of fencing, boxing, equestrianship, and gymnastics. Rizal's cohort wrote extensively about the reform of education institutions, advancing in their critiques what they perceived as the harm of Spanish clerical mysticism, superstition-laden ritual, and educational backwardness. Rizal's program for a new university—conceived during his exile in Dapitan—involved calisthenics, gymnastics, and other physical activity. To challenge the authority of the friars also meant to claim for themselves new bodies.

By the time of the majority of Aquino's writings, and certainly by the time her professional accomplishments had led to the nationalization of a distinctly Filipino folk-form repertoire, physical education as a discipline had been initially defined and shaped primarily by U.S.-trained, white physical educators. While the revisionists insisted on the romantic links to Rizal and a heroic nationalist historiography, it is the cohort of educators trained at the YMCA's Springfield College in Massachusetts who set the parameters for physical education in the Philippines. This does not seem to be a contentious point raised by the revisionists; it is merely a difference registered to allow revisionists to lay claim to a "pre-American" historiography.

What kind of discourse was physical education in the Philippines during U.S. colonization? Who were its authors? We turn to the birthplace of basketball: Springfield, Massachusetts, home to the International YMCA College. Founded as a school for Christian workers in 1885, it was also known as the YMCA Training School. It did not adopt the name Springfield College until after 1953. It was the self-described epicenter of the Humanics philosophy, an educational praxis stressing the integration of "mind, body, and soul." Four graduation theses written between 1916 and 1922 by Harry L. Kingman, Edward Mazurkiewicz, George Goss, and Serafin Aquino established an initial vocabulary for this second foundation of physical education in the Philippines.[77] Kingman's thesis highlighted the YMCA's Christian-centered service inflected with Western paternalism. YMCA trainers understood physical education's ability to provide access to the educated classes in several countries, developing a "friendly footing [with] the student population." Kingman often quoted the physical educator Dr. J. H. Gray, noting how such training was actually an evangelical movement married to the scientific premise of the disciplines of biology and medicine: "God has distinctly given this movement His approval and put His guiding hand upon it, and . . . therefore it should be utilized as an additional method or instrument for the upbuilding and extension of His Kingdom in the missionary enterprise. Does it not logically fit into the modern conception of religion—a religion that must save the whole man in this life as well as the life to come? Does it not coincide with modern scientific research which says that a man is an entity, and that body, mind and spirit are one, and not divisions antagonistic to one another or separated into water-tight compartments?"[78] In his comparative study of the YMCA's efforts in various parts of the non-white world, Kingman believed that it was possible to understand how climate affected physical training. Most of the study relied on observation, attributing native behavior and attitudes toward play, organized sports, and other forms of physical training to approximated notions of "culture." For example, Kingman's understanding of physical cultures in India was grounded in his perception of the "spirit of asceticism," which he claimed favored "the destroying of the body for the supposed glorifying of the soul." Consider also one of his observations on Latin America: "[Those of] Spanish blood are too selfish and indolent and their traditions are too deep set, to allow them to adopt a game that requires rigor or cooperation."[79] Yet for all his attention to the comparative differences in climate, Kingman could make no general claim for its relation to physical exertion. What Kingman was looking for, however, was not simply the presence of physical activity, but the outlines of "national games," to be generated by "a definite system of physical education": "Civilization and national development go hand in hand with the organizing and accepting of more elaborate forms and systems of physical education, and the civilization and forward progress of any nation can be pretty well measured by her national games, amusements and forms of exercise."[80]

Some of the first forms of U.S.-style physical activity were mostly accidental. Members of the Army YMCA conducted events and games for the soldiers without the supervision of a physical director, special equipment, or facilities. Complicating any effort to make this activity a mass form was the fact that several thousand U.S. soldiers were scattered throughout the islands, although many were stationed at Fort McKinley, in Rizal Province. Taking a break from the ongoing combat between the native population and the Spanish, U.S. soldiers played a game of baseball in 1899. Years later, one recalled how white men performed for their brown counterparts: "[Soldiers] dug out of their old kit bags, old dilapidated mitts, balls, and . . . baseball bats, [and] proceeded to thoroughly enjoy themselves in our great national game of baseball. One can picture the evident amazement that must have swept the faces of the Filipino youth who were privileged to witness, to them, the marvelously skillful manipulation of the ball from fielder to fielder."[81] Other writers would wax romantically about the importation of U.S. teachers, more popularly known as the "Thomasites": "These splendid specimens of our manhood and womanhood were then sent into every nook and corner to teach Filipino youth our language and to educate them so that in time they could shape the destiny of their country."[82] This trope of the pioneer teacher traveling to a faraway corner of the Earth to teach "little brown brothers" served as a powerful metaphor for the ongoing missionary enterprise. The physical educator Edward Mazurkiewicz put it in the following terms: "Of the romance of this true missionary effort on the part of the American 'Maestros and Maestras.' None of the comforts of ice, or of electrically driven fans were theirs; running the dangers of tropical diseases, for the present efficient Board of Health was only in its infancy; without the saving balm of companionship with their own kind, for they often operated alone, the only white persons for miles; under such conditions and handicaps did that brave and courageous group of teachers labor that our promises to our 'little brown brethren' might be fulfilled."[83]

Athletics proved useful in coaxing the young into play, and therefore into American trust, setting the stage for the expansion and formalization of physical education.[84] Under the direction of the U.S. Army and Navy Departments, a local YMCA was founded in Manila in 1905. Three years and forty thousand dollars later, a capital campaign funded an association building and gymnasium (whose property encompassed eight acres). Manila proved to be the key site for this work. It possessed a workable infrastructure for the YMCA's needs, which included graded streets, sewage and water systems, concrete buildings, churches, and homes servicing a robust and quickly urbanizing population of three hundred thousand. However, the initial group served by this association building would be ten thousand young men, more than half of whom were from the United States. Elwood Brown, the first physical director sent by the YMCA to the Philippines, arrived in 1911, signaling the most drastic change for the field. The first thing he noticed was the work that needed to be done with a gymnasium without a running track, equipment needs, and the raising of a membership base. He began by holding gymnasium classes mostly for U.S. businessmen or other professionals. The special Business Men's Class ran all year, three times a week, with an attendance of forty. Within the first year of Brown's operation, the gymnasium's attendance rose to more than eleven thousand a year, with at least two thousand eight hundred playing tennis. When other activities were included, such as bowling, swimming, handball, baseball, and basketball, the department's total attendance grew to more than twenty thousand. Gymnasiums, swimming pools, weight-lifting rooms, and tennis and basketball courts were busy. Businessmen, students, government workers, and private clubs had been organized into volleyball teams, baseball leagues, and tennis teams. The city's sports arenas and courts were packed with the overflow of spectators, some nearing the thousands. "Athletics and play have taken the Philippines by storm. It is longer a question of promotion, but one of direction and control." The Bureau of Education counted twenty-nine thousand girls organized into uniformed indoor baseball teams. That number doubled for boys playing the same sport.[85] These activities were largely segregated. Filipinos did not have access to their own facilities until their own city structure was built in January 1913. That same year, six Filipinos were trained as physical directors. Brown's work had produced some very tangible results for the YMCA's campaigns: the training of Filipinos in key administrative positions; the large participation of Americans and Filipinos in various activities; and the construction of several association buildings. But it would not be until Brown's visit to the hilltop summer capital of Baguio at the request of Governor-General William Cameron Forbes to organize summer athletic events that the marriage between the YMCA's work and the colonial government's policies would take place.

Brown was tapped to organize summer sporting events for the U.S. government employees. Those events included football games between rival colleges, as well as volleyball tournaments pitting Filipino teams marked the "Grays" against the "Blues" who represented the Bureaus of Education and the Executive, respectively. Thousands of fans raised a clamor from the sidelines with musical instruments, tin cans, and sheets of iron. Forbes' post-game commentary lauded the work: After having worked seven years in the Philippines, he observed that "the Filipino is extremely ready to take hold—this applies not only to the young men but also to the young women. I have a picture of a girls' baseball team which was organized somewhere in Luzon, and I have seen many places where the girls play basketball and tennis. I shall be very pleased to see the successful culmination of your plans for the construction of a building or buildings by your Association for use by Filipinos."[86]

Physical directors were spread out among various association offices throughout the Philippines, China, India, Japan, and Latin America—approximately a dozen primary instructors, not including the several native instructors being trained at that time. Also, YMCA boosters could boast of buildings and gymnasiums in as Peking (Beijing), Shanghai, Foo Chow (Fuzhou), Canton (Guangzhou), Hong Kong, Manila, Kyoto, Kobe, Yokohama, and several others in Mexico and India as more proof of a movement in need of dedicated physical educators from the United States. This phase of the YMCA's involvement in the Philippines would be marked by Brown's efforts to streamline a national physical training program.[87]

The Bureau of Education's director started an effort to organize athletic associations, which up to that point had been growing but largely under-coordinated. The key was to centralize authority in the bureau;

establish clear lines of authority, decision making, and curriculum planning; and map the organization of physical education in the Philippines. Prior to this, several interprovincial athletic associations had been formed, such as the Southern Luzon Athletic Association (1904), the Central Luzon Athletic Association (1908), the Manila Interscholastic Athletic Association (1909), the Visayan Athletic Association (1910), the Ilocano Athletic Association (1910), and the Southern Tagalog Athletic Association (1910). This burgeoning network of associations, private clubs, and school tournaments would claim to reach nearly every pupil in the public-school system while initiating a ranking system from novice to expert. The Bureau of Education reported rates of more than 95 percent of its students engaged in some game or sport on a regular basis. Legislative support came in the form of creating a minimum area for standard school sites, both in the central urban areas (10,000 square meters) and for outlying barrio schools (5,000 square meters). Brown also took credit for founding the Philippine Amateur Athletic Association (PAAA), as well as for organizing the Far Eastern Athletic Association (FEAA). These two associations—one focused on domestic and the other on international arenas—defined the most sophisticated elaboration of physical education as a national system for the Philippines. Brown's efforts did more to centralize Manila's role in the administration of this movement, as well as to more closely align the YMCA's, many religious communities', and the colonial government's interests in the administration of the Philippines.[88]

One of the issues to emerge from the growing movement for physical education in the Philippines was the need to train Filipinos to fill the positions that Brown and others held. The YMCA funded the education of a handful of Filipinos, among them Serafin Aquino. His early work marked a departure from the earlier writings of Kingman, Mazurkiewicz, and Goss. Less a booster for the YMCA and more fully realized as a native administrator under American colonial rule, Aquino's work was an example of the "Filipinization" of the discourse of physical education.

Serafin Aquino's graduation thesis was written for both U.S. and Philippine audiences. The former, according to Aquino, did not know much about "the play-life of the Filipino people."[89] But audiences in the Philippines—and here he was largely targeting the anticipated ranks of native physical educators like himself—had a different need for understanding physical education. "Children, in the public schools of the Philippines, in adapting and using the foreign and modern games, are fast forgetting their own. They have games and dances which, with slight modification to suit present conditions, will give the same amount of physical exercise and recreation. Why not use and preserve them for future generations?"[90]

Aquino's statements here are some of the first indications of how a generational need was identified: Physical education was necessary for "our" young folks, marking the internalized and adapted discipline of physical education. His study analyzed five hundred questionnaires completed by teachers. He was less interested in the games imported by Americans to the Philippines than in what kinds of games the students brought with them to the playground. Aquino's assumption took physical-education instruction further by marrying colonially structured pedagogy with the familiarity of native cultural forms.

Between 1918 and 1919, five government-sponsored students from the Philippines were sent to YMCA colleges in Springfield, Massachusetts, and Chicago for training in physical education. Aquino credited the colonial government with improving the educational levels of Filipino students and with providing a structured environment for physical education. The elaborate network of tournaments and events coordinated by Brown consisted of interprovincial competitors to advance through interscholastic meets. The most successful of these athletes would narrow to compete for positions at the Philippine Carnival and the Far East Olympic Games. Serafin Aquino lauded the campaign of bodily discipline. As one of the *pensionados* being trained by the Americans, he witnessed the changes in the youth of his home; they became a "new people": "In a comparatively short period of time, the physical education program of the Philippine Bureau of Education has been productive of good results. It has inculcated in the minds of the Filipinos the idea of right living, proper and nourishing foods, and good systematic forms of exercise. Twenty years ago the Filipinos were undersized, undernourished and disease-ridden. *Today, anyone can look at the Filipino children and realize that a new people, actually is in process of development.* . . . [S]chool athletics have given the young Filipinos the conception of good sportsmanship, sense of humor, moral stamina, self-control, regularity of life, and the healthful habit of play and recreation."[91]

Aquino's study presented several unpublished games that were popular throughout the Philippines. It described games suitable for playgrounds, games that involved small numbers of students, and games that were targeted to children from grade school through high school. Schoolroom games were also covered. For example, the *sungka,* Aquino wrote, has an ancient history, traveling through Africa and Asia. Here the discourse of physical education drastically changed with the publication of Serafin Aquino's material on folk dances. A photograph opens one of the sections of the master's thesis. It features hundreds of young girls arranged on a large, grassy courtyard. They all face in the same direction—toward a large building whose central entrance is accessed by a grand stairway. They stand akimbo at arm's length from each other. They await instruction from their teachers—men dressed in white suits and straw hats. They stand at attention in block formations while hundreds more watch from the sidelines. They are dancing the *cariñosa*. The girls wear white skirts hemmed past the knee, with white stockings and some sort of headdress. They are in the fourth grade. It is Manila's Annual Playground Demonstration day.

One of the published dances that Aquino included is the "Igorot Dance Step," which had been previously documented in the anthropologist Albert E. Jenks's comprehensive political, economic, and religious study *The Bontoc Igorot* (1905). Aquino also made use of other ethnological surveys undertaken by U.S. scholars, as well as the Philippine census of 1903, to document several other dances. It would not be until the publication of Francisca Reyes Aquino's thorough system of cataloging several hundred more dances that the term "national" would be historically appropriate to use. Serafin Aquino's thesis provided the link between the largely masculine-driven enterprise of physical-education reform in the Philippines and the anticipated turn toward folk forms (song, dance, costume) studied by Francisca Reyes Aquino.

Serafin Aquino's work, soon followed by the more detailed, ethnographically based, published writings of Francisco Reyes Aquino, shifted the historiographical roots of physical education away from the missionary enterprise of the YMCA and toward a nationalist orientation. The generation to follow these educators and athletes, Filipino educators trained after World World II, built on that nationalist historiography, first by emphasizing that the history of physical education did not begin with U.S. colonization. Rather, their more inclusive and broader definition recognized activity that was incidental to ancient life patterns, such as planting, fishing, hunting, tree climbing, tool and weapon making, and boat and shelter making.[92]

These nationalists turned to Spanish-language materials as far back as the seventeenth century, to Antonio de Morga's chronicle *Sucesos de las Islas Filipinas,* mining its pages for descriptions of the skills of hunters, forms of play, and ritual dance. Other documents dating to the early thirteenth century also held accounts of spectacular feats of physical prowess—catching fast-moving deer on hunts, lifting massive logs without aid, or skillfully targeting prey as an archer. And while Bocobo's biographer Celia Bocobo Olivar pointed to the general lack of physical training offered to the natives during Spanish colonial rule, Regino Ylanan and Carmen Wilson Ylanan linked José Rizal's recollections of his gymnastics classes at the Jesuit Ateneo Municipal de Manila to the eventual "progressive" reforms instituted by Americans. In the main, however, physical education was the province of the elite until the end of Spanish rule. In 1863, Spaniards established a normal school for men in Manila. By 1893, the normal school had granted permission to train natives for positions as teachers; one of the graduation requirements was gymnastics. Soon to follow was the hiring of a gymnastic teacher for four hundred pesos a year. In the last decade of the nineteenth century, Spanish authorities established a Superior Normal School for female teachers. Among the graduation requirements, a "room gymnastics" course. Rizal figured in this nationalist historiography with his plan for a *Colegio Moderno* in Hong Kong. His exposure to the gymnasiums of Europe convinced him of the benefits of activities such Swedish calisthenics, swimming, fencing, equestrian sports, and dance.[93]

The U.S. period starting with the establishment of a civilian government in 1901 and ending with the creation of the commonwealth in 1935 would be referred to by nationalist physical educators as the "golden age" of sports in the Philippines. In 1911, the Bureau of Education published the *Athletic Handbook,* designed to "systematize and give direction to physical instruction." By 1920, physical education was required in the public schools but was not counted in a student's grade-point average. To advance from the fourth grade, students had to score at least a 75 percent in the subject. Physical education was not averaged into a student's overall grade-point average until 1937. That year marked the point when physical education became a curricular subject in the public school.[94] Several Springfield graduates, *pensionados* sent in 1918 and 1919, including Regino Ylanan, Candido Bartolome, and Geronimo Suva, were appointed physical directors within the university system. In 1921, the university's Board of Regents created the Department of Physical Education. Francisca Reyes Aquino was sent to Sargent College in 1929. This department was divided into a men's and women's section. Francisca Reyes Aquino served as director of women's physical education from 1935 to 1940. Aquino's work on folkdance and games became a cornerstone of the nation's curriculum.[95]

## Composing the Nation

Francisca Reyes Aquino's work on folk forms, while grounded in and modified from U.S. discourses about the training of the body, harnessed another powerful stream in the construction of a nationalist aesthetic during the 1920s and 1930s—a resurgence in attention to the relationship between nationalism and musical repertoire. Filipino composers drew several cues from the works of critics, composers, and other performers based in locales such as Eastern Europe, Russia, Norway, and England, and in the works of the Czechoslovakian composer Bedrich Smetana, the Russian critic Vladimir Stasov, the Norwegian composer Edvard Grieg, the English folklorist Ralph Vaughan Williams, and others. Their music referred to the "blood," or a national music's "spiritual principle," and as owing more to the inexplicability of primordialism than to bourgeois culture's "vulgar sciences."[96]

The composer widely known for championing folklorism and the development of a "national style" is Béla Bartók (1881–1945). Trained in ethnomusicology and a tireless chronicler of folk music, he, along with his longtime collaborator Zoltán Kodály (1882–1967), collected thousands of folk tunes from his native Hungary, as well as from Turkey, Serbia, Romania, and North Africa. He signaled this turn toward folk forms as part of a more general cultural crisis among European composers working at the turn of the century. Hoping to find refuge from the claim that nineteenth-century "Romanticism" was leading nowhere, Bartók recognized the wealth in "peasant music," a resource that required *transformation*: "In my opinion, the effects of peasant music cannot be deep and permanent unless this music is studied in the country as part of a life shared with the peasant. It is not enough to study it as it is stored up in museums. It is the character of peasant music, indescribable in words, that must find its way into our music. It must be pervaded by the very atmosphere of peasant culture. Peasant motives (or imitations of such motives) will only lend our music some new ornaments; nothing more. The question is, what are the ways in which peasant music is taken over and becomes transmuted into modern music?"[97] Bartók wondered whether melodies should remain largely "true" to original rhythms and vocalizations while harmonies and accompaniments were allowed to take more creative liberties. Or should it be the other way around?

Filipinos working toward the establishment of folk forms—like Francisca Reyes Aquino and the nationalist composer Antonino Buenaventura—asked similar questions of their own repertoires. Throughout the "American period," composers like Buenaventura featured the national temper in their compositional styles Buenaventura took up his father's passion for music. His father was a military bandleader during the Spanish regime. Buenaventura's musical training started in the elementary grades. The first pieces he wrote were for a small orchestra made up mostly of friends banging on improvised tin or wooden instruments. His advanced training at the University of the Philippines in composition and conducting would place him under the tutelage of major figures in the music scene at the time. Upon his graduation from the university in 1929, he was hired as an instructor at the Conservatory of Music. In 1934 he was selected to join

Bocobo's Committee on Folk Songs and Dances. Notice how native elements are crafted for a national project. "My raw materials are everything that is Filipino. But mine is not regional in inspiration," said Buenaventura. "It's the Filipino spirit as a whole which I try to capture."[98]

The jazz and film composer Miguel Velarde Jr. is known for his popular "Dahil Sa Iyo (Because of You)," translated into English, Spanish, Japanese, Chinese, and local dialects. Born in 1913 and the son of a doctor, Velarde enrolled at the University of the Philippines medical school, which he did not find to his liking. He spent the afternoons at a local radio station. After a confrontation with his father, and after consolation from his mother, Velarde financed his own studies in music as a bus conductor. The musical training in school consisted of traditional, Western-based harmony and composition in the classical European idiom, but he found himself drawn to the American jazz music of Cole Porter and Irving Berlin. The job with the radio station would allow Velarde to perform his compositions over the air. He also taught jazz piano to several students. Business rolled in, and soon he was earning a living as a professional musician. With his own jazz band, the Mike Velarde Jazztocrats, he continued his success in the realm of the emerging Filipino film trade. He wrote songs for the movies as well as complete film scores. "I went into a series of experiments in my endeavor to discover a design which would project my musical messages," wrote Velarde. "My formula was first, be direct to the point. Second, inject the proper feeling. And third, convey ideas in the simple idiom of the masses. My motto, of course, was 'Think Filipino, write Filipino, and sound Filipino.'"[99] Most of his compositions were written largely in the vein of American popular songs. One of the more popular results of this approach was "Dahil Sa Iyo," sung by Rogelio de la Rosa, in the 1938 film *Bituing Marikit.* His film works would encompass the years 1935 to 1962.[100] Composers and performers like Velarde and Buenaventura remind us that Filipino musicians inherited a long Western tradition of imagining in national terms. Although these artists represented a range of musical tastes and idioms, both witnessed and were influenced by the more general movement in defining a distinctly Filipino national culture as directed by its Manila-based luminaries.[101]

THE WORK OF BOCOBO AND AQUINO is important for two reasons. First, this genealogy of folkloric forms and nationalism considers how educators in Manila invented and organized icons and symbols from the past to confer a unified national identity on their students. In anticipating the future of the Philippine nation during the commonwealth period, Boboco and Aquino demonstrated what Karl Marx warned in the

*Eighteenth Brumaire*: "Just when they seem engaged in revolutionising themselves and things, in creating something entirely new, precisely in such periods of revolutionary crisis they anxiously conjure up the spirits of the past to their service and borrow from them names, battle cries and costumes in order to present the new scene of world history in this time-honored disguise and this borrowed language."[102] The "new" Philippine nation was being choreographed by the patrician children of the *ilustrado* class. The inheritors of elite liberal tradition attempted to resolve the "incomplete" revolutions that concluded the nineteenth century.[103] Recall here Victor Turner's etymology of performance as the proper finale of an experience and that the romantic nationalists Bocobo and Aquino crafted the repertoire that would befit a sovereign body. Second, their invention of tradition was precisely what survived so many generations later as a repertoire that appeared to be anything but invented—timeless, unchanging, and authentically delivered from a distant past. Instead of dances and music emerging from a mystified primordial history, the national performance repertoire was bribed and cajoled into existence by anxious educators, nervous nationalists, and ambitious political sponsors. In the next chapter, I turn my attention to how a new generation of educators and artists in Manila extended Bocobo's and Aquino's work from the classroom and onto the international stage. With this new postwar choreography tightly identified with the Philippine nation, how would the repertoire play far from home?

# 2 "Take It from the People"

## *Dancing Diplomats and Cultural Authenticity (Brussels, 1958)*

*The Philippines, a Westernized Asian nation anchored by the accident of geography amidst powerful Asian neighbors, linked to the West by treaties and to Asia by fear of what the future would bring, would be in the awkward position of having to carry water on both shoulders, would have to talk Right to keep faith with Washington and to act Left to prove that she was still free in her heart and understood the language of her disinherited Asian brothers.*

—Richard Wright

## "More European than Asian"

A young university-trained musical scholar and composer based in Manila traveled with her fledgling dance company to Dacca in the winter of 1954 to perform at an international festival. Most of those taking the trip—six dancers and a guitarist—were students from the Philippine Women's University. The troupe joined companies from other countries, including Burma, Malaysia, Thailand, Indonesia, and Pakistan. Forty thousand attendees took in more than thirty-five shows. But not everything went as smoothly as planned, as the musical director and her students were accustomed to using a piano for accompaniment. The festival's organizers apologized for not having one available, and the dance troupe made do with a guitar. At first blush, the request for a piano seemed innocent enough. Yet it brought into relief a gulf between what Filipinos took for granted in their performance practice and what "outsiders" to that culture deemed "authentic."[1] The artistic directors found themselves protecting their young dancers from the festival's criticism. "What after all, would a Western instrument be doing in an Asian festival?" wondered one of the troupe's artistic directors. The dancers found that the use of the guitar was "frowned upon as being more European than Asian."[2] According to José

Lardizabal, the group's technical director, "It dawned on Dean [Lucrecia] Kasilag [the troupe's musical director] how heavily Western the look and sound of the Philippine presentation was in comparison with those of other Asian participants. By the time the festival ended, the shock of realization had spread to all the members of the delegation. They were faced with an *identity* crisis; among their fellow Asians, they were the outsiders. The delegates came home with a singular resolve: to probe deeper into *authentic* Filipino cultural heritage."[3] Kasilag offered her own oblique defense by stating, "Our dances and music surely impressed the audiences as unmistakably showing the influence of Western culture, not strange at all considering the curious mixture of influences in our nation's present-day civilization."[4] For Kasilag, a nation *possesses* civilization, evidence of a cosmopolitan and thoroughly modern sensibility. "[T]he Philippines—publicized as the land of happy, lively and delightful people—was represented by thirty-five folk dances, the *kundiman* [a native song form], and folk songs. The variety of folk dances ranged from the regional to the tribal and occupational." Kasilag admitted that her "first mistake was to ask for a piano to accompany the dancers—as was the practice back home."[5] The entire delegation recognized the urgency to deepen the research efforts. The young company found that other nations were also coming to their own conclusions concerning Asian nationalism in the era of decolonization and their relation to the West.[6]

In the years after World War II, the Philippines emerged as a nominally sovereign republic, and Manila's elites would not only continue to be the political and economic beneficiaries of a renewed relationship with Washington, but they would also continue to define the nation's cultural discourses. The aesthetic claims to an authentic Philippine performing subject paralleled, if not reinforced, the political tenor of the day. The quashing of the Hukbong Mapagpalaya sa Bayan (Huk) Rebellion; the undercutting of dissenters such as Claro Recto; and more broadly, the incorporation of the Philippines within the orbit of U.S. influence—all were obliquely buttressed by a centralized cultural nationalism from above that favored the progressive (i.e., "liberal") narration from the ethnically "uncivilized" to the nationally disciplined "Filipino," from the provincial margins to the metropolitan center.[7] The left was pushed to the margin, its impulses and challenges contained, and, in several instances, reorganized to legitimize the reconsolidation of native elite rule.

In the previous chapter, I examined how Manila's educators anxiously invented a national performance repertoire, anticipated the transition from colony to commonwealth to nation, and offered their students as surrogates for a nation-to-be. Pilipino Cultural Night organizers, working from the late 1970s to the present, bent the national repertoire to meet the needs and desires of students based in the United States. In doing so, they also crafted theatrical scenarios that staged their own presence in both U.S. and Philippine histories. These students did not create the repertoire; instead, they reinterpreted the Bayanihan's work. Indeed, the PCN performers of the 1980s have assumed the Bayanihan to be a synonym for Philippine culture itself, "often the first and only resource."[8] Yet the work by Jorge Bocobo and Francisca Reyes Aquino has largely been overshadowed by the Bayanihan's international career. This chapter focuses on the work of university faculty in Manila and their political sponsors of the 1950s and 1960s, the generation that followed the work of Bocobo and Aquino. I continue an investigation into the "special relationship" between the politics of nationalism and the development of performance repertoire that does more than reflect the interests of elites. How did elites construct a sense of themselves as Filipinos in light of the chaos and promise of Asian and other cultural nationalisms beckoning in Indonesia, Indochina, China, India, and Egypt? How was the construction of such identities both a political as well as a cultural project?[9]

We find part of the answers to these questions when we revisit the career of the Bayanihan. I rely on published writings by the troupe's artistic directors and reconstruct the chorus of criticism during the height of their career. Understanding how the Bayanihan came into existence—especially given the political history of the Philippines, with which it was intrinsically a part—helps to illuminate how culture anticipates and reinforces social and political aspirations. The Bayanihan's career demonstrates how culture was mobilized by a new generation of Filipinos emerging from the destruction of the archipelago during World War II amid the uncertainty of the region's aspirations for national liberation and cultural nationalism.[10] A post–World War II generation of educators in Manila built on Bocobo's and Aquino's work by "taking it from the people"—movements, inspiration, and authority—while further stylizing the folkloric for the new global tempo and acting as surrogates for a Philippine sovereign nation.

## The American and Philippine Half-Century

Two forces structure the political history of the Philippines in the post–World War II era: incorporation and independence. I refer to analyses of U.S. foreign policy after World War II in Asia—including, but not limited to, the anchoring of the Asian regional economy in Japan (committed to headquartering financial operations and the development of heavy industrialization and modernization) and the subsequent divisions of labor throughout Southeast Asia for the production of smaller commodities. This postwar story of incorporation (i.e., more thoroughly incorporating both underdeveloped and unevenly developed peripheral economies to the core, as well as the disciplining of dissent) would also require that various forms of Asian nationalism be policed in places such as Korea, Indochina, Indonesia, and the Philippines.[11] Simultaneous with incorporation was the granting of formal independence for the Philippines, peculiarly singled out as an example of U.S. hegemony gone right, a "showcase for democracy." While claims by the patron state were meant to discipline the Philippines, they were also used to do the hard work of U.S. hegemony in sustaining the legitimacy of the West in and through other nations, such as Pakistan, Thailand, and South Vietnam.

In 1946, the Philippines entered its first decade as an independent, politically sovereign nation. However, as several economic and political analyses reveal, Manila demonstrated that its continued relationship with the West, particularly with Washington, defined the persistence, if not the deepening, of U.S. hegemony in the Philippines. It was the aging generation of the elite Filipinos, whose children constituted one of the first cohorts raised under colonial rule, who triggered anxiety about and generation of "folk culture." By the 1950s, folk culture not only authenticated the "cultural" (or, rather, the anthropological or sociological) subject of Philippine culture but the "political" subject, as well. Nick Joaquin, National Artist for Literature called the 1940s the "decade of disaster." For young men and women of the generation who had come of age just a few years before the war, the decade would help to explain his generation's reticence concerning the consolation of survival. For those born in the 1920s and 1930s, surviving the war meant pushing through Manila's rubble, stepping over uncollected bodies and trash while learning to maximize and recombine available resources. They were children of the city's suburbs such as Pasay and Quiapo, where whole sections of the capital were hollowed out by strafing fire and bombing. Joaquin's assessment is appropriate here: "No decade in our history was more eventful than this one, during which we passed through four different governments; had six chief executives; inaugurated two republics; and underwent a total war, two invasions, and a great peasant uprising—not to mention a series of bloody elections in which the birds, the trees and the dead profusely voted. So vast now seems the difference between what we have become and what we were before disaster struck that, in the Philippine vernacular[,] the term 'peacetime' means exclusively all the years before December 8, 1941. There has been no 'peacetime' since then."[12] For common people who were not guaranteed opportunity by station, property, or education, U.S. "liberation" was less a choice than a reality made inevitable by native elites' bargaining. To maintain their strategic and economic advantages in the Philippines, military leaders such as General Douglas A. MacArthur instituted the mechanisms that restored native rule to the Philippine elite. In addition to military alliances aimed at pacifying dissent ("noncooperative" neutralisms and "hostile" nationalisms), the United States led campaigns to stabilize the rule of capital with the Bretton Woods formation of the International Monetary Fund and the World Bank.[13]

In the Philippine national elections of 1946, Washington officials backed General Manuel Roxas over the incumbent President Sergio Osmeña. Roxas was able to assure Washington that friendly relations concerning trade and aid would continue under his administration. While the much anticipated formal link to colonialism was severed with the granting of independence that year, the ties that bound the Philippines to the United States assured elites on both sides of the Pacific that profits and security would continue. The so-called postcolonial moment for the Philippines was hardly one for celebration. Rather, as the political historian Stephen Shalom has pointed out, the Philippines entered its neocolonial stage, or what the columnist Teodoro Valencia has called "colonization without an occupying force."[14] The U.S.–Philippine Trade Agreement, or the Bell Trade Act, was signed by President Harry Truman in April 1946, nominally extending free-trade practices between the United States and the Philippines. Key features included pegging the value of the peso to the U.S. dollar. Under the so-called parity clause, American citizens and businesses had the same economic rights as Filipino citizens concerning the operation of public utilities and natural-resource industries. The clause protected U.S. capital under the guise of attracting foreign investment, but such protections were not reciprocal. U.S. exports could enter the Philippines duty free for eight years, giving U.S. goods an advantage over other goods. Products from the Philippines, including sugar, rice, cigars, and coconut oil, were restricted. The U.S. president could also suspend all or any part of the bill if it could be demonstrated that U.S. citizens or businesses had been discriminated against. Also, the Philippine government was prohibited from imposing export taxes.

Military agreements were key in forging the closest of ties between the two nations. The passage of the Military Bases Agreement of 1947 provided one-sided benefits to the United States. Air Force and Navy facilities were excused from rent for a century. Military aid was used to "support the political orientation of the Philippines toward the U.S. and to strengthen its morale."[15] And the Military Assistance Pact provided that Washington would aid the Philippines by establishing the Joint U.S. Military Advisory

Group (JUSMAG) to train the Armed Forces of the Philippines (AFP). "Joint" referred not to the relationship between the two countries but to the branches of the U.S. military service.[16]

By the end of the 1940s, the Philippine economy was in near-collapse. The trade deficit between the United States and the Philippines had ballooned due to a glut of American goods coupled with a drought in cash reserves in Philippine banks. Monopolies, contrary to the oft-repeated defense that not all concentrations of wealth and decision making are anti-competitive, squashed smaller entrepreneurs' humble attempts to collectively invest and experiment, ensuring a generous distribution of wealth limited to elites and select families. While the sons and daughters of sugar barons studied at prestigious institutions and looked forward to promising careers, workers found themselves locked out of security and mobility. The stage was set for the emergence of radical responses in the form of Central Luzon's Huks, who were struggling for land reform.[17] President Ramon Magsaysay satisfied U.S. interests by crushing the Huk campaign with imported hardware. Combatants enlisted from the central and northern parts of the country were sated with homesteads, credit, health clinics, and cash in the southern Philippine region of Mindanao, a strategy that would help to sow the seeds of more violence as the predominantly Christian settlers wrestled with Muslim residents. More than fifteen thousand were arrested during the anti-Huk campaign. The Philippine Air Force continued to bomb Huk positions, flying two thousand six hundred sorties and expending two hundred fifty thousand pounds of explosives.[18]

Senator Claro Recto was one of the few national figures who registered dissent, from an incredibly isolated and unpopular position. He rejected the liberal nationalism of *burgis* dependence on the United States. However, Washington was already committed to shaping the discourse of postwar politics as a "choice" between communism and democracy. Critics have been consistent in naming the second half of the twentieth century as one in which a republic yielded to an empire with the erection of the "national security state." For Asian nationalists such as Recto, to be in the opposition often meant to be alone. Challenges to the legitimacy of the liberal Western order were met with McCarthyesque demagoguery or Central Intelligence Agency investigation. The Anti-Subversion Act, which outlawed communism, was one example of the narrowing of political possibilities for those to the left of the status quo. "To be anti-American," it was often repeated in Manila dailies, "was to be anti-Filipino."[19] These events should be understood against the larger aims of U.S. foreign policy after World War II—to economically integrate the Asian peripheries into the market economies of the core as sites for lucrative multinational investment in emerging markets and as cheap sources for raw materials and human labor. John F. Kennedy put a public face on the policy when he stated in 1961, "The great battleground for the defense and expansion of freedom today is the whole southern half of the globe . . . the lands of the rising people."[20]

As officials in Washington looked over the shoulder of their elite partners in Manila, they could also see the brewing crisis in China. By the time the communist revolution began in 1949, Washington's strategy was clear: "Every effort must be made to strengthen the overall U.S. position with respect to the Philippines, the Ryukyus, and Japan."[21] The entire region was subject to the calculus of containment of Asian nationalisms alongside the integration of economies. The number of countries in Asia and the Middle East that established sovereignty in some form was staggering. The 1940s and 1950s marked a turning point for the region, where several nations became at least nominally "independent"—for example, Jordan, the Philippines, Syria, India, Pakistan, Myanmar (Burma), Israel, North Korea, South Korea, Sri Lanka, Indonesia, Laos, Cambodia, and Vietnam.[22]

Members of the National Security Council (NSC), which was created in 1947, drafted key documents that described Herculean ambitions: to manufacture consent at home around what constituted a postwar threat to U.S. national security while disciplining the sense of possibility brewing in what the historian Geoffrey Barraclough has referred to as the revolt against the West. Stephen Shalom's analysis of neocolonialism, defined as the intimate identification of interests between elites in both nations, is on the mark: "In an age of nationalism, the National Security Council concluded, intervention by a Western power in Asia was likely to be counterproductive. The United States must work with, and even strengthen, a *moderate* nationalism as a means for opposing communism." The United States, the NSC noted, "should refrain from taking the lead in movements which must of necessity be of Asian origin." American propagandists expressed the strategic situation in sartorial terms: "[The United States] must present American ideas dressed in Asian clothes, coming from Asian mouths, if we are to succeed." U.S. policymakers found that clothing in the Philippines. As President Roxas had said in a speech in the United States in 1946, "We are not of the Orient except by geography. We are part of the Western world by reason of culture, religion, ideology, economics. . . . We expect to remain part of the West, possibly as the ideological bridge between the Occident and the Orient.'"[23] "Dressing up" the character to fit the role while another voices the part recalls ventriloquism; perhaps the theatrical reference is appropriate. While Filipino politicians saw themselves as bridges between the East and the West, U.S. policymakers understood the relationship in ways similar to lessons learned by the impresario and producer Malcolm McLaren—that "clothing" has always been less about "expressing oneself" than about acts of "disguise."[24]

A declassified NSC document, "A Report to the President by the National Security Council with Respect to the Philippines" (NSC 84/2), described the government's policy toward the Philippines, making clear that the nation's "independence" testified to "the recognition by the United States that nationalism in Asia is a basic reality which cannot be ignored. Failure of the Philippines to maintain independence would discredit the United States in the eyes of the world and seriously decrease U.S. influence, particularly in Asia.[25] What the authors of NSC 84/2 had in mind when discussing the "existing conditions" was the revolt by the Huks in Central Luzon: "the sole apparent military threat to the internal security of the Philippine Republic."[26] Likewise, another document, NSC-68, made explicit what kind of society the United States would need to be to take its position in the world as the premiere "superpower," one in which politicians were committed to the task of convincing the public of the threat of Soviet aggression and its satellites, calling for increased taxes as revenue for a continued arms buildup, as well as encouraging the overthrow of sovereign leaders who were not friendly to American interests.[27]

By 1950, the United States had provided the Philippines with $1.4 billion in aid. Several politicians, including U.S. Secretary of State Dean Acheson, echoed U.S. capital in claiming that such aid was doing little to stabilize the Philippines. U.S.-led economic survey teams reported that the Philippine economy was in near-collapse. Inflation, high rents, lack of credit, and rising interest rates had set the stage for the popular uprising of the Huks in Central Luzon. Huk strength was placed at twelve thousand to fifteen thousand armed personnel, with two million more mass supporters. Also in 1950, Edward G. Lansdale, a CIA operative, was sent to the Philippines as part of the reorganization of the country's intelligence agencies, becoming Magsaysay's right hand when he took office as secretary of national defense. The Office of Psychological Warfare set up under Magsaysay's authority was renamed the Civil Affairs Office and launched propaganda attacks against the Huks, including the dropping of thirteen million leaflets, reaching one and a half million people. The U.S. Information Service provided literature and films that lauded the "special relations" between the United States and the Philippines while demonizing communist-led forces. The turning point was October 1950, when several Huk leaders were captured in Manila. By the end of 1950, the AFP had increased from ten thousand to sixteen thousand battalion combat teams. From 1951 to 1952, the AFP's total strength increased 75 percent. The cost to the United States in supporting such a buildup was $10 million. A total of

$250 million in U.S. loans and grants was given to the Philippines in exchange for drastic reforms to the economy and a crackdown on the Huk movement.[28] A U.S. State Department official noted: "Much of the stigma of colonialism can be removed if, where necessary, yellow men will be killed by yellow men rather than by white men alone."[29] The defeat of the Huks had fulfilled the mission of the U.S. and native elite anticipated in NSC 84/2—namely, that "the Philippines [would] become and remain stable, anti-communist, pro-American, and an example for the rest of the world of the intention of the United States to encourage the establishment of progressive and responsible governments."[30]

The postwar period saw a diversification of these economic interests—members of families whose main economic interests had been in sugar would take up holdings in auto plants, import–export businesses, financing, transportation, or factory ownership, including increasing attention paid to the culture industries. One of the best examples of the importance of Manila for the growing and diversifying urban elites was to be found in the then emerging mass media. More than half of Manila's households had television sets. By the 1960s, seven of the Philippines' nine daily newspapers were published in Manila. Movies were offered in Tagalog and English, with one thousand movie houses scattered over more than two hundred seventy towns and cities.[31] Again, NSC 84/2 prophetically determined the shape of Philippine society, anticipating generations of political instability and the growing gulf between the rich and poor: "Leadership in the Philippine Government has been largely in the hands of a small group of individuals representing the wealthy propertied class who, except in isolated instances, have failed to appreciate the need for reform and the pressures generated among the less prosperous and more numerous groups of the population."[32]

## Staging Burgis Nationalism in Brussels, New York, and Manila

Writing for the New York *Times Magazine*, the music critic Howard Taubman noted that the 1958 World's Fair in Brussels was special because it promised to be "the place where the cold war, fought with the weapons of art and drama, music and dance, architecture, books and films [would reach] a climax."[33] Taubman was not alone in the widespread belief that culture should be understood as a tool of persuasion, that which could "win the good opinion and affection of peoples." For the Brussels presentations, the Soviet Union spent more than $50 million while the United States spent a little more than $13.4 million on orchestras, dance, opera, theater, and pop music. (Benny Goodman and Harry Belafonte performed in the U.S. pavilion.) The scientist T. O. Jones demonstrated a nuclear clock that measured time through the disintegration of radioactive substances, a symbol of the nation's "atoms-for-peace" program.[34] Taubman made plain the role that culture played during the Cold War, noting that even as "contending giants compete for attention," they "dare not forget the intangible things—the dreams and secret murmurings that speak from heart to heart more surely and swiftly than any guided missile."[35] These dreams and murmurings needed vehicles. Who better to guide them "from heart to heart" than performers who also functioned as "dancing diplomats"? The presence of the Bayanihan in New York stands as a powerful metaphor for the kind of exchanges and travel that Washington appreciated—movement and repertoire that masked U.S. expansion of power throughout Asia and attempted to tamp down the rowdy types in the region. These are the kinds of exchanges carefully considered by Christina Klein: "intellectual exchanges of conversation, economic exchanges of shopping, emotional exchanges of love, physical exchanges of tourism and immigration."[36]

At the heart of the fairgrounds stood the Atomium, a monument more than three hundred feet tall depicting the molecular structure of steel. More than forty-two million fairgoers visited the exposition between April and October 1958, the first to be held after World War II. A copy of the Soviet Union's Sputnik was displayed in the Russian pavilion. Each of the participating countries pitched pavilions on the fairgrounds; each had its own special day or days "to display . . . cultural identities, prominently in manners theatrical."[37] Italian, German, and Japanese cultures were on exhibit through song, fireworks, martial arts, folk arts, literary work, and food.

José Lardizabal, artistic director for the Bayanihan, noted that the "Philippine contribution, through an audacious pattern of contrivance . . . arrived in the form of 38 shyish individuals in blue-grey uniforms accompanied by a meager 4,000 pounds of props and costumes, a substantial portion of them in sun-dried bamboos."[38] Helena Z. Benitez, founder and executive producer of the Bayanihan (and president of Philippine Women's University), conceived of the troupe as evidence of Philippine culture to the world. As president of the Philippines, Ramon Magsaysay promised to the fair organizers that he would send a representative of the national culture. The theme of the fair was "Triumph of the Human Spirit over the Machine." Claiming that she and the Bayanihan traveled without government support, Benitez said that her staff "decided to bring a live exhibit—to bring our people as Exhibit A and demonstrate our folk dances and songs."[39]

On May 27, 1958, during the Philippine night in the fair's grand auditorium, the Bayanihan concluded its program with the crowd-pleasing *tinikling,* the iconic dance in which performers step through and jump between clapping bamboo poles.[40] Leticia Perez de Guzman, a staff member, remembered how the room "erupted in thunderous applause as the curtains fell; it was clear that Bayanihan had conquered Brussels." In the fair's competition for national dance-theater companies, the Bayanihan took first place in an international field of thirteen. Their presentation caught the favorable attention of the U.S. television personality Ed Sullivan, who featured the troupe on his show in a filmed tour of the fair on June 15, along with the Platters, William Holden, Sophia Loren, Brigitte Bardot, Maurice Chevalier, Jacques Tati, Mitzi Gaynor, and the Nitwitz.[41]

The presentations also impressed the Russian-born New York impresario Sol Hurok, a promoter of international acts and manager of the singer Marian Anderson. On October 13, 1959, the Bayanihan performed at the Winter Garden Theater on Broadway as part of Hurok's international festival, which included performances from Japan, Israel, Germany, and Hungary. The Bayanihan's successful debut at the Brussels World's Fair was followed with acclaim from the city's notoriously finicky dance and music critics. Walter Terry of the New York *Herald Tribune* wrote that the "Bayanihan is one of the newest examples of an ethnic dance culture which has gone beyond simple preservation (as important as that is) and into creative growth. . . . We are carried from the elemental, wild and free dances of primitive mountain peoples to the refined actions of those touched by Spanish culture, from the Orient-slanted gestures of the Muslim inhabitants to a wide selection of regional dances and rural scenes of work and play."[42] John Martin of the New York *Sunday Times* lavished praise on the organization of the program, costuming, lighting, and set design, as well as the musical accompaniment. Several other reviewers also strayed a bit from confining comments to dance criticism. Whitney Bolton of the *Morning Telegraph* wrote: "As any one who ever has known Filipinos is aware, these are a lovely people: lovely in face, in gesture, in speech and grace. They have a sunny, live sense of humor, a warmth of heart that is constant and they somehow seem to suggest the best of the eastern spirit. They had a magic of their own, with sudden, wide uninhibited smiles, deeply fetched laughter and a quick generosity of spirit. They have what most races have lost in the tensions of our times: human affection openly expressed."[43]

Soon after the Brussels performance, the Philippine government appointed the Bayanihan as its Official Cultural Mission to the Americas and Europe. Nothing encourages hometown praise more than the sound of foreign applause, as demonstrated by Morli Dharam's review in the Manila *Times*: "We have followed Bayanihan's development, seen it again at the Winter Garden in New York in 1959 and at the Metropolitan Opera in 1961. We have seen how in a few years by dint of effort, dedication and eclectic search for perfection, it has danced its way to the front rank of the world's best companies—the Habimah of Israel, the Moiseyev of Russia, the Ballet Folklorico of Mexico to name a few."[44]

How did the Bayanihan's directors craft a sense of the "authentic" in the first decade after nominal independence? How was cultural production mobilized by this cohort? How did the Bayanihan transform folkloric dance into dance theater? Several accounts of the company's history begins with the storybook images of the Brussels victory leading to Broadway acclaim. However, those accounts fail to emphasize the crucial events in the few years before their success. Lardizabal assessed what was at stake for postwar nationalist sentiment, identifying the troupe's function as critical to a nationalist project: "It was inevitable that after the Philippines proclaimed its independence from the United States in 1946, nationalist sentiments that had been momentarily lulled should be fanned afresh. For a growing number of the discerning Filipinos, it was time to go back to their roots, reassert national identity."[45] The task of postwar artists such as Lardizabal, self-described as "discerning Filipinos," was to do more than merely go "back to [the] roots." They invented traditions, asserted national identities through the presentation of the "folk," and edited ritual into palatable entertainment forms built for export.

We get an indication of how this work developed by tracking some events in January 1953, when three researchers from the Philippine Women's University (PWU)—Lucrecia Kasilag, Aurora Diño, and Jose Maceda—visited the Bukid Mangyan tribe of Bongabon, Oriental Mindoro. Lardizabal recalled a "shy burst of giggles" as the Manila educators saw members of the tribe huddled together on a hill across a gorge from the open field. Too bashful to meet their visitors face to face, the Bukid chose to have a look at the strangers from a distance."[46] The researchers presented the tribe's chieftain with a gift of beads and scarves, enticements to perform. "Giggling like children," the recollection continues, "the tribesmen were overcome with bashfulness once more. Eyes downcast, they kept their silence as the visitors made overtures of friendship and asked about their music."[47] This fieldwork was repeated with the Saklag in Mindoro, the Tagbanua of Palawan, and the Bontoc and Kalinga of the mountain provinces. In the research notes, we read the familiar lament of the metropolitan scholar witnessing a process similar to what had befallen the "vanishing Indian":

> The researchers were disturbed by the discovery that while most of the tribes had kept their culture intact, many had already begun to *lose their heritage to modern influence.* Among some tribes, only

> the elders could sing ancient tribal songs; the young, whose formal instruction was in the current regional dialect, could not speak the tribal tongue. The urgency of documenting ethnic cultures before they disappeared completely thus gave the PWU studies fresh significance. The researchers' findings became material for cultural programs showcased at PWU recitals. Significant as these were, it was soon realized that *a single journey into the Filipino's trove of cultural riches was not enough* to touch every treasure that lay there. They had barely scratched the surface. At no time would this sense of inadequacy be felt more than in a first cultural visit outside the country.[48]

With the embarrassment of the Dacca incident, recalled at the beginning of this chapter, the leaders of the Bayanihan committed themselves to the grounding of the troupe's work in the "folk." The PWU researchers redoubled their efforts and made "Take It from the People" their guiding philosophy. The data culled from the trips resulted in several test performances before Brussels: in Bangkok, Rome, Barcelona, and Madrid. By 1957, the PWU Filipiniana Folk Music and Dance Committee had been formally organized into the Bayanihan Folk Art Center, with the opening of classes in folk music and dance for children and adults. Members of the center also asked local tour operators to add the Bayanihan to their itineraries. Kasilag did not work alone. Her contribution as musical director was complemented by several others—most notably, the choreographer Lucrecia R. Urtula, the costume designer Isabel A. Santos, and the executive producer Helena Z. Benitez.

Urtula was then working as a physical educator at PWU. Occasionally she held classes in one of the many courtyards. She incorporated native folk dance into her physical-education lesson plans—games, singing, and movement. Her work was noticed by Leticia Perez de Guzman, who served on the faculty of PWU. De Guzman asked Urtula to organize a physical-education club and to pursue folk dance more intensely. Its growing popularity among the students and staff at the university caught the attention of President Magsaysay. The dances were performed at several events and ceremonies. With the group's growing reputation, Magsaysay asked university staff to produce a nationwide celebration. Urtula and de Guzman programmed dances that represented the archipelago's three major island regions in a show called "Glimpses of Philippine Culture."[49] Urtula's efforts resulted in the creation of a new genre of performance in the Philippine tradition: dance theater based on folk arts. She sought to "retain all those elements of the original material without which the authenticity of the new material would have been diminished; and two, to enhance the original material and structure it in such manner as to meet the requisites of theater."[50]

Urtula's essay "Keeping in Step with Yesterday" shed light on the kinds of challenges involved in her work with the troupe. She envisioned the guiding principle of the choreography to be "the adaptation of indigenous dance to the conventions and possibilities of theater." On the one hand, fidelity to the "cultural context" was intended as an act of preservation, to retain what was found during the ethnographic process and to accurately reflect the encounter with the "folk." In several programs, albums, cassettes, and videos, this claim to the authenticity of the presentation was a premium that is repeatedly asserted: "The Bayanihan from its earliest years recognized fieldwork as the basis of its existence and its success. We have made it a point *to take ancient lore straight from the people.* The production staff has toured the length and breadth of the accommodations in quest of the dance art. . . . It is, above all, essential not to lose the original flavor and feeling of the dance. It is likewise essential not to offend the sensibilities of the ethnic group from which the dance originated, an eventuality avoided by an understanding of social and cultural roots. For this reason Bayanihan has always kept in close touch with various consultants."[51]

Among the list of authenticators are scholars, dance teachers, and performers hailing from the various regions of the dances' origins. However, restructuring the original material into the modern and "sophisticated" spaces within which performance takes place represents the other major consideration, one that stresses adaptation rather than fidelity. Urtula identified three aesthetic dimensions that shaped the adaptation of the folk dance: *compression, enhancement,* and *highlighting.* Compression involved editing the flow of the original dance, sometimes ritualized for extended periods (days or weeks), to modern audiences sitting for no more than two hours. Dances were also edited from their folk presentation to make storylines clearer, crucial especially since the work would be presented far beyond its immediate, local context. Enhancement involved coordination with the musical director and costume designer by providing accent through rhythm or explicit melodic lines and by using contrasting colors to accentuate regional differences or transitions. Highlighting, for Urtula, meant clearly crafting suites that could be differentiated from each other. The Bayanihan model has reliably returned to the performance of separate suites, within which an infinite variety may be determined: the northern, Spanish colonial, regional variations, southern (or Muslim), and rural. Urtula identified venue as an important aspect in distinguishing folk dance from the dance theater. In indigenous settings, the dances were presented outdoors; open to the participation of performers and audience, they eliminated a strict division of labor between the two. In other words, with the exception of village officials, the dance was not an affair reserved for certain individuals. Proscenium-style spaces invited no such mingling. As the musician and scholar Ricardo D. Trimillos has noted, Philippine dance activity has been moving from a participational ("we-oriented") mode to a presentational one that emphasizes mutually exclusive roles of performer and audience.[52]

The costume designer Isabel A. Santos agreed with Urtula's vision of adaptation. In her essay "On Pins and Needles: Three Decades of Costuming Bayanihan," Santos discussed how their attempt to offer authentic representations of ethnic groups inevitably led to the need to play with tradition:

> As costume director, I always try to beg, borrow or buy their beautiful costumes, but ethnic tribesmen are not always willing to part with their treasured ceremonial garments. . . . Once we nearly had to provide two wives as the purchase price of a couple of intricately beaded and embroidered Bagobo costumes. Sharp bargaining brought the price down to six horses. . . . Costume design for national or traditional dances, like choreography, must respect the authentic, conform with tradition. This does not mean, however, rigid accuracy. Most of the costumes we collected or documented in our research sorties are, on close view, a handiwork of imaginative and exquisite workmanship. On stage, however, they lose a lot of their unique attractiveness. *To keep their original impact they must be restyled in deference to the demands of theater.*[53]

For Santos, the stage demanded practicability and wearability. The fast tempos of the dances meant that dancer needed to be able to make quick costume changes. She offered the example of the Bayanihan's version of the Maranao costume for women: Originally consisting of three pieces, Santos reconstructed it with one. "This particular costume proved to be quite a hit with the viewers, even with the Maranao ladies themselves, one of whom expressed a desire to have this modernized version made for them."[54] Two more dimensions of the aesthetic of stage performance were an important consideration: simplification and stylization. The attempt, according to Santos, was to achieve a certain "clarity" and "unity of effect":

> A costume is therefore studied in its original form for its principal features after which a central motif is lifted from the original and deliberately emphasized. . . . In dealing with ethnic costumes, the

> principle observed is one of enhancement; colors are modified to stand out, usually in vivid, intense hues, not forgetting fidelity to the color schemes particular to different ethnic groups, since these usually relate to religious and social values. The Maranao, for instance, have definite color schemes characterized by strong, even strident combinations, such as acid greens with fuchsia (as in the extravagantly plumed *sarimanok,* the Maranao totem bird).[55]

Repeating Urtula, Santos noted how the group has relied on consultants from various tribal groups and other organizations to ensure fidelity to the local subject. She also repeated other comments that underscored the urban–provincial dyad apparent in the work of the Bayanihan. She underemphasized the role that urban cultural workers have undertaken to both ethnicize the nation and nationalize the folk. Santos claimed that, in the "pursuit of authenticity, we have constantly kept in touch with original folk weavers and embroiderers. Some costumes which would be difficult to execute in Manila are ordered directly from distant regions."[56] Providing "appropriate" and "effective" renditions of the native does not involve re-presenting or re-creating the native. Notice how Santos and Cabanatan insisted that the theater's purpose involves *elevation,* a progressive logic that translated the tribal/provincial to the urban/universal: "The precise, photographic reproduction of the authentic original is neither necessary nor even advisable. When a dance is elevated from the tribal campfire to the stage, costumes no less than other elements of the dance—movement patterns, music and lights—undergo a sea-change: colors become more intense, details bolder, central motifs emphasized and unnecessary details played down, if not completely eliminated. This simplification and stylization results in a truer and clearer (because uncluttered) picture of the original."[57]

The audience was led to trust the enhancement—in the form of *intensification*—because the modern folkloric performer has performed the function of filtering out the extraneous and the ephemeral. "Some of the costumes in the tribal numbers come right off the tribesman's back," Helena Benitez said with pride. "And the instruments such as the bamboo nose flutes were also purchased from the source. We've performed their dances in front of the natives, and they quite enjoyed it."[58] Benitez's comments suggested that the approval of the native was necessary, not necessarily for the granting of permission from native to metropolitan to perform the dances, but for the metropolitan explanation to non-Filipino audiences: "The natives can be such sticklers for accuracy. There was a time when they insisted that some of their dance rituals must go on for five days.

But can you see us keeping people in the theater for five days? The pathways to the past have not been easy to follow. Barriers had to be overcome. Sometimes shyness, sometimes suspicion, even indifference. These from people who were almost untouched by civilization."[59] For Santos, the "past" was authenticated by "natives" while embodied by her metropolitan students. Trimillos noted how "the dancers are mostly students from Lowland regions and—more significantly—urban centers. They are accustomed to sitting in chairs, climbing in and out of jeepneys, and using a gait appropriate for the urban lifestyle."[60] And once again, the extant record of such researchers left the moment of the dance ethnography obscured. The rhetoric also constructed the metropolitan researcher as the proper and sole interpreter of the nation's patrimony, while the native flit about the jungleside, wary of the strange visitors.[61] Urtula echoes Santos's thoughts: "All told, the [Bayanihan] Company not only discovered new aspects of the Filipino race; it forged bonds with all Filipinos—Christians, Muslims and animists alike."[62]

In several instances, music, dance, and costume researchers for the group have discussed this process in heroic terms. Here is the figure of the Manila urban educator who made a fantastic and arduous trek to the "hinterlands" to learn from the natives. The nation was defined by reference from its metropolitan center, the eye that could see outward, itself unseen: "We had to climb mountains, cross treacherous water, edge our way into the remote hinter-lands to get to our sources. And when we did get there, we had to cajole, beg, or bribe (with little gifts) to get the folk to perform their dances for us."[63] Santos has her own account of the intrepid work: "The adventure begins with research. By air, land and sea—by plane, truck, jeep, bus, ship, motorboat, *vinta*, and on foot—we have traversed the length and breadth of the archipelago in pursuit of authentic materials to work on."[64]

The Broadway performance made clear that performance for the stage and not re-creation of ritual by the native would drive the group's work. Choreographers like Urtula found themselves with more questions than answers. After the Broadway run, Urtula visited with the choreographer Martha Graham, a pioneer in the use of folk material in modern dance, who attended the New York premiere. Because Graham had lived in Indonesia for some time and had been exposed to Southeast Asian cultural forms, Bayanihan leaders such as Urtula were especially interested in her opinion concerning the dance company's professional future. Urtula had asked Graham specifically about the "quandary" of reconciling the folk with the theatrical. "It's not all that simple," Graham said. "You can't favor one element and reject the other. When you choreograph you have to look at the totality of things. Continue doing what you've been doing. Continue studying. You're very lucky you have so much to draw from."[65] The musical director Lucrecia Kasilag pointed to similar tensions between authentic representations and adaptation to new forms. Her preference as a composer and arranger, she has said, has been to render folk themes in their "pure, pristine best." Yet being "faithful to the original traditions," as she has put it, is not possible since the group's work consists of taking indigenous and folk music and raising it to a theatrical level.[66]

## Dancing Diplomats

The task of aligning the Bayanihan's interests with that of the state fell to Helena Benitez, the group's executive producer. She was perfect for the role: well educated, a graduate of PWU and a student at George Washington University, with postgraduate training from the University of Chicago and Iowa State University. As a member of the Senate and the National Assembly, Benitez wrote several bills involving the promotion of Filipino national culture.[67] Among them was Republic Act 5871, an amendment to Republic Act 4165, which established commissions devoted to preserving cultural artifacts. The function of the commission would be to assist in the revival of "traditional" or indigenous arts and crafts through training, the facilitation of workshops, and the funding of institutions. With the passage of the Cultural Promotion Law, Public Act 3042, the Philippine Congress began to provide grants of 200,000 pesos for cultural groups that would represent the country while abroad. The Bayanihan Folk Arts Center, founded in 1957 at PWU, developed goals that would allow it to fulfill the functions described in the legislation's emerging cultural policies: "to conduct and coordinate research on Philippine culture and its development; to collect and preserve indigenous Philippine art form in music, dance, literature, arts, crafts and costumes; to encourage use of these indigenous art forms in modern crafts and industry; and to promote international goodwill and cultural exchange through performances abroad."[68]

Benitez's role in aligning the troupe's work to that of the nation's emerging cultural policy was evident especially during an incident that took place during the first years of the troupe's existence. Benitez turned down an invitation by the veteran pageant producer Helen Tieken Geraghty to have the Bayanihan perform at a major event in Chicago. At the time, Benitez was negotiating a contract with Sol Hurok for the New York performances. The contract imposed three conditions: the troupe would have to provide for its own transportation; it was to have the support of the Philippine government; and "no other similar Philippine group [would] appear in the United States before the Bayanihan."[69] Benitez secured a letter from Philippine President Carlos P. Garcia designating her "the official representative of Philippine interests in the presentation of the Bayanihan dancers in the United States and abroad." After receiving similar invitations to perform in Paris, France, and Cáceres, Spain, another dance troupe, based at Manila's Far Eastern University (FEU), secured its own presidential endorsement.

The FEU troupe was received well in France at the Théâtre des Nations International Cultural Festival, as well as at performances at the Théâtre des Champs-Elysée. Its successes were reported in the United States, and the talk made its way to Geraghty in Chicago, who extended the invitation to the FEU dancers on May 12. The troupe secured 50,000 pesos from its Board of Trustees for traveling expenses. Hurok demanded an explanation, and he informed Ambassador Carlos Romulo of the situation. FEU's President Teodoro Evangelista quibbled with Benitez, who was both president of the PWU and founder of the Bayanihan. What did Benitez and Evangelista make of Garcia's dual letters of endorsement? "I hereby formally designate the Bayanihan Philippine Dancer's group of the Bayanihan Folk Arts Center to officially represent the Philippines as a special cultural mission to the Americas and Europe." Benitez read this as an *exclusive* endorsement, while Evangelista read it more broadly—that the endorsement did not preclude other companies from serving as representatives. Benitez then sent two memos to Foreign Affairs Secretary Felixberto Serrano, "Suggestions for Policies and Regulations to Govern Cultural Policies" and "The Official Designation of the Bayanihan as Philippine Representative on a Cultural Mission to the Americas and Europe Specifically from July 1959 to July 1960." The memos argued that the shortage of foreign currency demanded frugality and that only "one group of similar programs be designated to represent the Philippines in any one area at any one year and that only the best offerings in the country be designated to represent the Philippines."[70]

The second of the memos stressed that having two companies perform similar material would risk the creation of an "unfavorable impression." Benitez was notorious for suggesting to newspaper and magazine correspondents that they avoid covering the FEU troupe's tours. Hurok delivered an ultimatum to Serrano: Either the FEU troupe would reverse its Chicago plans or Hurok would stop plans for the Bayanihan's performance on Broadway. Serrano capitulated. Conrado Benitez, dean of the Bayanihan Board of Trustees, wrote: "At this time, any competition for the American public between two Filipino dance groups presenting a program similar in nature would only indicate lack of national unity, coordination and discipline among us Filipinos and, in the opinion of good friends, might bring on us uncomplimentary opinion of the world."[71] Notice the implications: Only one agent—and not just any, but one formally acknowledged by name—can serve as representative for the state *during this time.* The dynamism of culture as a process is replaced by an aggressively branded and administratively sanctioned product.

Despite the possibility of generating unfavorable international opinion as the result of having multiple dance troupes perform abroad, companies other than the Bayanihan continued to travel to the United States. The FEU, Barangay, Filipinescas, Tambuli Cultural Troupe, and many other troupes crossed stages with the Bayanihan. Yet Benitez's work produced results: The Bayanihan would define the model for Philippine folk arts internationally in the postwar era. With its several audio and video recordings and performances—the group has made more than a dozen world tours and hundreds of shorter ones in more than sixty nations—the Bayanihan has not only presented Philippine culture. It has become synonymous with it.[72]

## Critical Responses

This section turns to the immanent critiques generated by the work of the Bayanihan over the past forty years. The first set of critiques holds out for the possibility that the Bayanihan performs a valuable service in representing Philippine culture abroad in national terms. The second is unconvinced by the Bayanihan's claim to authenticity while leaving itself open to charges of subscribing to essentialist thinking. The last set problematizes the categories of analysis by claiming that existing disciplines have provided few answers concerning the need for cultural critique.

The Bayanihan has had no shortage of defenders. Alfredo Roces understood the group's work in terms of the necessity of nationalism—to organize the heterogeneity of the local, to make sense out of the past by identifying with how other modern nations have done the same:

> The Filipino cultural problem has been one of fragmentation and synthesis. It has often been observed that what a particular artist may claim to be truly Filipino is nothing but a fragment of our diverse and varied personality. Our history has been largely responsible for this cultural fragmentation, which while seeking to weld various cultures into one was itself torn and fragmented by the invasions of foreign powers. Somehow, despite this large and rather constant fragmentation, some mysterious invisible force has always moved for synthesis. One revelation has been the folk dance groups,

> particularly the Bayanihan, because they have managed to depict the Philippines' best. This has been, to our mind, not only because the dance is a most expressive form for Filipinos, but because the numbers featured in the dance showed the distinct diversity and multiplicity of cultures in this country.[73]

Nicanor Tiongson, artistic director for the Cultural Center of the Philippines, took a step further than Roces's notion of the presentational: "The dances shown by Bayanihan were not only the Christianized dances, but included all our traditions: Muslim, ethnic, lowland, etc. When all these are presented in one performance, it contributes so much to the unity of the country. *Because it legitimizes all the ethnic dances which before were marginalized—the whole range of our traditions is legitimized, is synthesized—in the performance.* . . . [O]ur history has been so fragmented in terms of cultural traditions so that just putting them altogether and making them flow into each other already is such a big statement in terms of our cultural identity. In putting them together you realize that whether it is Muslim, Igorot or Christian—the basic sensibility is the same. There is a basic continuity between the dances."[74]

Roces conjures the idea of "invisible forces," obscuring the roles that elites have played in assigning specific cultural meaning to movement and sound and, according to one reporter in Manila, doing the "tremendous job of selling the Philippines abroad." Concealed from view are the purveyors and architects of national culture who attempt to filter the raw material of the "folk" with the technical specifications of contemporary performance. They are like the traditionalists and modernizers of Latin America that Néstor García Canclini describes: "They tried to construct pure objects. The former imagined 'authentic' national and popular cultures, and sought to preserve them in the face of industrialization, urban massification, and foreign influences."[75] PCN organizers in the United States have thoroughly invested in this federated model of understanding difference and diversity in Filipino culture. The histories of southern Philippine secession, of northern indigenous resistance to Catholicism and even the anti-Tagalog bias demonstrated in the central part of the country, like many other issues, are painted over in the contemporary Pilipino Cultural Night. Performers and organizers have fallen back on the familiar notion of seemingly unmanageable diversity that can only be expressed through its metropolitan center (Manila).

The second set of responses is critical of the Bayanihan's claim to authenticity. Foremost among them are those claiming to carry forward the work of physical educators and folk-dance instructors trained in the

1920s and 1930s. These critics point to the desire to theatricalize as the culprit—such aesthetic and performative choices remove the imprimatur of the folk. What is left, they argue, are only copies, not originals. Aquino, a pioneer of folk-dance education from the earlier generation, raised the ire of many younger choreographers when she exclaimed: "Let the folk dances be as they are—of the folk. We cannot sacrifice heritage for progress." In her earlier career, Francisca Reyes Aquino had organized the elements of a national repertoire to stave off the corrupting influences of American culture in the early years of the twentieth century—jazz, movies, comics, language, dance. "What was left of the Filipino?" Aquino wondered as she taught physical education to the first generation born after the U.S.–Philippine War. "Culture" for Aquino was not an afterthought to the social organization of the commonwealth regime. Rather, the repertoire she created became a bulwark against U.S. hegemony and the first step toward a new bodily discipline. Toward the end of her career, Aquino saw the rise of a young generation of artists, choreographers, and musicians. Rosalia Merino Santos, a founder of the Far Eastern University Experimental Modern Dance Group in 1958 and a former student of Aquino's, witnessed the changes to folk dance, as well. "Now, [the new choreographers] stylize [dance movements]. With so much stylization, you lose track of the real thing. Dances are being danced twice as fast. How can you savor the steps? How can you see the beauty of the dance steps if it's danced so fast? I admit, long ago, our dances were repetitious and slow-moving because [they were] written for schools and teachers, not for the theater. But the Bayanihan appalls me with its theatrical [presentation]."[76] Add to this a trenchant critique from one of the leading authorities on Filipino dance in the United States, the choreographer and author Reynaldo G. Alejandro: "The style of this internationally famous folkloric company has become increasingly theatrical over the years and *no longer lays claim to presenting authentic Philippine folk dance*. . . . The stylistically staged revue dancing of the Bayanihan presents an image of the Filipino people as eternally happy, carefree, childishly irresponsible, ignoring all sense of the hundreds of years of social struggle and suffering that have been the traditional inspiration behind the greatest works of Philippine literature and music. Dances are copied, then recopied from troupe to troupe, making copies of copies. Without truly inspired Filipino artists doing the direction, the flavor of the dance can become diluted, the spirit dissipated, and all sense of authenticity sold out in favor of the flash and color of theatrical extravaganza."[77]

Alejandro is joined on this point by others who claim that the international consumption of culture has compromised authentically complicated subjects, creating a "hostage economy where tourist industry employment means active participation in [one's] own degradation."[78] In "The Bayanihan: How Authentic Is Its Repertoire?" the ethnomusicologist Usopay H. Cadar both critiques *and* retains an "essential" subject. His attack rests on the assumption that such claims should be interpreted narrowly; some suites, movements, costuming choices, and musical interpretations of ethnically specific references either do not exist or are wholly "distorted" from the "original":

> The Bayanihan uses the *Hari Raya* as a category of a cluster of dances. Actually, *Hari Raya* is . . . an important Muslim festival. It is the commemoration of the fasting month. It is so strictly religious that all musical and dance activities are discouraged during the period of fasting. The only audible sounds characteristic of this period of time are those emanating from Islamic chanting and prayer. *Kzadoratan* has no place in this festival, nor has any other dance. There is no such thing as religious Maranao dance. A careless use of *Hari Raya* outside of its real context is bound to create inconsistency, such as the incompatibility between *kzadoratan* and *Hari Raya*. . . . [The Bayanihan should] label the "authentic" as it is and describe the "original artistic creation" as it is. This is the way the innocent people should be guided by the "outstanding educators" of Asia.[79]

The Filipino subjectivity actively defended in this quote differs from the kind staged in contemporary PCNs. For those who take up Aquino's and Alejandro's lines of argument, authentic Filipino subjects (presented in folkloric forms) are raised as bulwarks against both Western modernization from without and the Filipinized version of culture directed toward tourists and other foreigners. PCN organizers deploy another sensibility by virtue of their different location along one of the forward edges of the diaspora: They play with an improvisational form of cultural representation that reflects their need to define ethnicity and nationalism as minorities in a larger polity.

Aquino, Merino Santos, Alejandro, and Cadar make pointed critiques of the Bayanihan's claims. Yet they also are hemmed in by some familiar and popularly held assumptions that continue to rest on the notion of a "true" folk subject that awaits to be discovered or one that remains unchanged. Stuart Hall wrote about the analogue to this when he inquired about those who consider the "'oneness' underlying all the other, more superficial differences . . . the truth, the essence, of 'Caribbeanness,' of the black experience." These are powerful and longstanding commitments that many have shouldered—as artists, activists, students, and scholars—to think of cultural identities not in the plural but "in terms of one, shared culture, a sort of collective 'one true self,' hiding inside the many other, more superficial or artificially imposed 'selves,' which people with a shared history and ancestry hold in common."[80] Is not the search for such a unity the kind of "spiritual principle" that Ernest Renan lectured about in 1882, the kind of intangible bond that would forgive the barbarity of generations of tribal warfare so long as the true modern sovereign could be revealed?[81]

The last set of responses to the work of the Bayanihan takes the form of diffuse and symptomatically read commentary. While some of these responses take up the Bayanihan directly, others generate questions about folk art—how the categories of analysis need to be broadened and how lines of disciplinary inquiry need to be rethought. Renato Constantino's works guide this last section by offering historiographical interventions into Philippine studies, here reminding us to consider context as much as content.[82] "Many cultural presentations highlight the songs and dances of these tribes as representative of our rediscovered civilization. [T]his effort appears to be premised on a static view of culture. It assumes that national culture merely awaits rediscovery and that the principal source of the people's self-pride must be sought in the achievements of their pre-colonial ancestors."[83] We may read Constantino's comments with others making related points regarding how many of "us" in advanced, privileged positions consider "time and the other." Freezing tribes and natives into remote pasts congratulates the modern researcher for her actions but sheds little light on the specificities of struggles undertaken in these people's times and on their own terms. How might cultural analysis be different if we were to pursue Constantino's challenge to pay attention to what one theorist has referred to as the "structuring principle" of popular cultures? Rather than merely provide an account or tally of the popular, we can pay closer attention to how powerful interests in various institutions such as the state or universities actively pursue cultural repertoire for a host of reasons: to make ethnicities and expressions of locality commensurate with each other, to filter out what seems to be extraneous information from a heroic and singular narrative, to mirror the repertoires of other members of the global community of nations, and to secure for the native elite positions of authority to legitimate their need.

Claims to certain kinds of authenticity have concerned the registration of crisis: the recognition of threats to a group's survival or mobility; of feelings of dislocation, disruption, or loss that are experienced in periods of change that seem to overtake one's ability to make sense of it.[84] Appeals to authenticity are also sometimes latent critiques of one's host culture. Strident forms of contemporary nationalism performed by racial or ethnic minorities are not only occasions for extolling the virtues of one's own; they sometimes are also among the few ways that groups have to register dissent or simply to remind others that a raft of interlocking inequities persists despite the state's or the market's assurances that everything will be all right.

The Bayanihan's history invites us to link the troupe's performance choices since Dacca, Brussels, and New York to the state's work in disseminating the national patrimony. In the dioramic displays at the Ayala Museum of Makati, or in the miniaturized rendition of the Philippine archipelago's landscape at Ngayon Pilipino, or during the multiyear government-sponsored celebrations of the nation's centennials, we find the national patrimony disseminated to its public as part of the larger work of continually renewing hegemony. Such artifacts, the Bayanihan's program included, may be understood as state acts of benefaction, handed down from one generation to the next (usually), and perhaps preferably, without much question. In the Bayanihan program we are assured that the metropolitan center competently organizes what suspiciously lurks below the surface. Without the reliability of a national narrative (here in the form of the Bayanihan's ordered suites), national unity may be forsaken, fearing that the "ethnic" will undo the work of the nation. The Filipino will resort to what he or she trusts more than the metropole's agents: the tribe, the clan, the province.[85]

Local critiques are being forwarded. They help us refuse forms of cultural analysis or reportage passed off as in the "national interest." Arnold Azurin might easily be talking about the folkloric research undertaken by the Bayanihan, as well as the discipline of folklore, when he writes that much of folklore is in fact an active creation of elites who anchor their position by locking others into simplified pasts: "The political manipulators obviously know the viability and intricacy of folklore as a facet of the national culture and consciousness much more than the researchers and experts in our universities and scholarly circles."[86] Marian Pastor Roces's work on analyzing the gendered division of cultural labor between arts and crafts wryly problematizes what has been taken for granted in Filipino cultures, wondering how one of the leading folk dance companies can convincingly argue that it is the "conservator of authentic ethnic traditions" when "the artistic director does not consider their costuming, proscenium theater, international touring, choreography, research, or staging to be problems."[87] Roces suggested that more attention be given to how so-called indigenous communities, as well as metropolitan dwellers, "contend with the rupture [of Philippine colonialism]" and take on the task of "re-invent[ing] modernity."[88]

## A Side Trip to Batangas, 1998

While traveling with a dance troupe of mostly U.S.-based Filipinos from Southern California, I witnessed an example of how a modern community adapted cultural practices to its unfamiliar and new settings. Badjao families had migrated from their homes in the southern Philippines to places farther north, to the small village we visited on the outskirts of Batangas City, a major port approximately 70 miles south of Manila. Our host was a celebrated choreographer and dance educator who had been taking visitors on exposure tours and master-dance seminars to learn some of the roots of Philippine dance. When we arrived at the settlement, we saw that the families had brought few material possessions. The *datu,* or chief, dragged out to a central clearing a *karaoke* machine powered by a small generator. He inserted an audiocassette and played the tape. Several of the Badjao women started to dance, encouraging the American students to join in. The music was blaring and distorted but familiar. Leaning in more closely, I recognized the tune: It was one of the many versions of the Los del Ríos hit "Macarena."[89] In a seaside village on the outskirts of the Philippines' second largest port, our Los Angeles-based troupe, led by a champion of ethnographically informed folk dance, learned movements from a displaced southern tribe with a tune mass-produced for the dance floors of Sydney, Belgium, Rome, Seville, and Paris. If some of us were having trouble that day in Batangas with what was supposedly an authentic rendering of the dances, it is not through any fault of the Badjao. Rather than regret that they did not have their instruments or costumes, as a couple of the U.S. dancers lamented on the way back to Manila, the Badjaos' sharing and hospitality demonstrated a larger lesson: that cultural expressions are rarely pristine, unpolluted, or unresponsive to the times. Instead, the Badjao reminded us that culture also represents a transactional space in which the things that matter to us so much—our songs, dances, lyrics, poems, stories—find ways to live on in the present by embracing compromises and discontinuities and to continue to make substantive meaning wherever one may call home. I doubt if any of the U.S.-based choreographers and dancers I traveled with would ever think of "faithfully" staging their own version of the dance we saw in the Badjao settlement. I imagine that much of the event would be deemed too far outside of what the overseas performers and audiences would expect—certainly if jerry-rigged machines blasting garbled dance beats were used. How authentic would that be, after all? Those privileged enough to authorize Philippine culture in the diaspora make those kinds of decisions about repertoire all the time. What we saw in that remote village would have to be actively forgotten or perhaps even lamentably dismissed as an occasion demanding charity or pity. And rather than seize the opportunity to draft a choreography (an embodied writing) of survival, organic adaptation, and utility to share with our audiences and communities in the United States, some of us would prefer instead to rely on the timeworn movements sanctioned from above. How convenient for us that, after "taking it from the people," heralded dance companies sell their repertoire in video and music stores all over the world.

IN THE NEXT CHAPTER I turn to an example of how the national performance repertoire is once again reinvented, this time by overseas cohorts of Filipino college and university students in the early 1980s. The Bayanihan's popularizing of Philippine folkloric forms becomes an essential element in what would become a wholly new genre unto itself, the Pilipino Cultural Night. The students, using the dance and movements as familiar signposts to an immigrant culture, also crafted a compelling narration that was a mirror of their own lives as young people at the forward edge of the Philippine diaspora and the U.S. multiculture.

# 3 Dancing into Oblivion

## *The Pilipino Cultural Night (Los Angeles, 1983)*

*There was a lot of family, friends, and people from the community. It was all through personal ties. It was something that we did on our own. I don't recall having an instructor guiding us along.*

—Helen Toribio

THE PILIPINO CULTURAL NIGHT is the most popular mass-based expressive form of culture organized by Filipino American students. Starting with a modest estimate of the number of participants—say, one hundred cast and crew members multiplied across two dozen campuses and mounting shows for at least twenty-five years—that conservative figure still represents a dramatically large cohort that has shared complex performance experiences and a largely improvised kinetic education in Philippine and Filipino American cultures. Some casts and crews swell into the hundreds while the number of campus student organizations no doubt exceeds my calculation, especially given the sprawling network of public and private colleges and universities (and even high schools) in California that have been a kind of ground zero for the PCN. Again, take that initial, rather low estimate of sixty thousand participants since the early 1980s and multiply it against another modest figure—the one hundred or so hours of rehearsal spent by each student per show—and the notion of how much time is committed to the performance of "Filipino-ness" is nothing less than astonishing.

By the mid-1980s, the PCN had developed into a familiar stage show consisting of folkloric dance wedded to an asynchronous theatrical narrative. Prior to this, community groups, student organizations, and other performers had mounted culturally themed presentations or festivals. For example, Arleen de Vera has traced the emergence of pre–World War II Rizal Day Queen festivals in the United States, narrating an intricate story of an immigrant community's performance of the "ideal Filipina" in relation to a nascent understanding of nationalism.[1] In New York, Bruna P. Seril organized her own folk-dance group and presented such work as early as 1943.[2] In the wake of the massive strike at San Francisco State University in 1968 that produced the first college of ethnic studies, student organizers created curricula deemed relevant for a global education and included proposed courses in Philippine history, economics, and dance.[3] In Hawai'i, the *Gabi ng Pilipino* (Filipino Night), sponsored by the Fil-Am Club at the University of Hawai'i at Mānoa, which featured dance and musical presentations, had been popular from the late 1970s through the mid-1980s but eventually was sidelined by events performed exclusively in Tagalog or Ilokano.[4]

In the United States, performing the national repertoire of the Philippines represents a complicated set of responses to living "stateside." Students have bent and extended Philippine cultural forms to meet the needs of an overseas Filipino population to document its own reckoning with American as much as Philippine history. The PCN takes up the burden of answering questions about Philippine and Filipino American culture that are not adequately addressed institutionally on campuses and informally at home. The shows take up too much time and labor for anyone to seriously think that the students are merely looking to entertain themselves and their families and friends. At the heart of the PCN experience are what Kimberly Alidio refers to as "productive problems" attending to absence, silence, and invisibility. Yen Le Espiritu's informant Pablo Barcenas attested to the lack of institutional structures to formally learn about his family's culture, citing only a cursory mention of the topic in class, followed by the dismissal, "Okay, let's move on."[5] Barcenas's experience at school has been reflected at home, with parents claiming that it is important for their children to "know about the Philippines" while stating, in response to a survey, that they rarely celebrate or observe Filipino special days.[6]

The productive problem that Alidio referred to—historiographical and familial gaps in knowledge—has been addressed countless times by thousands of students tending to hours of planning, rehearsal, and production. Raul Calderon, a PCN participant, "found a passion in it. . . . [T]his is when I really made connections to the Filipino culture and my cultural identity."[7] To appreciate connections made in the absence of curricula, mentors, and parental encouragement, I understand Calderon's situation of realizing just how disconnected Filipino Americans occasionally feel. On the one hand, Filipino student organizations encourage the adoption and reclamation of cultural practices, languages, histories, and even radical political traditions. On the other hand, Filipino parents often push their children to adopt the dominant culture's reward system while in college, with the expectation that their young will become less like them, less Filipino. They hope that the children will become better-educated versions of themselves and no longer associated with misunderstood cultural practices, seemingly obscure languages, forgotten histories, and even an embarrassing or potentially damaging accent.[8]

In this chapter, I examine the Samahang Pilipino's *Kasaysayan ng Lahi* (History of the People) at the University of California, Los Angeles, in 1983—an early and influential PCN—as a case study to consider closely what the repertoire can tell us about the kinds of choices young people made when the PCN was relatively new. *Kasaysayan ng Lahi* provides an excellent place to examine the beginning of a unique genre of Filipino American expression neither as a static Philippine import nor simply as a different version of "American" culture.

## The Golden State

The 1960s and 1970s represented a moment in U.S. culture in which public space seemed to widen under local and global influences. The 1980s, by contrast, have come to represent a rightward response, crucially narrowing the spaces in which racial minorities experimented with and pledged cross-cultural support for international struggles. Consider the final scenes in Duane Kubo's documentary on Asian American music, *Cruisin' J-Town* (1975). The narration moves from the bustling, multigenerational urban and working-class setting of Los Angeles's Japantown to El Teatro Campesino's construction of a politically informed and community-based arts center in San Luis Obispo. Shortly after Dan Kuramoto and Daniel Valdez reflect on how the Chicano *rasquachi* aesthetic resonates with American funk, Valdez sings "America de los Indios" accompanied by members of the jazz fusion band Hiroshima. Consider also the recording of "Somos Asiaticos (We Are Asians)" on the album *A Grain of Sand* (1973), by Chris Iijima, Nobuko Miyamoto, and Charlie Chin. Singing in Spanish, three Chinese and Japanese American activist artists vow to talk, sing, and fight *siempre juntos* (always together), *yo para tu gente / tu para la mia* (me for your people / you for mine). Those two examples, within a wider constellation of thousands of expressive moments, performed the artists' political commitment to each other—Asian Americans and Latinos *in concert.* Also, while both the cultural-nationalist and cultural-reactionist periods of the 1960s and 1970s share critiques of prior generations, the 1980s are often characterized for their rootless and narcissistic creative output—expressions of popular, not professional, forms of entertainment and socialization.

We can try to correct that kind of thinking by problematizing "multiculturalism," the cultural logic of the day, with Avery Gordon, David Theo Goldberg, and James Lee as our guides. While the promise of multiculturalism was that differences could be represented, consensus sustained, and resources better distributed, this was far from the reality.[9]

In the years after World War II, many Americans witnessed an era of rising expectations. From 1945 to 1973, the United States was paying its workers some of the highest wages among the industrial nations, allowing many to take seriously the possibility of fulfilling the suburban dream. Millions would take advantage of massive investments in public schooling. The number of students pursuing higher education more than quintupled, from a little more than two million in 1947 to more than thirteen million in 1988. The proportion of female students jumped from 29 percent to 54 percent, and by 1988 almost 20 percent of all college students were racial and ethnic minorities.[10] Those rising expectations would be challenged by two events: the advent of mass-based social movements of the late 1960s—a coming-of-age cohort that could not reconcile the First World's strategic and economic ascendance during the 1960s with continued racial injustice at home and struggles for national liberation by the world's African, Asian, and Latin American majorities—and the world economic crisis of the mid-1970s.

Over a twenty-year period beginning in 1973, the incomes of production workers would fall from $12.06 an hour in 1979 to $11.25 an hour in 1989 to only $10.83 in 1993. The greatest losses occurred in families with children younger than eighteen and in which the head of the household was younger than thirty. For young Latino families with children, the decline during these years was 27.9 percent; for young African American families, the drop was a devastating 48.3 percent. By the time President Ronald Reagan and President George H. W. Bush completed their terms in office, a massive national redistribution of wealth upward had taken place. The top 1 percent of households would control 16.4 percent of all incomes and 48 percent of the total financial wealth of the country. The bottom 95 percent would take 27.7 percent of the nation's total financial wealth.[11] Adding to the hyped success of so-called model minorities, commentators often noted low rates of Asian American employment while missing the more nuanced picture unfolding between the constituent ethnic groups. In her detailed assessment of employment during the 1980s, Anna Madamba concluded that Filipino Americans with educational levels higher than the national average were encountering high levels of underemployment, exhibited by job mismatch, the result of one's overeducation relative to the requirements of their occupation.[12]

In the 1980s, conservative nationalists re-coded how race, class, and gender were to be interpreted in the United States, and contradictions re-emerged between an economic logic that accentuated class differences in the form of union busting, supply-side economic policies, and corporate bailouts and the state's logic of managing and recasting cultural difference, as seen in the rhetoric of Margaret Thatcher's "A New Britain" and Ronald Reagan's "It's Morning Again in America."[13] If the student strikes of 1968 represented the leftward shift in national political culture—its emphasis on antiestablishmentarian and progressive thought and praxis—then the 1970s and 1980s represented a period of conservative reaction and repositioning.

The year 1978 marks a watershed in California politics, a harbinger for political discourse in succeeding years, especially in how the politics of redistributive justice would continue to be challenged. Around the issues of taxes and education, working-class white men and middle-class white homeowner activists pressed the notion that social investment had gone awry and that the nation needed to check concessions made to recent immigrants and racial minorities. The passage of Proposition 13, a popular California state initiative, limited the raising of property taxes and spurred similar "tax revolts" in several states. More significant, the initiative was a popular referendum on how state revenue was being allocated in the rapid "Third Worlding" of California's inner cities and suburbs.[14] In the same year, the Supreme Court's decision in *Regents of the University of California v. Bakke* drew attention to working-class white men who claimed to victims of "reverse discrimination."[15] Both issues reflected the growing anxiety of white working-class and middle-class Californians, fueling the perceptions that state investment had swung too far to the left and that racial minorities were to be held accountable for declining wages and opportunities.

Recounting the politics of racial division among the working and middle classes should also take into account how such discourses not only resonated with but were managed from above.[16] Conservative nationalism of the 1980s was in face, quite bi-partisan. In a report to the Trilateral Commission, European, American, and Japanese intellectuals and government officials meditated on the "ungovernability" of Western democracies. Among those assembled for this effort were advisers to the Kennedy and Carter administrations. Published not quite ten years after the strikes of 1968 and the mounting of mass-based movements, the report draws attention to how some bemoaned the signs of the times. It blamed those

> who assert their disgust with the corruption, materialism, and inefficiency of democracy and with the subservience of democratic government to "monopoly capitalism." The development of an

> "adversary culture" among intellectuals has affected students, scholars, and the media. . . . In some measure, the advanced industrial societies have spawned a stratum of value-oriented intellectuals who often devote themselves to the derogation of leadership, the challenging of authority, and the unmasking and delegitimation of established institutions, their behavior contrasting with that of the also increasing numbers of technocratic and policy-oriented intellectuals. In an age of widespread secondary school and university education, the pervasiveness of the mass media, professional employees, this development constitutes a challenge to democratic government which is, potentially at least, as serious as those posed in the past by the aristocratic cliques, fascist movements, and communist parties.[17]

Containing that threat involved well-worn tactics of divide and conquer. The war on poverty had shifted into a war against poor folks as social services and investment were drained from inner cities and ethnic enclaves. One of the pernicious subtexts of the assimilation paradigm has been the notion that a group's unassimilability into mainstream American life can be explained pathologically, shifting attention away from structural inequality and emphasizing, instead and exclusively, personal behavior.[18] Reagan's presidential victory in 1980 was the result of a dramatic political realignment. The winning conservative coalition was held together in no small part by the way in which racial differences spoke to and across various constituencies: to Christian fundamentalists on the far right and to conservative Democrats, many of them white male industrial workers. The union of these disparate groups was purchased with racial coding.[19] In the 1976 presidential campaign, Reagan bandied about phrases such as "welfare queen," conjuring indelible images of women cashing in their food stamps and welfare checks while cruising around town in Cadillacs. During his first presidential bid, Reagan's successor, George H. W. Bush, used dramatic imagery of Willie Horton to scare people into thinking that his rival, Massachusetts Governor Michael Dukakis, would let other convicted felons loose on the population. Both media strategies brazenly demonstrated how the leading conservatives of the day married fear with race and appealed to the electorate's worst impulses. The subtext is that the Democrats' social and economic policies were actually responsible for poverty and criminality and that the Democrats could not discipline the "welfare cheats" and criminals they helped to create or depended on. Rather than exclusively drawing attention to the racial bodies themselves, conservatives launched attacks on what they characterized as a bloated liberal welfare state. For example, Governor Pete Wilson worked hard to win the loyalty of staunch anti-immigrant supporters by blaming "misguided immigration policies" for California's economic sluggishness, poorly conceived systems of preferential treatments, welfare systems that created dependency, and bilingual-education programs that impeded assimilation.[20]

"The triumph of Reaganism represented a cruel and paradoxical conclusion to part of the rebellious impulse of the late 1960s," Manning Marable has observed.[21] Part of the paradox to which Marable refers is the fact that several intellectuals and leaders in the African American community, including Eldridge Cleaver, had placed their hopes in the conservative nationalism that Reagan offered. Counted among Reagan's supporters were activists such as Hosea Williams, a member of the Southern Christian Leadership Council, and Ralph Abernathy, once an aide to the Reverend Martin Luther King, Jr. They would blame the administration of Jimmy Carter for the continued economic slide of non-white communities in the 1980s.[22]

Political rearrangements would also signal larger developments along the cultural divide. The organizing and aesthetic strategies developed by racial minorities would continue to be discredited, and in their place the premium placed on ethnic universalism would be reinvigorated. The corresponding cultural logic of the day—cultural nationalism from above—would be reissued as "multiculturalism," a token acknowledgment of difference and a revalidation of the ethnic paradigm. During this period, Filipino American performing arts and cultural production underwent a disidentification with previous attempts and promises of cross-cultural linkage that echoed the difficulty of sustaining broad-based political coalitions across racial minorities in California. What survived in the midst of the government's programs of austerity (governors George Deukmeijian and Pete Wilson at the state level, and presidents Ronald Reagan, George H. W. Bush, and Bill Clinton at the federal level) were turns toward ethnic and cultural essentialism, or the persistence of cultural forms of expression marked by their efficiency in communicating heroic, unified, and essentialized histories. The narrowing of the public space for the arts in general would also mean that cultural performers would have to push through leaner times. With funders investing in works, projects, or artists that could be expected to turn a profit, experimental and marginal works found it difficult to grab popular attention (unless they were fetishingly sensationalized).[23]

A number of developments take hold in the 1980s that are worth noting. Filipino American families continued to slowly to make their way out of the central cities and into more spacious suburbs, while many of the more recent immigrant families built communities without direct familial reference to earlier generations' working-class experiences.[24] Funding for ethnic studies courses fell under politically charged scrutiny. University administrations tightened requirements for hiring, restricting positions to candidates with training from research institutions and excluding community activists, artists, and other specialists without "proper" credentials. And with the influx of Filipino immigrants into the United States, college-age children of the post-1965 generation found themselves on college campuses with the help hundreds of student organizations serving ethnically, nationally, or culturally specific themes. Funding for student services became the primary financial means on campus for developing relevant and meaningful "cultural programming."

In this scenario of diminishing and shifting resources, especially away from hard-won battles for semiautonomous ethnic studies curricula and structures and toward more socially acceptable activities promulgated in student services offices, college students constructed the first PCNs out of the remnants of a waning Filipino American student movement and a hunger to stage their histories on their own terms.[25] They reconfigured the role culture would play after the advent of the mass-based social movements. They would start in the context of a public culture that, for racial minorities, was shrinking, especially given the contrast to the prior generation's use of the discourses of cultural nationalisms to fuel art making. By the 1980s, however, the hard-won lessons of cross-cultural political and creative work gave way to the privileging of ethnically exclusive forms of cultural production.[26] Multiculturalism, according to one literary critic, became the "nation's operative fantasy."[27]

## Setting the Stage: *Kasaysayan ng Lahi*

In this section I provide detail Samahang Pilipino's *Kasaysayan ng Lahi.*[28] Part of the problem of researching this type of mass form is in determining definitive "origins" for the show. Mass forms such as the PCN do not lend themselves to tidy histories. For example, many early scriptwriters and dancers referred to shows produced in the mid- to late 1970s. They would talk about large crowds; long rehearsals; the elements of the shows, such as dances and music; and audience participation.[29] It was tempting to allow each of the interviewed performers to take credit for coming up with the idea of the PCN, but popular forms of culture like the PCN force us to consider not simply the origins of a dynamic form of culture but its various "beginnings"—to seek out not merely the logical succession of events, but to identify moments in time where individual actions, statements, objects, or performances resonate with a context in need of interpretation.[30] I find helpful the work of cultural critics who analyze discrete texts as part of "macro-textual" commentaries.[31] Let's start with the opening act.

## *The Warm-Up and the Emcee*

Gary Bautista was billed as a "popular Pilipino singer/entertainer" on the evening's program. A year after the performance, he joined the musical variety group S.O.S. (Society of Seven), based in Las Vegas and Honolulu, of which he would be a member until his death in 2006.[32] For the *Kasaysayan ng Lahi* performance, he donned the costume of a lounge lizard—a white, shawl-collared tuxedo jacket, black slacks, white shirt, and a pink bowtie and cummerbund set. He began with a note-for-note rendition of Al Jarreau's "We're in This Love Together." His moves were professional—smooth, polished, and reminiscent of a bygone era caricatured by comedians from Steve Allen to Bill Murray. When he turned from stage right to left and back again, he tossed out the microphone with a wide flourish while holding on to the cord, as if to give him even more room on an already bare stage.

His accent pointed to his Tagalog-speaking roots. Bautista dubbed himself "the Man with a Thousand and One Voices" and claimed to be able to perform 168 celebrity impressions. He got his start, he explained, by copying the voices of his teachers and fellow classmates: "It's all muscle-control, really." Bautista delivered impersonations of Louis Armstrong, Dean Martin, and the Filipino singers Carmen Rosales and Rogelio de la Rosa. He interviewed himself, playing both *Nightline*'s Ted Koppel and Philippine President Ferdinand Marcos. In Koppel's voice, he asked whether Marcos would ever give up power. "Never!" Bautista exclaimed as the late dictator. Still in character, Bautista/Marcos welcomed the audience, sending them into fits of laughter. His dictator's tone also eerily echoed the slurring swagger and folksiness of cowboy movie legends such as John Wayne. "Long live your Philippine roots," Bautista/Marcos said.

Consider the timing of the performance. Marcos's martial-law regime was eleven years old, and Marcos was the only president of the Philippines the PCN organizers had known during their lifetime. For anti-martial law activists in the United States, the threat of a president for life was no punch line. Rather, those events both galvanized and split several overseas communities.[33] President Ronald Reagan also surfaced, chatting with his wife, Nancy, about a boy who stopped to look at a painting of George Washington hanging in the White House. "Did you know that was our first president—George Washington?" Bautista answered with a non sequitur as "Tattoo" (the character played by Hervé Villechaize on the television series *Fantasy Island*), delivering his lines on his knees: "The plane! The plane!" Bautista then called for his "maestro"—a friend operating a tape player on stage behind the curtain—and launched into the Filipino ballad "Kailangan Kita." During the instrumental break toward the end of the tune, he wondered aloud how others would have finished the song. Like jazz musicians trading short passages to slip in improvised statements, Bautista's characters fired off a line at a time. Marcos surfaced again, followed by Paul Williams (with Bautista on his knees), then Bautista finished the tune in his own voice.

In the next routine, Bautista's did a rapid-fire delivery of a one-man children's show in which Popeye, Cookie Monster, and Kermit the Frog made appearances, then sang another ballad as Julio Iglesias. Ballads gave the impersonator a chance to demonstrate vocal control and intensity over long arcs and phrases; the form's sentimentality and romanticism also conveyed a sense of gravity that offset the comedy bits. Bautista returned to a comedy routine with another slate of characters (starting with a pixie wearing extra-large sunglasses and an exaggerated bowtie) before launching into "The Rainbow Connection," sung as a rapid-fire succession of characters, including Johnny Mathis, Jose Feliciano, and Elvis Presley. Toward the end of the tune, characters from the early part of the act jumped in, completing each other's musical phrases—Reagan, Popeye, Mathis, Kermit and Bautista himself, although it was not apparent that it was him at first.[34]

After a brief pause, Bautista was followed by the evening's emcee, Dom Magwili. In presence, tone, and demeanor, the two could not have been more unalike. Magwili's accent was "American"—Californian, really. He wore a dark double-breasted suit. His eyeglasses lent him a certain intellectual propriety over the evening's proceedings. He landed a few laughs with the line, "Gary Bautista did everything I was going to do." Magwili opened the show with a tune that he called the "Pinoy Blues," explaining that "the Blues does not have to be a sad thing. The blues can be happy too." Accompanying himself on harmonica, he soon had the audience keeping a steady and rousing backbeat. The song's overall structure bore a striking resemblance to Jerry Lieber and Mike Stoller's 1962 track "I'm a Woman," originally released by Christine Kittrell in 1962 and recorded by Peggy Lee, Maria Muldaur, Ruth Brown, Koko Taylor, and Bette Midler. In the 1970s, the song was used in television advertisements for Revlon's Enjoli perfume. By 1983, the audience might have forgotten the original song but probably was familiar enough with the form and melody to delight in Magwili's lyrical play.

*I get up in the morning*
*I wake up my son*
*He says, daddy, what's happening?*
*I say let's go for a run*
*and on the road*
*I ask him what he want to be*
*and* Jesusmariajosep[35]
*He want to be like me*

*A Pinoy*
*P-I-N-O-Y*
*I said a Pinoy*
*P-I-N-O-Y*

*I like my* pancit *[stir-fried noodles]*
*Over hot rice*
*I like my* lumpia *[spring rolls]*
*With beer and ice*
*and when I want to gamble*
*To Vegas I fly*
*I always go first class*
*'cause I always go in style*

*I am a Pinoy*
*P-I-N-O-Y*
*I am a Pinoy*
*P-I-N-O-Y*

*You ask me this question*
*"What's my responsibility*
*To be American and Pinoy*
*To my community?"*
*Well you know that question*
*Got to make me stop*
*'cause all I know, brother, is don't mess up, 'cause*

*You are a Pinoy*
*P-I-N-O-Y*
*I said a Pinoy*
*P-I-N-O-Y*

In an interview, Magwili explained that his tune served as an answer to Bautista's slick song styling, a self-conscious attempt to root the evening's performance in what he understood to be an explicitly Filipino American context.[36] The troubadour accompanying himself on a harmonica referenced histories and the blues aesthetic of pre–World War II men and women of anonymous trades in a way that the disembodied stylings of random celebrities could not. Magwili's tune indirectly drew the audience's attention back to the utility of cultural performance not for its own sake but for its ability to create a resonance between the immediate audience and the narratives of working-class communities. While Bautista's impersonations were committed facsimiles of popular song, Magwili's tune suggested deep linkages to the gutbucket "immigrant blues" that writers such as Bienvenido Santos attempted to document—the song of the student, the migrant, the worker looking for the America they had been promised before making their way out of the Philippines.[37] The impersonator allows us to escape into our former identifications, to recall our memories of celebrity, yoking disparate voices into the performer's sometimes absurd settings. Magwili's blues perform a critical function that Angela Davis identified in *Blues Legacies and Black Feminism*, when a subject perceived to have been a problem is named: "The process of *nommo*—naming things, forces and modes—is a means of establishing magical (or, in the case of the blues, aesthetic) control over the object of the naming process. Through the blues, menacing problems are ferreted out from the isolated individual experience and restructured as problems shared by the community. As shared problems, threats can be met and addressed within a public and collective context."[38]

## The Show

*Kasaysayan ng Lahi* featured live and recorded music to accompany the dancing and play. Two forms of live music were presented. One took the form of a *rondalla* ensemble (stringed instruments playing Philippine folk tunes) and percussionists highlighting non-Spanish-derived musical and dance forms (e.g., *kulintang*). The first suite began with a courting dance performed by a male and a female dancer. Both were garbed in traditional clothing representative of particular regions. As the dance concluded, the dancers hitch-stepped off-stage while a solo flute played. Drums and gongs rolled lightly at first and then rose to a thunderous crescendo. From this, a steady rhythm was established for the next dance, this one featuring six men. The percussive music droned on. The men exited, and six women took their place in the next part of this suite. Magwili commented on the southern Philippines' Muslim populations, pointing out how their costumes, music, and dances presented "a different culture from the other groups" in the central and northern Philippines. The emphasis in this narration was on the ability of the southern Filipino to resist Spanish religious conversion and political domination. The *singkil* dance was a spectacularly imperial and mythic showcase. All of the folkloric elements were on display; and the dancers carried it off full of attitude and stoic bravado. The dance was mesmerizing, comprising slow and at times *rubato* (out-of-time) chanting and contrasting with the dirge-like pace of the percussion of the opening sequence. Male pole bearers created an arch through which female dancers wearing scarves and bearing gilded fans moved slowly toward the front part of the stage. The chant shifted to a lilting melody carried by the slowly measured *ostinato* (repetition) of the drum and *kulintang.*

As the women left the stage, the men repositioned themselves into two quadrilles. They lowered poles toward each other into crosses. A single drumbeat signaled the command for the pole bearers to snap into a crouched position. They waited silently as the princess and her attendant slowly made their way through the crossed poles laid flat on the floor, stepping lightly, pausing, and then moving once again. From the mythic story on which the dance is based, both stepped through a forest of felled trees. The princess followed an attendant carrying a parasol. With a stamp of her heel, the princess issued the command to begin the slow clapping of the poles. Her movement was shadowed by the attendant. A strike of a gong signaled the clappers to change rhythmic pattern. Both princess and attendant moved through one set of clappers while another cue called out the rest of the princess's entourage to begin its ensemble movement at a faster tempo through the quadrilles. Her entourage exited as a prince made his entrance. Banging his sword against his shield, he stepped lightly through the clapping poles. The accelerated rhythmic pulsing of the bamboo signaled an earthquake shaking the forest. The prince guided the princess and attendant to safety.

This dance is part of a larger so-called "Muslim suite." More than any other in the repertoire of the PCN genre, this suite emphasizes a martial and highly romantic view of southern Philippine culture (part of a reference to a history of anti-Western resistance) and a gendered code of protection. The prince tames the unstable and wild so his princess may pass safely. This popular dance serves to reinforce the narrative of masculine protection of the docile and demure yet beguiling female presence. It narrates privilege amid the exotic and percussive reality that is imagined about life in the southern Philippines, about its reputed "danger." Ultimately, the dance also is part of young Filipino Americans' projection of a nascent anti-imperial critique. The "Muslim suite" represents more than an ethno-regional group's folkloric performance. It also represents that part of an identity to which the young performers aspire—an example of a heroic, unconquered, and imperial "past."[39] I will return to other iterations of the *singkil* in subsequent chapters.

The next segment of the show moved forward to the era of Spanish colonization of the northern and central part of the archipelago beginning in the sixteenth century (between 1521 and 1898). The narrator emphasized the brutality of colonization rather than the liberal benevolence of discovery, countering the privileging of European authority. The narration pointed to the presence of a culture already at work on the islands. The text, though, provided a weak counter to what was next presented on stage: a suite of dances demonstrating strong Spanish and European influences on performance and folk forms.[40] As a direct contrast to the presentation of the unassailed southern Philippine subject, the narrative supporting the display of central and northern cultural forms emphasizes the technical mastery of movement as well as the deft incorporation of the West's major religious system into a syncretic colonial culture. A very clear example of this influence is in the conversion of northern and central natives to Catholicism. The narrator pointed to the strong presence of religion for the lowland Filipinos represented in this particular suite of dances, represented on stage by a priest leading a small delegation through a candlelit prayer processional.

These folk forms do more than demonstrate the assimilation of New World choreography and performative rules. The PCN organizers also found normative gendered codes in courtship dances such as the *cariñosa* and *la jota*. According to the narration, these dances display the "secretive, demure, traditional Filipina."[41] Three couples slowly entered from stage left, the women outfitted in long, flowing gowns reminiscent of Spanish colonial culture, with butterfly sleeves, their hair tied into buns, and flittering fans to hide shy faces. The women approached their male dance partners, who were wearing *barong* (usually an untucked and semitransparent long-sleeved shirt traditionally made of piña cloth). They danced in three-quarter time to the *rondalla* ensemble. Once again, the narration made explicit the contradictory nature of the presentations. As if to counter the heavy colonial debt registered in this suite of dances, the narrator pointed out that, not only do the Christianized Filipinos of the central regions have "grace, style and musicality," they "also have fierce tempers." He pointed out that Filipinos could take credit for the invention of phrases taken for granted in the U.S. vernacular such as "running amok." The text attempted to balance the message that natives could so easily assimilate European cultural forms against the strain of resistance to colonial elite culture. The narration continued with histories not embedded in the dance—unfair taxation of lands by the Spanish, the nascent nationalism fermenting in the late nineteenth century, and the sporadic revolts against civil authorities throughout the archipelago.

The next segment consisted of a series of monologues featuring some of the leading figures in Philippine history. The first vignette featured Andres Bonifacio, who is credited with launching the secret anticolonial organization popularly known as the Katipunan. Bonifacio's heroic rhetoric captured the temper of the modern political sensibility, calling on concepts such as "freedom, equality, fraternity" that echo the French Republican motto. His was the voice of the uncompromising nationalist hero, a masculinism that identified the "proper" role of the young nationalist male as protector of the "motherland": "My fellow Filipinos, the hour has come to shed our blood."[42]

Next was the character of Apolinario Mabini, a major intellectual figure in the Philippine revolution, offering a more personal testimony: "They [the Americans] have raped our women, and stolen our lands." The actor playing Mabini simply sat in a chair at center stage, which amplified his cerebral nature by deemphasizing his physicality. The Mabini character was followed by Melchora Aquino, known also as Tandang Sora. An octogenarian by the late 1890s, Aquino was portrayed as an elder thundering about the failed revolution to unite Filipinos against Spain. She addressed the audience as *katipuneros,* imploring it members to "defend the rights of the Filipino people" and "the preservation of the Philippine heritage." The characters functioned similarly, reenacting how exemplary leadership spoke to the masses against Spanish and U.S. rule. But they also served another purpose: to collapse time, as if to recruit the audience for the cause of Filipino grievances to be carried forward to the United States. The quartet of heroes was rounded out with a monologue by the propagandist José Rizal, at the end of which he claimed: "We know how to die for our duty and principles." Much of the monologue lamented the escalation of violence in the Philippines as the Spanish desperately struggled to hold on to colonial rule. The character walked to center stage and paused. The sound of a gunshot rang out, and Rizal slumped forward in his final step. Rizal's death here summed up the narration of a decidedly nationalist version of Philippine history that emphasized anticolonial critique, the martyrdom of a nonviolent activist, and the cultural adaptation of folk forms. In this, the PCN emphasized the arc of the grand tradition of Philippine historiography, which places a premium on burgis elite male leadership hailing from a particular time period (1872–1898) as the crystallization of sentiments that had surfaced from generations of grievances in the colony. Reynaldo Ileto cautions against this historiographical framing, troubling the "founding moment" of the revolution by challenging the assumption that the peasant-driven anticolonial movements understood "nationalism" and "freedom" in the same way that their elite *ilustrado* counterparts did.[43]

In the next section of the show, the narration shifted from heroic proportions—histories centered on leading figures—to the lyrically personal by focusing attention on a specific geographic region, lowland scenes depicting Christian celebrations of Christmas and Easter, and idyllic representations of *barrio* life during the fiesta.[44] The jaunty *maglalatik, sakuting, pandanggo,* and *tinikling* were all prominently featured by dozens of dancers accompanied by folkloric music. The dancing set the stage for a young couple's courting scene that played with the audience's contemporary recognition of the precarious nature of securing immigration visas to the United States.

CARMEN: Do you really love me? Really really love me?
ROGELIO: Do you have a green card? (He is leaving for America.)
When I come back, I'll build you a big BIG nipa hut.
CARMEN: How long are you going to be away?

While setting the action against an idyllic provincial backdrop, the scriptwriters made a temporal jump and had the characters speak to a common contemporary anxiety: the difficulty of obtaining legal passage to the "States." It is an exchange that played with the audience's awareness of splitting family members apart for years, sometimes indefinitely, and often without knowing exactly all of the reasons. While wrenching, it was a scene played for laughs. Rogelio and Carmen held each other close to share a goodbye kiss and were interrupted by comic relief provided by another character, Carmen's *ate* (sister). The crowd laughed and sighed familiarly at the sister's Tagalog accent. But in this passage, the comedy wore thin, as the punchline seemed only to be the disjunctive timbre of the accent itself rather than a character's attempt to work through some absurd premise. At this moment, the script allowed the audience members to reassert their identity as relatively well-educated U.S.-based Filipinos listening to their Filipino "other." The scene never raised the possibility that *everyone* has an accent. With the sister character positioned linguistically as Filipino by virtue of her "foreign sound," the couple's bond was reinforced to each other and to the audience. Rogelio and Carmen stood in for a Filipino nation with which the audience could identify, a heteronormative reminder of the journeying man's role in the protection and care of the homebound woman.

Loud crashes marked the transition to the next scene, and the stage went dark. The narrator announced the coming of the U.S.–Philippine War (1899–1902), and part of President William McKinley's speech was recited: "We could not turn them over. . . ." Addressing a delegation of Methodist leaders, McKinley wondered aloud about the role the United States played in the wake of the Spanish–American War, at first seeming to come to the aid of Filipinos in their revolution against Spain. "We could not turn them over" meant that the United States would conduct military operations in disparate parts of the globe simultaneously, rejecting a potential windfall for other empires such as post-unification Germany.[45] The narration then juxtaposed the expectations of immigrants rhapsodizing about American streets "paved with gold" against harsh labor conditions found in pre–World War II Hawai'i and in the United States. The context of this early-twentieth-century history served another crucial purpose in the show: It established for the PCN organizers the material link between the United States and the Philippines. The script drew loosely on Philippine histories under Spanish colonial rule to reckon with some interesting juxtapositions wrought by modernity. When referring to the Spanish-influenced dance suites, dancers and choreographers lauded the Filipinos' ability to assimilate cultural forms. But the choreo-history would also elide the oppression of colonial rule and the dispersed acts of resistance throughout the archipelago during the same period.

In turning to the early decades of American colonial rule, the PCN organizers made sense out of the U.S. colonization of the Philippines by viewing Filipinos as part of a cheaply paid reserve labor pool. The action on stage consisted of students miming the repetitive movement of stooped agricultural labor in Hawai'i and along the U.S. West coast. The narrator made plain the contrast between the dreams of securing an education in the United States, learning skills to improve their economic lot, and returning to their homeland, with the reality of a "land . . . paved with hard labor," the insult of antimiscegenation laws, the crush of the Great Depression, the formalized racial regime buttressed by the U.S. Supreme Court's decision in *Plessy v. Ferguson,* and the climate of Asian exclusion that resulted in panic at the border.

The PCN organizers' main reference for this era was the "personal history" of Carlos Bulosan, the rich tapestry of personas and circumstances drafted in *America Is in the Heart.* The work has had at least two distinctively different audiences. On its initial release in 1946, *America Is in the Heart* was lauded by mainstream reviewers as a paean to the liberal orthodoxy of American assimilation and as testimony to the guiding and durable myth of personal achievement over adversity in the United States. In the pages of *Pacific Affairs,* Catherine Porter wrote that "Filipinos and Americans alike who believe that honesty and understanding are the roots of good international relations will welcome this book." A year later, Paul F. Cressey read Bulosan's text as a "story of thousands of his countrymen" fired by "idealism" and "hope."[46] When the book was re-released in 1973 by the University of Washington Press, a new cohort of readers—activists and academics seeking narratives for a usable and heroic Asian American literary history—drew inspiration from it. In the same year that Ferdinand Marcos declared martial law in the Philippines and four years after the massive strikes that resulted in the establishment of ethnic studies at San Francisco State College; the University of California, Berkeley; and the University of California, Los Angeles, critics such as E. San Juan Jr. could take up Bulosan's text as an offensive weapon, "enabl[ing] us to perceive the nature and direction of the class struggle in the Philippines and our historic mission as participants in it."[47] For the editors of the landmark literary anthology *Aiiieeeee!* (1974 ) and for several others teaching in the early years of the revisionist disciplines, Bulosan's text spoke eloquently to young people's growing identification with international radicalism and a nascent cultural nationalism.[48] For PCN organizers in the 1980s, Bulosan's *America Is in the Heart* was one of the few available texts that provided a moving portrait of life for Filipinos in the United States. Its rhapsodic moments (e.g., his gorgeous description of his first dancing experience) complemented the melancholic eloquence and unimpeachable credentials of a Popular Front–era writer.[49] Back on stage, the PCN drew directly from Bulosan's text. The tableau involved the building of Agbayani Village, low-cost residences for several aging Mexican and Filipino farmworkers in central California, where Depression-era writers and union activists set up workers' schools.

The post–World War II era—when Bulosan's narrative ends—became more difficult to narrate on stage for the students. The organizers of the show did not have the luxury of being able to rely on many historical works. For these stories, students relied on the recovered histories from their parents' generation. These performers were only one generation removed from the characters they portrayed on stage, narrating migration and settlement in the 1940s, many as returning soldiers or their wives.[50]

In a memorably staged farce, the players depicted a scene in which young Filipinos recruited into the U.S. Navy were not permitted to rise above the rank of steward. Here they pointed to the absurdity of the recruitment process, the culture clash of "naive natives" shouted down by humorless officers. Three young recruits met Captain "Guapo" (Tagalog for good-looking) and his Filipino aide. Downstage left, the captain and his aide were seated at a table:

CAPTAIN: Next! (*Baduys* [a colloquialism for buffoonish characters] push and shove each other to go first, acting scared. Pedro is finally forced to go first, cowardly approaching the desk.)

CAPTAIN: (Tough) What's your name?

NARIO: My name is Pedro Isidro Prodigalidad Espiritu Santo Salagubang Batumbakal, Ser. . . . But you can call me Boyet. (Starts to take a few steps back)

CAPTAIN: Come back here boy!

NARIO: (Turns to audience) See, he knows my name already! (Walks back to table)

CAPTAIN: Have you ever had any serious illnesses?

NARIO: (Acts confused; doesn't understand English) Ah, no espeaking English. . . . (Turns to aide) *Ano yung sinabe niya* (What did he say)?

AIDE: (Repeating the captain's question) *Nag karon ka na nung malalang sakit?*

NARIO: *Nung maliit ako yung kuya ko ay nagka bulutong pero hinde ako nahawa. Yung ate ko naman nam ka beke pero hindi na hawa. Yung nanay ko naman namatay sa jabetis pero hinde pa ako patay. Malusog ako.* (Flex muscle)

CAPTAIN: (Turns to aide) What did he say?

AIDE: He said "no."

CAPTAIN: (Confused with the first answer, he then asks) Where do you live, boy?

NARIO: Bukawi, Ser.

CAPTAIN: (Turns to aide) What did he say?

AIDE: He was born on Kapis, but when he was five they moved to Tondo. When he turned twelve they moved to the Babuyan Islands. But now he lives in Bukawi.

CAPTAIN: He said all that, huh?

AIDE: Yes, Ser.

CAPTAIN: Congratulations! (Shake Nario's hand) You're in the Navy!

NARIO: (Acts excited) Oh thank you, thank you, thank you. (Starts to kiss captain's hand. Turns to other *baduys* and starts to show off. Other two get excited and try to beat each other to be first. Manuel finally goes first.)

CAPTAIN: What's your name, and quit eyeballin' me, boy!
MANUEL: My name is Manuel Ebanquel, Ser.
CAPTAIN: Spell "Ebanquel," boy.
MANUEL: "Ebanquel": "E" as in Ibon (Tagalog for bird), "B" as in Bibby Ruth, "A" as in "you're Adorable" (Pinches the captain's cheek)
CAPTAIN: Don't you pinch me again, boy!
MANUEL: Yes, Ser. "N" as in Envelope, "Q" as in Cuba, "U" as in Europe, "E" as in another Ibon, and "L" as in Elephant.
CAPTAIN: "Ebanquel"—are you sure that's you real name, boy?
MANUEL: (Hurt by the question, Manuel starts walking away, hand on forehead, shaking head)
CAPTAIN: Come back here, boy. Are you sure that's your real name?
MANUEL: (Walks back, angry, almost crying) Of course Ebanquel is my real name. What do you take me for . . . granted? (Snubs captain. Juan butts in, very cocky, thinks he is better than the others)
JUAN: Do not paying attention to him, Ser. He is stupid. (Turn to Manuel, ridiculing him) You are so estupid. You do not eben know how to spell your name!
CAPTAIN: What's your name, boy?
JUAN: My name is Juan Desoto.
CAPTAIN: Spell "Desoto," boy!
JUAN: "Desoto"—"D" as in Desoto, "E" as in Esoto, "S" as in Soto, "O" as in Oto, "T" as in To, "O" as in O—"Desoto!"
CAPTAIN: Congratulations! (Shakes their hands) You are now all in the Navy!

The scene allowed the audience to share in the recruits' laughter and in their play with authority, recalling for so many families countless scenes of indignity and insult weathered during military service. The characters parodied the absurdity of determining qualifications for jobs with no hope of promotion. Filipinos served in the U.S. Navy as early as 1901, under an executive order signed by McKinley, but the crucial years for the enlistment of Filipinos as U.S. naval personnel would be during the Korean and Vietnam wars, as more than five thousand five hundred were recruited between 1953 and 1958 and more than one thousand two hundred recruits enlisted each year between 1959 and 1976. The policy of not allowing Filipinos to work in an occupational specialty other than steward was modified in 1971 and discontinued three years later. Responsibilities for the steward position were reclassified into others, such as mess management specialist. The staged folly of the PCN Navy recruitment scene originated in San Diego, as many of the student performers and scriptwriters came from military families and had heard their fathers and uncles tell stories about being passed over for promotions and other benefits, often leaving them with only everyday forms of resistance—indirect verbal jabs, jokes, and innuendo. What is more funny than the over-the-top accents was how the characters playfully switched codes, sometimes leaving their would-be bosses in the dark. The scene ended with a routine involving several more cast members and choreographed to the Village People's song "In the Navy." One of the dancers swabbed the deck and wildly swung a mop to turn directions, nearly taking off the head of the dancing captain, who was also a part of the routine. Several audience members were pulled from their seats to join on stage.[51]

From that playful sequence, the narrator returned to describe the "third wave"—family members and underemployed professionals who came to the United States after the watershed immigration-law reform of 1965. A few figures were posed on stage, not interacting with each other but miming their professional tasks—a medical doctor, a businessperson, a lawyer, a sales clerk, a housekeeper. Conceived primarily to liberalize the international image of the United States as a beacon of democracy against its Cold War rivals, the 1965 Immigration and Nationality Act was initially designed to manage what was expected to be a large influx of Southern and Eastern European migrants whom Congress believed would seek relief from the devastation of World War II. Legislators and social scientists did not expect migrants from Latin America and Asia to take up the offer in the large numbers they did. The act abolished the existing system of fixed quotas per country. The reform allowed the immigration of twenty thousand people per country, with upper limits set per hemisphere. The act would also be key in helping to set a pattern of growing class differences and heterogeneity of Asian American communities. The sociological literature reveals the emergence of essentially two "Asian Americas," the first composed primarily of relatives petitioned by people of Asian descent. The newer immigrants, especially those from the Philippines, had fewer ties to the generation of laborers and students who had emigrated in the early part of the century. Able to secure migration status largely by filling U.S. labor shortages, these newer immigrants of the "third wave" were those who possessed technical skills needed by various sectors.[52]

The tendency in the existing Filipino American historiography is to laud the post-1965 generation for its relatively stable and upwardly mobile class status. This has the effect of vindicating a liberal view of history, privileging individuated access to material wealth. Those who celebrate the third wave's achievements draw on the colloquial telos of "rags to riches" in narrating Filipino American history, coddling bourgeois aspiration while turning away from civic and community accountability. Whereas once there were colonial subjects, insurrectionists, and underpaid and disadvantaged students and laborers, now there are teachers, doctors, engineers, and other so-called professionals to testify to the hard-won (and individuated) victory of achieving the American dream. The logic cherished in so many historical and performative narratives pats the author on the back, reminding "meritorious" individuals that they do not need preferential treatment or "handouts." The authors of this kind of logic reward the post-1965 immigrants for their apolitical presence. And often they present a history that seems to conclude in the present, with entertainment awards, elected office, victories in beauty pageants, or corporate sponsorship.[53]

In this section of the show, the action and narration turned intensely personal and lyrical again as the students projected some of their own family stories onto the stage—including lost promotions, job discrimination, and frustration in the midst of a nation's booming economy. They did not broach the history of the later 1960s when rising material wealth and the continued promise of prosperity exploded from criticism by the new social movements. Instead, the show closed with the character of Rogelio, now much older, reciting a letter to Carmen back home in the Philippines. He never made enough to return after years of earning depressed wages as a farmworker in California. He wrote from the retirement home built by young activists, lamenting the fact that he would see his last days in the United States and not in the country of his birth: "Maybe I won't ever be a rich man. But there is one thing I am proud of: I am Pilipino." It was bittersweet, but hardly a resolution for the character. Rogelio was a projection of the student's reckoning with the historical memory of men and women like the aging laborers and former students they would come to know—folks who were passing away. The long and hard work of mounting the PCN and finding a way to narrate Filipino American and Philippine history on stage would continue almost as a direct response to being removed from those earlier communities.

Just as the show opened with a blues call-and-response, with Dom Magwili on vocals and harmonica, the evening ended with another troubadour, the student Mel Ilomin, accompanying himself on an acoustic guitar on a song he had composed that became the student organization's theme. Another student at the time, Augusto Espiritu, recalled the song and the singer: "I was quite struck by it when I first heard it because it was, in my mind, the best rendition of the song. It was very powerful. [The students] were getting exposed to the struggle of the manongs/ . . . [Marcos's rival Benigno] Aquino had been assassinated. [The song's lyrics] say something. There's a message to it. It connects Samahang [Pilipino] to something larger."[54]

The 1983 show demonstrated how the repertoire for the PCN was being crafted: *impovisationally,* as with Magwili's "Pinoy American" blues shout to Bautista's polished impersonations, as well as *formally,* out of the scarce knowledge about Filipino culture and the Philippines readily at hand. *Kasaysayan ng Lahi* offered a unique and hybrid matrix: (1) a performance that was critical of dominant presumptions that immigrant children born and reared in the United States should abandon their parents' identification with the "homeland"; while also (2) a celebration of the multiculturalist goal of acknowledging Filipino culture as commensurate with other nationalities and therefore deserving of adequate representation; (3) an obliquely pejorative statement regarding certain aspects of Philippine culture deemed complicit or beholden to a "colonial mentality";[55] and, finally, (4) a romantically nostalgic paean to earlier cohorts of Filipino migrants to the United States and Hawai'i, especially agriculturally and industrially bound laborers. As Espiritu noted, students indeed connected to something larger with songs and stories of their own creation. But how would this newly inaugurated PCN genre fare over the years? How would it continue to connect biography, history, and nation through performance? That is the subject of the next chapter: the extended life of a show that, over the course of a generation, has become a thoroughly reliable and downright intransigent expressive form of Filipino American culture.

# 4 Repetitive Motion

## *The Mechanics of Reverse Exile (San Francisco, 1993)*

*Are Filipino Americans becoming more visible? To combat the collective Filipino identity crisis, some Filipino Americans are fighting for visibility by promoting cultural awareness and ethnic pride. For example, the mostly Filipino Kababayan Club of the University of California at Irvine (UCI) recently staged a play that showcased Filipino cuisine, music, dance, and customs, and portrayed a Filipina American discovering her cultural heritage. Due to the Kababayan Club's efforts to increase awareness about Filipino culture on campus, a course on Filipino Americans is now offered regularly at UCI.*

—Lan Cao and Himilce Novas

IN THE SAME YEAR that Filipino students helped to launch a popular performance genre, two academic works were published that would change how we think about the relationship between repertoire and cultural identity: Eric Hobsbawm and Terence Ranger's *The Invention of Tradition* and Benedict Anderson's *Imagined Communities.* Nations—and the repertoires associated with them—have very specific histories; are bound to specific times, cultures, and places; and have been subjected to endless amounts of editing, meddling, and experimentation. The essays in Hobsbawm and Ranger's volume challenged seemingly ageless cultural practices, especially claims to authority that had long been enjoyed by elites and affirmed by everyone else—from the augmentation of the trappings of the British monarchy for its Indian and African colonial subjects to revivals of Druid ritual and the performance of Celtic music. The supposedly long histories of bagpipes, kilts, and clan tartans, according to one writer in their volume, rested on creative scholarship aimed at providing symbolic rejoinders to British advances being made on Welsh and Scottish political autonomy.[1]

In previous chapters, I described how the Philippine national repertoire was invented in the 1930s to anticipate the granting of sovereignty to the colony. By the late 1950s and early 1960s, the choreography had left the schoolhouses where Aquino had trained legions of physical-education teachers for the international stage in a movement that mirrored the dispersal of the Filipino diaspora. Pilipino Cultural Night casts and crews in the United States have often become the kind of communities Anderson described in which no individual can know all of the people in his or her community and yet "in the minds of each lives the image of their communion."[2] In a patrimonial sense, the organizers are the inevitable inheritors and stewards of enduring, if beleaguered, cultural practices. To forestall the "loss," the custodians renew that patrimony every year, reminding themselves of tradition's vitality.[3]

In this chapter, I point to several theatrical elements that have become staples of the PCNs on numerous college and university campuses (although the activity is not carried out exclusively at the college level) since the 1980s. I identify the basic structure of the show, which has tended to harden over time. The PCN continues to enlist stand-ins not only for heroes of yore (iconic as well as undersung) but also, now, as *reproductions of productions.* How did the diffuse cultural productions of a seemingly heterogeneous group of Philippine- and U.S.-born Filipinos become standardized, replicated, and, ultimately, predictable?[4]

The production of PCNs since the 1980s reflects the larger changes in immigration from the Philippines and changes within post-1965 Filipino American families. The 1980s saw large numbers of Filipinos immigrating to the United States, with the population growing 126 percent between 1970 and 1980.[5] When Filipinos settled in the United States in this period, they did so along a pattern of dual-chain migration, revealing the community's cleavage along class lines. On the one hand, working-class families petitioned for relatives with similar life chances and choices. Many of these families had known the migratory life of labor camps or the urban experience of single-resident-occupancy hotels. Some would find their second and third generations moving out of the central cities and Manilatowns historically located in Los Angeles, Stockton, or San Francisco to the outlying areas or districts—to Daly City, San Leandro, or Carson, California. On the other hand, another cohort of what has been described as professional and technical workers—especially those working in the medical and information-technology fields—found that their migration to the United States would be facilitated by the reform of immigration laws in 1965. Another Filipino America began to form outside the traditional urban cores, built on the middle-class expectations of dentists, nurse practitioners, insurance brokers, real-estate agents, software engineers, and attorneys. They made their homes in places like Milpitas, Hercules, Pinole, California, as well as in the suburbs of Chicago and Houston and in Jersey City, New Jersey.[6] Not only were Filipinos coming the United States, but the children of the generation of post-1965 immigrants were also coming of age, attending colleges and universities in increasing numbers. At the University of California, the number of undergraduate degrees conferred on Filipinos more than quadrupled between 1982 and 1992. Many of these students spent their time in chemistry and engineering labs, business programs, social-science lecture halls, and life-science facilities.[7] The development of friendly rivalries among campuses has also necessitated the creation of master calendars to allow organizers to help plan around each others' shows.[8]

To understand how the PCN has become so durable, we have to begin with the important role played by Filipino student organizations on college and university campuses.[9] Many Filipino student organizations have histories that coincide with the political awakening of students on college campuses in the late 1960s and early 1970s. For example, San Francisco State University's Pilipino American Collegiate Endeavor (PACE) was founded in 1967; the Pilipino American Alliance (PAA) at the University of California (UC), Berkeley, was founded in 1969; Samahang Pilipino at the University of California, Los Angeles (UCLA), was founded in 1972; and Kababayan at the University of California, Irvine, was founded in 1974. During spring academic terms, the organizations' memberships elected officers for the following year. Certain positions were reserved for coordinating PCN logistics. Some organizations preferred to have a "cultural coordinator," the de facto PCN coordinator, sit on the group's executive board. Others preferred to staff that position with a broader mandate, sometimes titled "political and community coordinator" or "special events coordinator." In either case, those vying for the elected or appointed positions realized that their work would be devoted to the planning of a very complicated performance. Beginning in the fall, students were delegated various production tasks—designing sets, making costumes and props, catering, choreographing dance, arranging music, and so on. Several students sacrificed many hours of planning and rehearsal time. For the most part, each organization's leadership relied on what it recognized as its core members—those unelected and highly motivated individuals who volunteered time, labor, and out-of-pocket funds for several months ahead of the show's run. The number of cast and crew members grew as the production neared. This was especially true for rehearsals of large numbers such as the dance suites, where it has been typical to see more students in the few weeks before a show's run.[10] On some of the larger campuses where productions have demanded several hours of rehearsal time each week, organizers have created tutoring programs for their members, justifying time spent on the show as community building and retention. This has been the subject of some internal criticism.

Members have also shouldered out-of-pocket expenses, usually the printing and reproduction of handbills, posters, and programs. But funding for the show has also been a long-term and sometimes complicated task. Students have tapped special student government programming grants from student activities offices (on most campuses, under the direction of the dean of students) or the office of the university president. The amounts granted for such shows have varied wildly, from a student organization's budget at a small campus laying out $300 to more than $30,000 for one evening's worth of entertainment. The group's finance officer generally has tracked major expenses, such as securing the venue, purchasing or renting costumes, and paying for choreographers, caterers, and printers. For example, in 2006 student legislators at UC Berkeley passed "A Bill in Support of PAA's 30th Annual Pilipino Cultural Night of UC Berkeley," allocating $1,500 to the show's coffers. The budget submitted for review included $14,180 to rent the venue; $800 for dance props, music, and costumes; $1,300 for publicity; $3,500 for programs; $1,200 to rent practice venues; $1,000 for set design; $3,000 for the "PCN Afterparty"; and $3,500 for miscellaneous expenses such as food, flowers, and pressing DVDs. The group's resources included a $4,000 allocation from PAA for the show, $1,000 from tentative sponsors, $18,000 in ticket sales, and $2,700 from "participant packages" ($30 per student for ninety students).[11]

## Native Elements

The efforts of student organizations, the influx of college-age Filipinos and Filipino Americans throughout the 1980s and 1990s, and the encouragement of friendly intercampus rivalries and support point to the further development of a "PCN genre," according to the choreographer Joel Jacinto. UCLA's Samahang Pilipino, he says, "had a lot to do with moving the genre forward or establishing the format of the genre and setting precedence in terms of the different types of productions that we did on campus. We helped give birth to the genre."[12] Joel and Ave Jacinto co-founded a folkloric performing-arts troupe in Los Angeles and have returned often to their alma mater as consultants.[13] Jacinto understands the PCN genre within contexts that emphasize presentation over participation in the Western sense of separating audiences from performers. Presentation modes assume a passive audience, with performers remaining detached (conventionally barred from breaking the "fourth wall") and usually accentuated with defined play spaces on stages and by distinctive costuming, lighting, and so on. The PCN genre can be contrasted with the more organically and highly ritualized exchange out of which folkloric forms are based. In the participatory settings from which folk forms emerge, dances and songs are not done for others so much as they are done *with* others.[14] Jacinto and his classmates helped to set in motion performance standards, elements, and expectations that have been hammered into predictable conventions since the 1980s. His reference to a "genre" is appropriate. Since the 1980s, student performers have insisted on key elements to distinguish PCNs in several ways. As past chapters have demonstrated, the PCN has been closely modeled on a particular kind of dance-theater presentation made popular in the 1950s and based on a national repertoire in the 1930s. Like other invented traditions that have dubious roots in an "authentic past," the Pilipino Cultural Night has become a static and seemingly unchanging and unchangeable artifact.

PCN participation has become a rote activity, what the actor and director Dom Magwili has referred to as a rite of passage. Richard Schechner, building on the work of Arnold van Gennep and Victor Turner, helps frame Magwili's experience with his young charges. Schechner clarified that the movement through life's various well-defined stages (e.g., birth, social puberty, marriage, parenthood, social advancement, job specialization, retirement, and death) would be punctuated with a host of rituals.[15] Not only are rituals "memories in action," but they also help people deal with "difficult transitions, ambivalent relationships, hierarchies, and *desires that trouble, exceed or violate the norms of daily life.*"[16] With desires that trouble, exceed, or violate the norms of daily life, the PCN as a ritual is loaded with significance precisely at the time that students become more Filipino than fellow classmates who choose not to participate in the shows while also becoming less Filipino as they adopt consumption patterns, dominant cultural codes, and reward systems that often are in conflict with their immigrant parents' histories.

Victor Turner's concept of liminality can be applied here: "Liminal entities are neither here nor there; they are betwixt and between the positions assigned and arrayed by law, custom, convention, and ceremonial."[17] It come as no surprise, then, that colleges and universities have been what Schechner would refer to as "hotbeds" of invented rituals, with an array of activities that range from hazing, graduation ceremonies, and processions to sporting-events cheers. "The fact [that] there is a quick turnover in the student population helps establish new rituals swiftly," Schechner notes.

"In real life a generation takes 20 or 30 years to turn over; at college it is four years."[18] To be neither here nor there can also mean, in a ritualistic sense, to be neither this kind of person nor that, an in-between time in which one is vulnerable and directionless. That is the moment one recognizes that one is at a crossroads, where being lost is not far from being found. The PCN as a *rite*—or as a profoundly Filipino American ritual—is as much about a mode of entry into dominant culture as it is a passage from ignorance and indifference to awareness and expression.[19]

The PCN genre features two halves: folkloric forms and a theatrical narrative. I will discuss those two elements in greater detail later. First I want to highlight secondary aspects that mark the PCN in unique ways. The first concerns the use of flags and national anthems; the second is the deployment of Tagalog as the presumptive default language within the presentations.

Almost without exception, PCNs since the 1980s have opened with the singing of both the Philippine and U.S. national anthems. The former is uniformly sung in Tagalog, led by a soloist or a choir. This comports with the "Flag and Heraldic Code of the Philippines," which states that the anthem must be rendered in "the national language."[20] The act also stipulates that "the singing must be done with fervor."[21] Like other invented traditions that seem to have unvarying histories, the Tagalog anthem is actually a mid-twentieth-century phenomenon. The composer Juan Felipe wrote the music to "Lupang Hinirang [Our Land]" in 1898 in the form of a military march without words. The poet Jose Palma's added Spanish lyrics a year later concerning a beloved land (*Tierra de amores*) that would refuse to surrender to invasion (*No te hollarán jamás*); although there is comfort and sweetness there (*En tu regazo dulce es vivir*), her children would die to right any offense (*Es una gloria para tus hijos, Cuando te ofenden, por ti morir*). In the 1920s, during the U.S. colonial period when nationalist symbols and songs were banned, an English version, "The Philippine Hymn," was commissioned and adopted by the commonwealth. Consider how such an adjustment—the creation of a hymn rather than an anthem—would suit the situation. Hymns are generally songs of praise or love of a deity. Anthems, by contrast, derive from an antiphonal style of singing; connote a secular practice; and involve groups in singing with each other, trading passages, or enjoining call-and-response. Hymns acknowledge the submission of authority to the divine. Anthemic singing allows for the sovereign to be reconstituted at the performance. With Philippine sovereignty in the hands of a foreign power, a hymn refers to an ethereal authority, somewhere other than in the presence of its colonial moment. It would not be until well into the 1950s that a Tagalog version would be commissioned and embraced by an "independent" Philippines. At several PCN productions, the choir deftly merges "Lupang Hinirang" and the "Star-Spangled Banner" into a seamless medley.[22]

Related to this are the presentations of the two national flags on the stage, in printed material distributed to audiences, and in other publicity. The placement of the flags connotes a correspondence between the nations—that is, emblems of comparable sovereign entities, each with its own separate and equal standard. The Philippine flag's symbols refer to foundational stories and a conception of what or whom is included under the banner: eight rays emanating from a sun to signify the regions that rose up against Spanish rule in the late nineteenth century, three stars indicating major regions in the country, and colors representing peace (blue in the top half) and patriotism (red in the bottom half). Interpretations of these signs have changed over time. At the signing of the Declaration of Philippine Independence in 1898, the colors "commemorat[ed] the flag of the United States of North America, as a manifestation of our profound gratitude towards this Great Nation for its disinterested protection which it lent us and continues lending us."[23] The presentation of both the national anthems and the flags at the opening of PCNs suggests that U.S.–Philippine relations have been unambiguous and resolved with the granting of independence, despite what one scholar has referred to as their "entangling" for most of the twentieth century.[24]

Tagalog has occupied a central role in PCN productions. Hundreds of shows have rendered their titles in a Philippine language—for example, *Fiesta Sa Ating Bayan* (Celebration at Our Town), *Pagsasama sa Pamamagitan ng Cultura* (Unity through Culture), and *Ang Nawalang Kayamanan* (The Lost Treasure). In a study of language use and preservation by the grandchildren of contemporary immigrants, researchers justified the exclusion of U.S. Filipinos due to the "high rate of English monolingualism, attributable partly to the status of English as an official language of the Philippines," despite the fact that Tagalog was the sixth most widely spoken language in U.S. homes. When the question was narrowed to the ten languages most frequently spoken at home other than English and Spanish, Tagalog rated fourth, ahead of Vietnamese, Italian, Korean, Russian, Polish, and Arabic and behind Chinese, French, and German.[25] The use of Tagalog—in show titles, untranslated asides, the dynamic idiomatic play of Taglish puns delivered by characters on stage, and various publicity materials—has done more than merely reflect the popularity of speech patterns and preferences. Such usage may also be understood in the performative context as projections of aspirations and a rooting of diasporic sensibilities in a homeland vernacular to capture and play in public spaces amid recurring and anxious calls for "English Only" and "English First" initiatives.[26] This process is also reflected by the popularity of Tagalog-immersion courses in the Philippines and in the dozens of campaigns on campuses to offer instruction in the Tagalog and Ilokano languages. More than preservation, interest in native languages in places as disparate as Davis, California; DeKalb, Illinois; Mānoa, Hawai'i; and Virginia Beach, Virginia hewed closely to concerns shared by Filipino intellectuals after World War II who, according to Augusto F. Espiritu, "validated not only the vernacular but also the Philippines' indigenous, pre-Western, and especially oral cultural legacies."[27]

As noted earlier, the PCN genre has consisted of two essential features. In the first feature, Filipino folkloric forms such as song, dance, music, and costuming, PCN organizers have unwittingly drawn from two competing schools of thought. On the one hand, they have relied on the repertoire invented in the 1930s by educators in Manila that authenticates an understanding of "Filipino culture." That is, the folk forms helped to ground the students' experimentation with fashioning identities and crafting a sense of transnationalism from within the context of the United States; through the shows, they became a different kind of "Americans" as well as "Filipinos." On the other hand, the repertoire has drawn heavily from the highly stylized rendition of the dance-theater work popularized since the late 1950s. Samuel Gilmore notes, "For the average dance coordinator, the Bayanihan is often the first and only resource. It is not only readily accessible, it is also clearly a professional representation of traditional choreography. It thus functions as a widely accepted referent for traditional dance, and its use will generally deflect criticism from most sources or inquiry as to the source of particular dance movements. . . . In practice, the Bayanihan tapes serve as a legitimation resource for dance coordinators that helps to differentiate them from their peer group."[28] As I recounted in the previous two chapters, Bayanihan choreographers such as Lucrecia Urtula were taken to task by the traditionalist standard-bearer Francisca Reyes Aquino for speeding up tempos, liberalizing costuming choices, and performing dances and songs out of context or sequence. Aquino and her students, who were self-styled traditionalists, criticized this postwar stylization. Dance theater was not folk dance, Aquino would claim, and therefore did not have a claim on authenticity. The tension between these two streams remain blurred in the PCN genre.

The second feature is an asynchronous theatrical narration that performers refer to as the "skit." It is in the theatrical narrations that the PCN has been more fully defined as a genre not originally from the Philippines and later adapted to U.S.-based needs, but rooted in and reflective of students' anxieties and aspirations. While the performance of the national repertoire aimed for the epic, aspiring to the telling of the grandest tales and the demonstration of the homeland's patrimony, the language of the PCN's play was that of the lyrical—personalized and intimate testimony of undertheorized cultural identities and national affinities.[29] While the performers played the roles of royalty, ritualized animals, and even gods in the folkloric suites, they embodied different versions of themselves in dramatic scenarios. These mini-plays allowed organizers to explicitly raise concerns about their experiences in the United States, including poking fun at their parents' reticence concerning family histories, the latent homophobia found in their peer groups, anti-gang exhortations, organizing to support affirmative-action and equal-opportunity programs, and celebrating the Pinoy boxers of the 1930s, and retelling the stories of Flor Contemplacion, Benigno Aquino, Ferdinand Marcos, "mail-order brides," the campaign for benefits waged by World War II–era Philippine veterans, the struggle for Filipino American and ethnic studies on college campuses, young people's challenges to their parents' traditional views on a whole host of issues (especially marriage and courting), and the prevalence of (and silence about) domestic violence. Contrasting genres of poetry, Max Harris posed the epic poet as a bearer of "impersonal and sacrosanct" traditions, while the lyric poet "writes of the personal and present."[30] Leaning more toward exposition than analysis, PCNs—and, in particular, the theatrical narrations—have represented imminent and incomplete arguments for how cultural memories were to be preserved by this generation.

Perhaps the most widely used device in the shows has been the "reverse telos." The PCN genre has been both an imminent critique and a symptom of the assimilation paradigm at whose heart is a story of or proposition for how conflict among ethnic groups will be resolved. Assimilationists have recycled the popular metaphor of the "melting pot," which is also the title of a play written by Israel Zangwill in 1909 that was influential for dramatizing how recent immigrants could cast off memory, language, and their insistence on intraethnic marriage to realize a "New World Symphony."[31] The assimilationist's premium has been built on the liberal expectation that immigrants, and especially their children, would sever their allegiance to the Old World to conform to the New.[32]

How has this been reversed in the PCN genre? At the beginning of the show, the protagonists do not know their history or "culture," a situation that produces consternation and humor among their on-stage friends and family. In a familiar "quest" motif, the characters meet guides—elders, spirits, or parent figures—who "transport" them from safe, privileged, and increasingly suburban and apolitical settings to an idyllic Philippines.

During their journey, the characters encounter sounds and visions that are dramatized in the form of folk-dance suites, and they marvel at their new knowledge of aspects of Filipino culture that had been unexplained. They have "gone native." The bird dances, courtship waltzes, warrior chants—all confirm for the characters the sanctioned repertoire of the Filipino. They rely on the visceral engagement with bodies for their authentication—costumed, armored, dancing, playing, and, often, praying. The protagonists are confronted with a test of some sort, a choice to be made or a task to be achieved, as the source of dramatic tension. Stay with the abusive boyfriend or risk the consequences of a public breakup? Leave behind one's *barkada* (close-knit group of friends) or follow an elder's stern judgment? Throw the fight to cash in against your "countrymen" or see the match to the end? By the end of the show, the characters reached an epiphanic state of cultural awareness and pride that they could carry back with them to the United States. This motif—of the quest, a "reverse exile"—has been the most familiar one deployed throughout the genre. For young characters, "something" was missing: that which was replaced by an imagined return to the Philippines where the "crisis" of Filipino American identity could be solved. "Reverse exile" is bracketed here to call attention to the problematic of American-born Filipinos who do not "go back" to a place where they have never been. Compare Oscar Campomanes's explication of the exilic motif in Filipino literature where he situates Filipino American literature in a "reverse telos."[33] The tacit assertion made here was that the Philippines—as represented in its folkloric repertoire—could be understood as a sturdy repository of knowledge, a warehouse of unchanging, static, and therefore "authentic" representations of Philippine life. The exercising of the "reverse exile" motif refused to acknowledge the fact of cultural change, indeterminacy, and reconstruction at work in *both* the Philippines and in the United States.[34]

Assimilationists advance the liberal expectation that succeeding generations will intermarry with other ethnic and racial groups. They will move out of cloistered ghettoes; change their eating patterns, patterns of dress, speech, and diet; and attain higher levels of education by breaking admissions barriers. And while such designations were merely taken for "extrinsic" manifestations of cultural change, the premium of assimilation would be best manifested in a cohort's move toward out-marriage and one's "primary associations."[35] The teleology of American assimilation ends with the children of immigrants no longer dreaming of the *homeland* as their parents did. Rather than having less significance for succeeding generations, ethnic articulations of cultural identity, such as the PCN, continue to be popular. The PCN is both an oblique challenge and a symptom of dominant culture's call for assimilation. As such, PCNs have resonated with the more politically and socially charged articulations of Afrocentrism or Chicana/o nationalism. Calls for communities to laud "mother Africa" or "Aztlan" as homelands and to claim the lineage of ancient kings and queens over and against so-called democratically elected present-day leaders registered an implicit critique of contemporary culture. But it is not much of a leap to see that the embodied reference to the Philippines was also at its root a nascent critique of what has been available for Filipinos to make sense of themselves in the United States. The attention (*obsession*, even) to homelands for U.S.-based racial and ethnic minorities outside the nation suggested how the dominant national narrative of freedom balanced with equality was deferred rather than realized.

The PCN genre's use of this imagined return to the Philippines stands in stark contrast to the sophisticated transnational work of Filipina activists based in the United States whose multigenerational stories are beginning to be documented. For example, working on issues that range from analyses of the Philippines' labor-export policy to the fate of Amerasian children living near former U.S. military installations in the archipelago, groups such as the Gabriela Network USA articulate a keen sensitivity to respecting the sovereignty of Philippine-based leadership while enjoying a degree of freedom in undertaking innovative approaches to globalized organizing work. While the PCN protagonists have taken for granted travel and mobility as part of a journey to discover and then collapse the distance between past and present, between here and there, activists and other cultural workers outside the PCN genre have acknowledged their limited efficacy by virtue of not being in the Philippines while forging ongoing connections and conduits for political activity.[36]

The PCN genre has also reversed the reticence of Filipino parents about personal histories. For a host of reasons related to shame or self-loathing, or simply to safeguard their children against feeling "different," parents have made specific choices about what aspects of the culture are available. For example, Victor Merina recalled what happened when he was taunted as a young boy for his Filipino accent: "[My parents] didn't want us to learn Tagalog [the main language of the Philippines] or a dialect from their islands, which is called Ivatan. At first they spoke both dialects at home with my sister and me. But after the incidents of language at school, they made a conscious decision not to mix the languages. So they didn't speak any Tagalog to my sister or [me] when we were growing up. In retrospect, we all regret that now."[37] In so many shows, students have played out Merina's frustrations. Playing the role of one's parents on stage has made for easy laughs. Filipinos rarely see or hear themselves as Filipinos in popular media. "Anything but Filipino" could easily be a mantra for the hundreds of actors of Philippine descent auditioning for work in Los Angeles's film and television industry or in New York's theater district: Mexican rockers, Chinatown cooks, Koreatown gangsters, Vietnamese shop owners, even the occasional off-world creature such as an Ewok. The initial burst of laughter stems from recognizing the unrecognizable: an aunty, a cousin, or an elder with an exaggerated accent. When the accent becomes the punchline, it usually is not funny at all. Marivi Soliven Blanco observes that a sense of superiority is at the root of the humor of some Filipino American comedy. Reflecting on a comedy show she saw in Berkeley, she wrote, "I realized that all those jokes about the bizarre nicknames, dysfunctional plumbing, quirky media, and assorted freaks in the Philippines implied a sense of cultural (or at the very least, technological) superiority: 'Look how absurd/backward/pretentious they are in the Islands! Aren't we lucky we don't have to live there?'"[38] Often, though, the humor has revealed a keen insecurity on the part of the students, a resentment even directed toward elders for not having communicated more cultural knowledge.

As the show's format and presentation have become more elaborate, so, too, has the criticism raised internally among organizers and externally among observers. Critics have argued that the PCN genre reinforces static constructions of Filipino American identities and that the origins of the folk forms need to be more concretely historicized or subjected to experimentation and play. Some have pointed to the "Orientalizing" function of the Muslim dance suites in several PCNs, particularly how students have undertheorized their importation of folkloric forms from the southern Philippines, opening themselves to the charge of being sloppy interpreters of "native" cultures.[39] Even though shows have been produced regularly, some voices have become critical of "new and entering students" who "may not realize that people before them had struggled to provide many traditions/programs in existence."[40] A veteran choreographer and performer described the mindset of the student performers who took up the show after his class. Referring to to campaigns specifically aimed at the recruitment and retention of Filipinos, he said, "I think they are losing the purpose of why we're doing this. . . . [T]here were other people that really fought very hard to keep the doors open."[41] The performer railed at students' sensibilities, which were also reflected in the larger community, that recognized only those hardships that were consigned to "history." The danger, he said, was that the young students saw struggle not as marking them personally but as belonging only to the past. Theirs was a moment simply to be recognized on stage as they congratulated themselves as members of a meritocracy.[42]

By the late 1980s, PCN performers and organizers were beginning to do their own research and hold out for the possibility that the show could be a means to achieve community organizing around access to higher education. Filipino admissions to UCLA, for example, had dropped 44 percent by the end of the 1980s, with only 141 people self-identified as "Filipino" admitted. "That means less Pilipinos coming in, less Pilipinos graduating, and less Pilipinos returning to the community," according to Arleen de Vera, a former coordinator of Samahang Pilipino's Affirmative Action Student Task Force.[43] Access to higher education would continue to be an issue well into the 1990s because of the rise of both conservativism and consequent politicizing of admissions policies and the increasing cost of education in general. When the Regents of the University of California banned race-conscious admissions policies in 1997, applications to graduate school by Filipino students fell by 10 percent, and the admission rate for the same group dropped by 14 percent.[44] Rising tuition at the traditionally working-class San Francisco State University had a negative impact on those who were supporting themselves or family members. Between 1991 and 1993, tuition for a full-time resident undergraduate student averaged $491. The following year, that cost would more than double, to $1,070.[45] How relevant were cultural productions given these material changes in the lives of students? Several others took PCN organizers to task for simply regurgitating familiar plot lines from previous years or from other campuses, offering contrived resolutions to weighty topics or even relying mechanistically on social realism as the prevailing aesthetic of the presentations. In other words, the criticism homed in on the point that the entire show had become an epic—a grand and bloated restatement of Filipino American culture.[46]

## *Cultural Evidence*: Rethinking the Genre

Criticisms raised by student organizers over the years have led to some modest changes and, occasionally, open challenges to the genre. Large campuses, especially those with more than twenty years of production history, such as UCI's Kababayan, have conducted post-show "wrap-up" sessions in which cast and audience members discuss problems related to the production and solutions to them. The dialogues generally have avoided openly tendentious comments and veered toward providing constructive criticism that the next year's crew could use. UCLA's Samahang Pilipino and UC Berkeley's Pilipino American Alliance helped to argue for and staff credit-earning courses in which students can take a broader view of performance, history, and culture as well as the mechanics of event production. But talking about change is much different from actually carrying it out.

In one instance—*Cultural Evidence,* a show produced by PACE at San Francisco State University in 1993—the organizers emphasized nontraditional approaches to narrative through theater, music, film, and poetry by tapping the creativity of members and the surrounding community in an effort to break from the PCN's hardened conventions. "Cultural Evidence" presented a series of shows over three days. The first evening included a film screening that featured works written, directed, and produced by students. It also featured a spoken-word event that drew on the city's large community of writers. Young poets were invited to share the stage with veteran activists and artists such as the poet Al Robles and short-story writer Oscar Peñaranda, who founded the original Kearny Street Workshop, the Manilatown Senior Center for Self-Help, and other community-based organizations. Part of the program included a one-act play accompanied by a jazz trio.[47]

The second evening presented local hip-hop artists such as DJ Qbert, Bubala Tribe, Urban Soul, and Lani Luv, who represent a mix of disciplines and activities, including scratching/mixing, dance, rap, and graffiti styles. Filipino American hip hop is not merely a miming of African American style; it demonstrates how young segments of the community are struggling and coming to terms with the most vital cultural forms of late-twentieth-century America. Filipinos have taken part in other aesthetically innovative moments in American culture: Consider, for example, the zoot suiters and beboppers of earlier generations. Today's Filipino American hip hoppers not only participate in but also rearticulate the form through a distinctive and improvisatory soulful style.[48] The third night featured a finale of sorts, a concession to organizers who wanted a more "traditional" cultural-night show involving folk-dance presentation. Perhaps the most significant aspect of the show concerned the organizers' decision to retain only the so-called mountain and tribal suites, which in effect drew more attention to the pastiche of monologues and vignettes. The pieces written, directed, and performed by the students represented an eclectic mix of interests and talents, including a reading of a poem featured in a literary journal; a meditation on Filipina American adolescence and personal maturation; a lengthy "epic-documentary" of Philippine history, with the Magellan-slaying narrator-(Lapu Lapu)-as-prophet; a play raising the problem of intergenerational conflict; and a dialogue set to the rhythm of two young Filipino men circa 1934 talking about how one of their countrymen created jazz.

Having displaced the PCN's traditional attention to dance form, the show's organizers left open the problematic of their editorial decision to highlight certain suites. Left out of the program were the barrio suites (featuring the signature *tinikling*) and the Muslim suite's *singkil.* The *tinikling* has become a de facto "national" dance because of its popularity and recognizability outside the Philippines. The *singkil* has been a staple of several PCNs for the same reason but also because of the implicit anti-Western narrative that can be read into its origins. In her reading of fictional works by the Filipino writers N.V.M. Gonzalez and Bienvenido Santos in which the dance figures prominently, Gertrudes Ang surmised that the "bamboo dancers" might represent "globe-trotting Filipinos . . . especially those in the States, caught there by [World War II] while in the midst of their studies or who were simply there as travelers with pleasure in mind."[49] Ang favors another angle: that the dance represents a blending of both "indigenous" or "autochthonous" (the bamboo) with the "imported" or "foreign" (as seen in the Western-based waltz music that accompanies the dance).[50] Barbara Gaerlan saw the reliance on the *singkil,* a dance based on an ancient southern Philippine epic, by many of her Filipino American students as a reflection of a need to embody dancing characters that are "regal," "proud," and "unconquered" in marked contrast to the historical setting of the dance's scenario, which involves a martial warrior prince attempting to rescue a princess in a forest of felled trees and presents enslaved people as attendants.[51] Omitting these two iconic dances made a strong editorial statement and an implicit critique of two kinds of subjectivities often associated with the dances: on the one hand, the smiling, naïve, accommodationist; and on the other, the unsmiling, imperious slavedriver. The former feared rocking any boat, while the latter wielded a masculine authority by conflating violence, sovereignty, and romance.

This eclectic, sometimes unfocused, and largely uneven finale to *Cultural Evidence* lacked the presentational unity of PCNs typical of the genre. In strategizing *with* essentialisms rather than receiving them uncritically, the organizers of *Cultural Evidence* set the static inventory of dances aside (while not wholly jettisoning them) and opened creative spaces for its members to engage in a conversation about what they felt was important and how they viewed their "culture." Rather than merely reproducing fixed structures, they highlighted the *process* of cultural production as an unfolding set of contradictions and possibilities. And yet, *Cultural Evidence*'s format did not have a lasting influence. In subsequent productions at the same campus, PCN organizers returned to the familiar conventions of Bayanihan-derived folkloric dances interspersed haphazardly among theatrical narrations.

In the next chapter, I turn to a production that focused less on enlisting audiences to reform the sturdy repertoire. Instead, satirists mocked the venerated performance. While *Cultural Evidence* aimed to rethink the PCN genre with an eye toward reform within the setting of a college or university campus, a group of artists—themselves veterans of dozens of PCNs—lobbed a parody from inside an independent black-box theater space.

# 5 Making a Mockery of Everything We Hold True and Dear

## *Exploring Parody with Tongue in a Mood's* PCN Salute *(San Francisco, 1997)*

*Authorities, any authorities, fear above all other things laughter, derision or even the smile, because laughter denotes a critical awareness; it signifies imagination, intelligence and a rejection of all fanaticism.*

—Dario Fo

WHEN DARIO FO, the Italian playwright and performer, was awarded the Nobel Prize for Literature in 1997, he heard not only cheers but also jeers. "I doubt that Fo is an author of the first rank," said Mario Vargas Llosa, wryly adding, "Even in the Nobel, as in other prizes, mistakes happen." Maurizio Gasparri, a member of the Italian Parliament, referred to Fo as "a clown who is worthy of a circus, but not of a prize of this significance." In the pages of the Vatican's *L'Osservatore Romano,* a writer noted that "Fo is the sixth Nobel from Italy after Carducci, Deledda, Pirandello, Quasimodo, [and] Montale. After these sages, a clown."[1] Performers like Fo, who draw inspiration from a long line of popular European entertainers such as "mummers, jesters, clowns, tumblers and storytellers," insist on the change and play of meaning, even recasting the context through the alteration of one's appearance, costume, gait, accent, gender, origin, and age. Fo's critics attack along two fronts. First are those who do not share his politics. Consistently over his long career Fo has hurled jokes into the teeth of the powerful, refusing to take seriously those who wield power indiscriminately or unjustly. And they were listening. Fo and his wife of more than fifty years, Franca Rame, a noted performer in her own right and descendant of a long line of respected actors, have been denied entry into several countries, including the United States between 1980 and 1986, and were banned from appearing on Italian television and radio from 1962 to 1977.[2] "A clown can't always be smiling," wrote Fo. "There has to be passion behind the red nose. You have to have anger—anger at the injustice and oppression in the world. And the anger has to be supported by hard work. A clown has to have virtuoso technique, an understanding of the grotesque, and an extraordinary sense of generosity and love of the people."[3]

A second set of critics does not believe that Fo is, in the strict sense, a "writer." They uphold a bias for written over performed or oral texts, elite culture over the popular, and the tragic or dramatic over the comic. Fo sees himself as "freed from conventional literary writing" and chooses to express himself "with words that you can chew, with unusual sounds, with various techniques of rhythm and breathing, even with the rambling nonsense-speech of the *grammelot.*" A satirical vocal technique and speech style dating to sixteenth-century European performances, *grammelot* is augmented with gesture, singing, and sparse use of actual words in native tongues. It facilitated communication across multiple dialects and languages while evading censorious power from above. Fo's work serves as an analogue for how artists take seriously the work of cultural criticism through parody.

This chapter steps into an intersection of the parodic and Filipino American cultural forms. Asian American performing artists are a growing area of interest, with texts focused on theater and popular culture and expanding to dance and music.[4] While some of that work analyzes comedic elements in the form of asides or specific moments that break narrative flow; rarely is comedy studied as its own genre.[5] Nerissa Balce has offered a detailed treatment of Asian American comedic narratives, where folk laughter can be understood as acts of "defiance and courage against fear, organized religion and the power."[6] Rather than providing a distraction from serious issues or attempting to escape from harsh realities, the postcolonial author and performer turns directly to one's immediate circumstance for the source of humor. This is a powerful and yet a delicate resource, one that can produce "critiques of an author's or performer's own culture viewed through the lens of alienation and defamiliarization."[7] As an expressive form of culture, comedy mediates Filipino American subjectivities whose function, according to another commentator, is to "[respond] to colonization through processes of cultural identity formation."[8] In the same year that a comic performer was awarded the Nobel Prize, a literary journal in San Francisco published a bitingly funny script by three Filipino American writers/performers, a parody of the Pilipino Cultural Night called *PCN Salute.*[9] The writers I discuss in this chapter take up Dario Fo's insistence that passion and anger—and not just a knowing smile—must also be behind the clown's red nose.

The U.S.-born stand-up comedian and writer Allan S. Manalo served as the primary author of *PCN Salute,* supported by the actor/performers Patty Cachapero and Kevin Camia. The three became the primary writers for the comedy theater troupe Tongue in a Mood, formed in 1992 by Manalo, Rex Navarrete, and Ron Muriera. By 1997, Navarrete was carrying on as a solo act, and Muriera continued to perform his lounge act as the character "Enrico," a slick "ladies man," accompanying himself on accordion. Manalo returned from a forty-eight-state U.S. tour and assembled a new and larger cast demonstrating an eclectic bag of skills: sketch comedy, comic monologues, live music, shadow (Indonesian *wayang kulit*) and live-action (Japanese *bunraku*) puppetry, stilt walking, clowning, and Laban-notated movement. Tongue in a Mood writers were heavily influenced by television shows such as the Wayans brothers' *In Living Color* and the stage work of the Chicano sketch comedy trio Culture Clash.[10]

Tongue in a Mood's work can also be understood as part of a larger history of Asian American theater that has attempted to answer dominant cultural representations of Asians in the United States but also, and more important, to feed the imagination of artists, writers, producers, promoters, and others passionate about proposing alternatives to what is often taken for granted as entertainment.[11] Mixing skills as an anthropologist and dramaturg, Dorinne Kondo reminds us that Asian American cultural production has often placed premiums on what she refers to as the "narrative production of home." Especially for theater artists of color, producing a home on stage means undertaking a bittersweet experience where one can occupy a "safe place, where there is no need to explain oneself to outsiders; it stands for community; more problematically, it can elicit a nostalgia for a past golden age that never was, a nostalgia that elides exclusion, power relations and difference."[12]

Tongue in a Mood's work can also be traced to the longstanding network of Filipino artists anchored in the San Francisco Bay Area who have called communities into being through examples of socially and politically minded art making. Several examples are not yet adequately documented and are in need of further study and reflection. Al Robles, the poet and Manilatown activist, recalls sneaking into Jimbo's Bop City in the Fillmore to listen to the pianist Flip Nuñez during the 1950s and 1960s.[13] The painter Carlos Villa performed a ritualistic incantatory piece and was inspired by his jazz-loving cousin and abstract expressionist Leo Valledor.[14] The choreographer Pearl Ubungen created site-specific work that commemorated the struggle for affordable housing at the foot of the International Hotel and at clearings on the Presidio that launched thousands of troops into the U.S.–Philippine War.[15] Activist writers and directors such as Ermena Vinluan staged historical plays about farmworkers and nurses with a political organization based in Oakland.[16] The poet and bandleader Jessica Hagedorn called out the United States for being a "gangster society" while fronting her funk band at a poetry-center taping.[17] The Maguindanao master musician Danongan Kalanduyan trained students in traditional *kulintang* at Skyline College and San Francisco State University.[18] And Bindlestiff Studio, a survivor of gentrification of the South of Market district, hosted Pinoy rockers from Manila, Daly City, Houston, Jersey City, and Manhattan.[19]

While building on the Asian American narrative production of "home" or carrying forward generations of artistic commitments by Filipino performers anchored in the city, Tongue in a Mood's material has been directed primarily toward satire—what one reporter has dubbed a "wild mix of physical comedy, movement, video and shadow puppetry, with a touch of Philippine-style political street theater." The shows had the feel of *bodabil* brought up to date—bawdy, loud, obnoxious and usually *bastos* (Tagalog for uncouth or impolite). When Linda Lucero, the performing arts curator for San Francisco's Yerba Buena Center for the Arts, booked the troupe for a show at her venue, she described ticket pre-sales as "phenomenal." "We don't really host Rolling Stones-type things. It was nice to see young people want to see theater."[20] The critic Brad Rosenstein pointed to the troupe's "sharp, irreverent, and sometimes deadly comedy" that "jumps headfirst into the space between 'Filipino' and 'American.'"[21]

In this chapter, I offer an annotated analysis of one of the troupe's more successful sketches, *PCN Salute*, written and published in 1997 by Manalo, Camia, and Cachapero. The writers of the sketch demonstrated that the PCN genre has generated its own cultural critique, as all three were veterans of dozens of shows. Their sketch also pointed out that seemingly static repertoires and identities are—or, at least, should be—always in *play. PCN Salute* skewers the genre's form and content, boiling down what has become on some campuses a six-hour event into a twenty-minute send-up. On the group's work, Patty Cachapero said, "We're all on the same page about not pounding a message on the head. The message is still to look at ourselves with affection and humor."[22] Elizabeth Pisares, a literary and cultural critic, wrote, "'PCN Salute' is remarkable not only for its enumeration of Filipino American anxieties about race and identity . . . , but for its incisive yet affectionate representation of the post-1965 Filipino American's sense of invisibility amidst other racial identities."[23] Just as the Italian comic Dario Fo played with conventional approaches in narrating histories and amplifying the absurdity of clinging to orthodoxies and moribund cultural practices, so did Manalo, Camia, and Cachapero question the venerable repertoire of the PCN with their backhanded salute.

## Anthem and Welcome

*PCN Salute* opens with the singing of the Philippine national anthem by characters named Chicanoy, Afronoy, and Chad, who serve as versions of Filipinos in the United States and are racially identified through language, clothing, and speech. A voiceover introduces them: "For the young Filipino American college student, the search for cultural identity is often one of frustration, confusion, and utter disappointment. Many of them look to stereotypical Afrocentrics as a way to identify. . . . Some try to claim they only identify with the *vatos* of Daly City. . . . And, of course, there are those who believe that being American, is being red, blue, and . . . ahem . . . white."[24] Two of the three characters (Chicanoy and Afronoy) throw up gang signs, mimicking dialects and marking themselves racially through television and references to music.

Tongue in a Mood performers used dialect-inflected accents and, occasionally, *grammelot* to bring their characters to life. Audiences, especially young Filipino Americans, immediately picked up on regional, linguistic, generational, and even class-based ways that Filipinos sound different to one another. This marking of difference through the presence of accents has been problematized by some critics and refers to a longer history of ethnic and racial minorities' bearing the brunt of discrimination for the use of "home" languages or having traces of denigrated accents.[25] Those criticisms help keep comics and theater artists in check concerning the fronting of a U.S.-centric attitude that reproduces prejudice and ridicule at the expense of immigrants, FOBs (for "fresh off the boat"), or JOJs (for "just off the jet"). For example, Marivi Blanco Soliven, an essayist based in the United States, wrote about a stand-up show she attended in Berkeley: "Jokes about white people and Filipino Americans [drew] laughs, but the real hysteria [was] generated by stories about the Philippines itself. . . . For those who'd never gone back, dippy fantasies of the 'old country' with its jungles and grunting natives conveniently confirmed everything their immigrant parents or clueless Caucasian historians had told them."[26] Perhaps there is some continuity between Soliven's response and Lawrence Levine's analysis of what he termed "black on black humor": "To laugh at the rural ethos that had enveloped most of the race at the beginning of the century accomplished several ends. Obviously it was a way of denying the immediate southern rural past and of encouraging acculturation to northern and urban life styles. It was also a way of laughing at oneself and one's peers, but it was a comparatively easy way. There were more complex and meaningful techniques of accomplishing the serious and necessary end of gaining perspective on oneself and one's situation and black humor utilized all of them." The joke is derived from, and speaks to, that transition, or a supposed sense of mobility, from the Philippines to the United States (for Soliven) and from the rural South to the urban North (for Levine) and allows audiences to laugh at the "idiosyncrasies of behavior" engendered by such movement, pointing to the "limits of northern deliverance."[27] Tongue in a Mood's accents and dialects; spare use of "Taglish"; special idioms, and other linguistic cues to the audience stood in stark contrast to culturally chauvinistic formal instruction given to actors in preparation for those auditioning for "foreign" roles.

Consider the following passage from Lewis Herman and Marguerite Shalett Herman's *Foreign Dialects: A Manual for Actors, Directors and Writers* on preparing for the delivery of a "Filipino Dialect": "In some respects, because of the use of bare key-words in the speech, the Filipino dialect resembles Pidgin English. In fact, it has, for this reason, been called Bamboo English." In addition to learning that the dialect features a monotonous intonation "which is varied only under emotional stress," the eager auditioner also learns that "because the Filipino speaks so that his lower lip does not make the proper contact with the cutting edge of his upper front teeth, he has difficulty in pronouncing *our* 'f' properly."[28]

*PCN Salute* continues with a welcome by the "headcore," an abbreviation of the title "head coordinator," or a lead organizer for the Filipino student organization. Here the performance takes a shot at the formal, stilted, and at times self-congratulatory language and style some leaders have deemed necessary to use during the opening of a PCN. The headcore is played effectively by the Ramon Abad, whose gestures are intended to seemed forced and unnatural. To punctuate his delivery, Abad extends his arm fully and draws a circle in a slow, roundhouse motion while hopelessly anchored by his notes. He does not appear flustered; he simply performs the role of the leader whose job it is to bring a certain gravity to the ceremony: "Tonight, we would like to address these issues, so that to nurture an awareness of the problems: the problems of gangs, the problems of drugs, the problems of a high teenage-pregnancy rate, the problems of a misrepresented history, the problems of homelessness, the problems of prostitution, the problems of pollution, the problems of national deficit, and, of course, the problems of problems. So tonight, we prove to you, we are not a bucket of crabs pulling down our brothers and sisters, instead, we present to you crabs, brown crabs that raise the roof, pushing up our brothers and sisters toward empowerment, pride and *mabuhay*!"[29] Abad delivers his welcoming comments in a shrill monotone, repeating the role that nationalist educators such as Bocobo, Aquino, and the Bayanihan had played in previous generations by imploring the audience to envision "unity" in the "community."

## The Family

The scene opens with a *lolo* (grandfather) reminiscing with his grandchildren as they pore over a photo album—apparently, an idealized tableau of intergenerational communication and reminiscence that lies at the heart of the PCN genre. Abad plays the *lolo* as a stereotypically hard-of-hearing and curmudgeonly *manong* (elder or older brother).[30] Rhoda Gravador's characterization of the grandchild Pinky emphasizes the amateurish acting in many student productions: She delivers her lines in a loud monotone, inserting long pauses and breaking words apart incorrectly as if to suggest that she is visualizing the script, and her gestures are ham-handed and exaggerated. Against the culturally knowledgeable *lolo* character, the children are racialized as "white" (Pinky and Heather) and "black" (Jimmy).

*PCN Salute* spoofs the PCNs' clumsy transitions between skits and folk-dance suites. The first dance suite is presented by a (supposedly) Bontoc (northern tribal) warrior. Instead of a large supporting rank of dancers, however, the piece is presented by Rene Acosta alone. *Lolo* provides no context or explanation for the transition:

> PINKY: Yes, this is fun. (Looking at the photos.) Oh my God, *lolo*, is that you? You look so handsome. And what a nice suit, you must have been rich, *lolo*.
>
> *LOLO*: No, we worked hard, very hard for little money, we worked hard. Like the warriors on the mountains of the Philippines. . . . (Enter Bontok [*sic*] Warrior, who dances across the living room floor, passing in front of the couch where everyone is sitting, then exits.)[31]

Acosta returns to perform in another dance suite representing Spanish influences on Filipino culture. Again, the *lolo* summons the dancer with an awkward transition. (*LOLO*: We were conquered and colonized by the Spanish, who oppressed our people for hundreds of years. That's why you may find similarities in our cultures. . . . GRANDCHILDREN: Similarities in our culture? Really?) The grandfather gestures upstage to the dancer. Acosta, this time wearing a *barong Tagalog* (a transparent shirt or tunic worn by men). He dances in three-quarter time, spinning gracefully and smiling as if he is performing in an idyllic *barrio fiesta*. Again, Acosta dances alone and not for more than a minute. The comic touch he adds is in his costuming: In addition to the *barong*, he sports the same *bahag* (woven G-string) that he wore during the Bontoc routine. The two ethnic costumes are not meant to be worn together, and Acosta does not let on to this, but the audience recognizes the incongruity. Acosta's layering of costumes instead of making a complete costume change saves time and makes great comic sense, but it also jabs at the ways in which the metropolitan center has managed the aesthetic appearance of "natives" for presentation to "foreign" audiences who most likely will not recognize errors.

## Heather's Crisis

As the grandchildren continue to reminisce with their *lolo*, Jimmy calls attention to Heather's supposed lack of cultural knowledge:

> JIMMY: Hey, Heather, why do you call him "Grandpa" and not "*lolo*"? Are you ashamed of our language?
>
> HEATHER: I don't speak Tag Log.
>
> *LOLO*: That's Tagalog, *apo ko.*
>
> HEATHER: *Apo ko*? But my name is Heather.
>
> *LOLO*: *Apo ko* means "my grandchild." Your language is part of your heritage. You should learn your language and show pride in your heritage.
>
> HEATHER: But I don't even know what my heritage is![32]

Cutting to the heart of a PCN protagonist's beleaguered "search for identity," Heather's last line, in delivery and sentiment, echoes a line repeated throughout the Chicano comedy troupe Culture Clash's show *A Bowl of Beings*: "I'm confused . . . and full of rage!"[33] Both productions make light of the protagonist's angst in the "ethnic identity play." In "Chicanos on the Storm," produced in 1991 as part of *A Bowl of Beings,* a straitjacketed character played by Richard Montoya pleads in earnest: "Brothers and sisters run, run for the hills—have you heard Madonna wants to play Frida Kahlo in a movie. Man, I finally find myself a hero and she's gonna fuck it all up for me—I hope they let a Chicano play Trotsky at least. What the fuck are you looking at up there? Haven't you ever seen a multicultural nightmare coming unglued right before your eyes, man? 'Cause I'm Spanish, I'm Indian—American Indian, a 'Dances with Wolves' kind of Indian—ahooo!"[34] *PCN Salute* plays up this staple of the PCN genre—the protagonist wallowing in navel-gazing torment about identity. Manalo, Camia, and Cachapero enlist the audience to move beyond the idea that Filipino Americans can be represented only in crisis.

In *PCN Salute,* a male authority figure checks the ignorance of supposedly assimilated *Pinays* such as Heather. Even though Jimmy speaks no

Tagalog, except when he refers to his grandfather using an elementary honorific, his Afro-centric mannerisms can be taken as a kind of provisional cultural authority. The commentary here about how young Filipino Americans adopt African American style targets the PCN audience again. The *PCN Salute* script criticizes the uncritical substitution and acceptance of African American culture as at least something more valuable than having no cultural knowledge (i.e., being "white" like Heather). This sentiment reiterates the attitude in Vince Reyes's poem "For My Stylin' Brothers" (1975): "Sometimes I close my eyes and I'm / In a roomful of Black sounds / And when I open them again I'm in a / Roomful of brown papier-mâché figures / With Huey Newton motors inside of them / And it's cool / And we can all dig it. . . . / So when we act like Bloods / Hey, man, it's cool / But like—you know / Don't forget our struggle is OUR struggle / And even though we is US. / And that Right On is really *Makibaka* / And that Cleaver is really Guerrero / That '45 is a bolo / And that black leather jackets are really / just old / Ilocano made rags."[35]

In performance, the actor Esperanza Catubig delivers Heather's line—"But I don't even know what my heritage is!"—by dropping to her knees, signaling a lighting cue. She steps forward into a spotlight while the rest of the stage goes dark. Another spotlight appears next to her, cueing the appearance of the late-nineteenth-century propagandist José Rizal, played by Mark Marking, who makes his entrance to the theme music from *The X-Files.*[36] (RIZAL: "Please come with me. And enter into my dream sequence.") Heather's only knowledge of Rizal comes from recognizing his likeness on Philippine ("their") money. The sketch writers revised history by having Rizal speak to the possibility of a "Filipino American" identity.[37] This portrayal of Rizal also highlights how a critical historical figure has become imagined, even worshipped, as a cult-like character shrouded in mystery and a supernatural ethos (otherworldly and unattainable)—the very things for which Rizal criticized Catholic clerics during his time.

RIZAL: You mean "our money." You are a Filipina, too, aren't you?

HEATHER: Well, I consider myself more American. I don't mind when someone calls me a Filipino, but I really don't eat that much pork. Hey José, have you ever seen *Friends*? You kinda look like Ross.

RIZAL: Listen. You don't have to be white to be American. You can be a Filipino American. Here, just read this. Never forget me. (José hands her a copy of *Noli me Tangere* and takes her back to the couch as dreamy music comes on.)[38]

Like Moses in Cecil B. de Mille's film *The Ten Commandments,* Heather returns from her "epiphany" bearing an authoritative text, Rizal's propagandist novel. She even peppers her speech with Tagalog words, such as *lolo,* to her family's amusement.

## Thugs

Jimmy has had enough of family fun time around the photo album. The opening strain of Snoop Dogg's "Who Am I (What's My Name)" is heard as Jimmy leaves the living room to hook up with Payat (a Tagalog adjective meaning "skinny" or "lean") and Tigas (a Tagalog adjective meaning "hard"). The three greet each other using aggressive, vulgar, and childish mannerisms associated with the gangsta stereotype. In the middle of their "conversation" (TIGAS: "Yeah, yeah, don't call him dat, ignant mutha fucka." PAYAT: "Hey shut up! Shut the fuck up, you Pinto-drivin' dick-breath mutha fucka!"), an unexplained drive-by shooting takes out Jimmy.[39] The two "homies" cry over Jimmy's slumped body. The filmmaker John Manal Castro's mock-umentary *Diary of a Gangsta Sucka* (1993) skewers Filipino American men's romanticization of the "thug life" to great comedic effect, asking why Southern California Filipinos—outfitted with cell phones and imported cars parked in front of suburban homes—find it necessary to join gangs. After a game of dominos in the park, Castro's characters reply: "To protect ourselves against our enemies!" They look to one another for confirmation. "You know . . . the system."[40]

The opening bars of the Eric Clapton song "Tears in Heaven" start up as Payat and Tigas continue to grieve over Jimmy's body. Rhoda Gravador as Pinky moves to center stage and, using her operatic vocal training to comical effect, delivers the tune in a grand, *bel canto* form, with her arms fully extended and shaking. In another version of the sketch, the actor Gayle Romasanta transforms Pinky into a diva long on melismatic effusiveness but short on accurate pitch. The appearance of the diva is not in the published version of *PCN Salute* but has been an occasional feature in several PCNs, especially in the "pre-show," a space that allows acts to be featured that do not belong in or could not be incorporated into the PCN proper. Countless Filipinas have tested the patience of audiences with renditions of power ballads in Whitney Houston or Mariah Carey style. Especially since Lea Salonga won a Tony Award for portraying a gold-hearted Vietnamese showgirl, the solo female singer at the PCN pre-show has represented the promise of mainstream acceptance as much as a demonstration of one's mastery of the contemporary song form.

At the close of Pinky's musical eulogy, the sketch returns to Payat and Tigas for another jarring scene transition: "PAYAT: Damn, Jimmy, why did you have to get shot? You're a hella good dancer, too. TIGAS: Yeah us Flips. . . . We can dance!" House music starts up, and the cast members perform a Michael Peters choreographed routine that resembles the synchronized squads in 1980s music videos. The routine ends with everyone rushing downstage and striking a tableau that recalls a sunburst.

## The White Boyfriend

Pinky's boyfriend, Elmer (played by the dancer, costume designer, and choreographer Billy Conti) drops by the family home with plans for the couple to watch an episode of *Friends*. Before they leave, though, the gangstas and *lolo* register their disapproval. Elmer apparently represents a "violation" that has enough force to wake the dead, causing Jimmy to come back to life as a "ghost in white face."[41] In the production, a cast member shadowed Jimmy by draping transparent mosquito over him as he spoke:

> JIMMY: What the hell is this? Fuckin' punk-ass white boy.
> *LOLO*: Hoy, Pinky, where are you going?
> PINKY: Elmer is taking me to watch a show.
> *LOLO*: Why are you going out with that *white guy*? (The Filipino males sneer the last two words.)
> JIMMY: Yeah, don't be stupid, Pinky. You're *Pinay*.[42]

As Jimmy recites that line, other cast members smash their fists into their hands, a masculine threat to hold Pinky in check regarding her supposedly ethnically transgressive choice. The scene highlights the community's internal politics over interracial relationships, posing dates like Pinky's as a threat to the Filipino (male) nation. It also invites an oblique reexamination, and somewhat of a reversal, of the anxiety felt by white male workers during the 1930s who saw Filipino men as threats to the sexual (national) order.[43] Elmer, now in a tough spot and looking around in fear, smiles with a child's confidence and delivers a non sequitur response, emphasizing words in all the wrong places: "*Magandang gabi, ho. Kumusta ka sainyo lahat!* (Greetings and good evening to you all)." Incredulous and insulted, the cast members throw up their hands. (Think here of the scene in Spike Lee's *Do the Right Thing* [1989] in which a white yuppie scuffs the sneakers of the irascible community activist Buggin' Out. When Buggin' Out calls the yuppie out for being in the "wrong" neighborhood, he replies:

"I was born in Brooklyn!") After an initial flash of anger, Jimmy melts in the sentimentality of the moment: "Hey! That's so patronizing . . . ! Yet, so beautiful!" Jimmy's culturally nationalist authority allows the family to claim Elmer, the white boyfriend, as one of their own. Elmer's inelegant and superficial display of the language has gained him acceptance as an "honorary" Filipino.

As Elmer woos Pinky, the *lolo* waxes on about romance, saying that Filipinos "know how to express love. We have always been romantic. It all started with this prince who saved this princess." This is the cue for the final dance by Acosta, who performs a condensed version of the *singkil,* a fable of southern Philippine royalty stepping through a menacing forest rocked by an earthquake. He poses menacingly with a tin-wrapped sword and chants indecipherably while the other cast members murmur along. To close his routine, Acosta tucks and rolls downstage, pushing the cardboard weapon toward the audience and punctuating his stop with a curt bark that startles the cast. He takes a quick bow, smiles, and dashes off stage. The spoof of this popular PCN suite resonates with Barbara Gaerlan's observation that the portrayal of a Moro dance she saw at a PCN in Southern California was "particularly striking because of its remarkable Orientalist flavor—something I was surprised to witness coming from an otherwise progressive and activist Filipino American student body."[44] Gaerlan traces the students' desire to present a heroic version of Filipino subjectivity through the "unconquered" Muslim cultural forms of the south. Her interviews revealed an uncritical and naive incorporation of Bayanihan aesthetics. The students

> perceived the dances as an anthropological window on Philippine culture. At the same time, without observing a contradiction, they appreciated the modern theatricality of the Bayanihan genre, saying that it gave them a venue for expressing Filipino culture in the United States of which they could be proud. They seemed unaware that, in addition to theatricality, the Bayanihan included another "modern" feature, Orientalism, highlighted in their presentation of the "Muslim" as exotic, autocratic, slave holding and patriarchal.[45]

The *PCN Salute* cast forms a half-circle and, with hands clasped, sings one round of the chorus to "That's What Friends Are For," mocking the earnest delivery of a "PCN song" in which the entire cast joins in what is supposed to be an inspirational moment but instead seems more like a simplistic resolution and an act of self-congratulation. After the tune,

Elmer hushes everyone and shouts a popular Tagalog curse: "*Putang ina mo!*" (a grave insult hurled against an opponent's mother). Everyone cheers and runs off stage.

## Off Stage

In the last chapter, I focused on the work of *Cultural Evidence* as an attempt by one group of students to wrestle with the terms of the PCN genre's primary conventions by doing away with a large narrative arc and substituting a jumble of vignettes, monologues, and other experimental theater pieces; by expanding the format of a single night to multi-night presentations of film, spoken word, and music; and by significantly reducing the role of certain folk-dance suites. The result? A Jamesonian pastiche: "a field of stylistic and discursive heterogeneity without a norm," a show that "randomly and without principle but with gusto cannibalize[d] all the architectural styles of the past and combines them in overstimulating ensembles." *Stimulating,* yes. Performed *with gusto,* most definitely. But on the promise that *Cultural Evidence* would make a lasting impression and one that would serve as a catalyst for other experimentation on other campuses, the show fell short.[46] Organizers returned to well-worn formats, reissued dance suites interspersed with the "skit," and continued to find clever ways to have their protagonists traverse the reverse exilic route plied in hundreds of other scripts.

In *PCN Salute,* the writers developed a parodic cultural critique, demonstrating what Linda Hutcheon recognized as part of the process of "how present representations come from past ones and what ideological consequences derive from both continuity and difference."[47] For the parody to succeed, the performer or author provided the audience with an opportunity to recognize and venerate "the original." Alessandro Portelli has reminded us that, for the parody to have a bite, the intended target must "never entirely disappear"; rather, it should linger.[48] The sketch writers' parodic sense echoed Dario Fo's understanding of the comic's discovery: "There is . . . the *great pleasure* of de-sanctification, of tearing down the sacrosanct monuments of sacred tradition, everything that the canonical texts have supported, codified, blessed and glorified."[49] Taking Portelli and Fo together, the object of parody is always nearby, never wholly jettisoned or discarded but still very much held close in a kind of grudging admiration. A critical difference between Fo's understanding of the comic's vocation and the function of *PCN Salute* is that the latter attacks not an institution or office of the dominant culture but a phenomenon that has taken on significance within a dispersed network of Filipino Americans in the United States.

*PCN Salute* named a nationalism hobbled by its paternalism. It opened by positioning the audience to help three college men regain their "lost identity," yet the men were never seen again in the sketch. Instead, Heather, the granddaughter character, was "corrected" by Rizal, who stood in as the absent father, while her sister Pinky risked losing the approval of her (male) family. Both female characters were redeemed, to an extent, by gaining the approval of "family"/"national" figures. This squares with Cynthia Enloe's understanding of how men have masculinized concepts such as the nation, security, labor, and power: The nation "will be a community in which women sacrificed their desires for the sake of the male-led collectives."[50] Just as *PCN Salute* implied a crisis in patriarchal authority in various attempts to discipline female characters, the text problematized the PCN genre's ability to credibly represent complex subjectivities. The "nation's" ability to tell its story through an authoritative repertoire—from dances that have little relation to the arc of the theatrical narratives to inattentiveness to historical detail and accuracy and the romanticization of "identity" (whether historical or contemporary)—has been called into question: By condensing "Every Filipino Cultural Night You've Ever Seen in Your Life," Manalo, Camia, and Cachapero laid bare the charge that the PCN has become predictable and ossified. Through citation, borrowing, and re-citation, they emphasized a mode of cultural production and presentation that never stops moving; refused static definitions; and showed that they were open to asking difficult questions about power, place, and imagination.

# Conclusion

*I have to believe in a world outside my own mind. I have to believe that my actions still have meaning, even if I can't remember them. I have to believe that when my eyes are closed, the world's still there. Do I believe the world's still there? Is it still out there? . . . Yeah. We all need mirrors to remind ourselves who we are. I'm no different.*

—Leonard Shelby

MY AIM has been to trace a genealogy of an expressive form of culture developed by Filipino Americans against a century of Philippine–American "special relations." In each of the periods, I place the voices of the actors at the center of large contexts: the anticipation of Philippine sovereignty (1930s), the reconsolidation of American hegemony in the Pacific (1950s), the conservative, "fear-of-falling" reaction from California's middle-class whites (1980s), and the development of rigid performative conventions and the creation of parodic critique (1990s to the present).

These performances have not always confirmed what we have known or wanted to believe about how cultural productions function. We find that expressive forms in every period were actively worked on, even at times bribed into existence. And in each period, teachers and students reshaped familiar repertoires for their own needs while their claims to an "authentic" past could best be described as tenuous. Educators in Manila authorized folk forms while anticipating Philippine independence. Choreographers and impresarios positioned one dance troupe as the internationally sanctioned face of the post–World War II nation. Filipino Californians coming of age in the Reagan era and during Marcos's martial-law regime re-mixed their parents' imported cultural practices. Finally, loyalists, reformers, and comics venerated a durable repertoire in their own ways.[1] In this book, I have stressed that folk and popular forms of culture are not simply handed down from one generation to the next. Instead of symbols, practices, and expressive forms that were replicated or reproduced faithfully, we found discontinuity. Within one generation, Francisca Reyes Aquino, the founding mother of Philippine folk dance, implored her successors to stop distorting the repertoire she had helped to invent. Those born after the mass-based social movements of the 1960s wrestled with the terms of their own performance genre while less critically adopting Philippine folk forms as "authentic."

Earlier in the book, I discussed how, according to veterans of the form such as Dom Magwili, the PCN is a rite of passage. It functions as an important ceremony for marking entrances and exits in the lives of young Filipino Americans. But let us turn to how an anthropologist such as Victor Turner thinks through these moments of passage. For him, such moments come when one is betwixt and between, vulnerable because one is essentially identityless and powerless in the face of what one may still become. Approaching ritual in this way does not mean that outcomes are necessarily guaranteed. For those of us who have performed in the PCN, many perils and pitfalls come with the promises and possibilities that the show has had to offer. For example, rites offer the possibility of achieving the long-sought-after transformation—finally getting over being a novice, landing decisively with a pitch-perfect performance, and gaining acceptance among one's supposed peers. There is also the promise of successfully meeting the demands of a community's reward system, knowing that there are actually outcomes for the attainment of cultural knowledge in a culture that has sought the laboring Filipino body while also refusing social, cultural, and political incorporation of the same. And yet the challenge of PCNs has also been to be wary of the peril of individual participants' failing the ritual's demands—missing the mark, standing out when that is not called for, adding drama to the drama. Rituals can conceal a great deal through selective scripting choices about topics relevant to contemporary diasporic and ethnic lives and about facile treatments or trite resolutions to weighty matters and by rewarding certain kinds of orthodoxies, conventions, and prejudices while holding the experimental, contingent, and idiosyncratic aspects of our cultural traditions at bay.

Pilipino Cultural Nights demonstrate how invented traditions play with time and allow performers to work with repertoires of surrogation. While tracking the nostalgic reconstructions of those in transit and others looking to imagined homelands, Svetlana Boym provides a helpful anchor in our interpretation: that the presentation of cultural-night events are not mere longings for a place (i.e., an idyllic version of the Philippines or the sepia-toned Depression-era Filipino America) but are yearnings for a *different time*—"the time of our childhood, the *slower rhythms* of our dreams.

In a broader sense, nostalgia is rebellion against the modern idea of time, the time of history and progress. The nostalgic desires to obliterate history and turn it into private or collective mythology, to revisit time like space, refusing to surrender to the irreversibility of time that plagues the human condition."[2] The PCN can hold out for the possibility that neither Philippine or U.S. official histories should go unchecked; the performers nominate themselves for roles that neither national formation expected—actors desiring alternative narrations or, at least, the endings to stories left out of history's frame. These are the stories of home-care givers beaten and raped; sailors consigned to menial tasks; inexplicable hate crimes directed against letter carriers, students, and others; the self-serving or self-righteous claims of those who demand that we refer to them as our "leaders"; and so many more. *Yearning for a different time* is to desire temporalities other than those set by factory clocks, office managers, deadline enforcers, and war planners who have narrow windows for *their* targets of opportunity. PCNs are not just about looking directly backward; they are about looking *sideways,* as Boym points out, in an effort to express oneself in *elegiac poems and ironic fragments, not in philosophical scientific treatises.*[3]

With time apprehended in the space of the PCN, the performers address themselves to what Joseph Roach understands as acts of surrogation. Reflecting their polity's anxiety during the late 1920s and early 1930s amid the reordering of an American colony into a sovereign nation, romantic nationalists such as Jorge Bocobo and Francisca Aquino turned chaos into continuity. Their generation witnessed a familiar arc of cultural importation, imitation, and localization. White performers from the United States who had been imported to the Philippines to perform for white colonial administrators were followed by native/brown educated student bodies aping versions of the metropolitan culture (e.g., the "Filipino Fred Astaire" and the "Filipino Laurel and Hardy"). These performers were substituted finally for more brown bodies singing in the vernacular who redubbed vaudeville "*bodabil.*" Bocobo and Aquino insisted also on replacing the choreography: out with the tuxedoed fox-trotters and in with the natively attired "folk dancers," merging the technical proficiency of modernity's anxiety-ridden physical education with an improvised ethnography of the *folk.* They transformed what they believed to be the diversion of imported U.S. popular culture into the destiny of Philippine sovereign reference by authoring folkloric forms in both quasi–"Asian" myth and modernity's push toward rationality and progress.

The Bayanihan Philippine Dance Company and other companies that emerged in the 1960s arrested the irreversibility of modern time by apprehending the native and the indigenized body—idyllically tamed, disciplined, costumed, choreographed, and rehearsed—for touristic purposes. The young bodies traversed the globe in the jet age—from Brussels to Broadway and back to Manila for more rehearsal. PCN organizers performing in the metropole have been concerned with the *absolute truth* of their movements, the authenticity of the performative regime ("*Our* costumes were recently imported from the provinces" or "Our *rondalla* rehearsed from the original recordings *in the field*" or—the apex of cultural authenticity among young performers—"Our choreographers performed with the Bayanihan!"). PCN organizers reconstruct, with painstaking attention to detail, all of those emblems and rituals of the home to which many have never been, or knew only as children, to, as Boym would have it, "conquer and spatialize time" itself. The performers arrest the rushing telos of their American present by hurling themselves into a mythic time out of time—to substitute oneself for plucky heroines and incantatory messiahs. Finally, Filipino American comics (who are also veterans of the cultural-night presentations) stage their own versions of the whole enterprise by refusing to be literal and, instead, being lateral, offering up the trickster—this time into what they perceive to be a calcified form, a sideways substitution into time's breach—to pull down the invented tradition with parody.

More work remains to be done, especially in the following areas of comparative cultural analysis. First, Filipino American cultural forms may be more thoroughly compared with those developed by other racial and ethnic minorities such as Chicano, Latino, African American, Native American, Pacific Islander, and other Asian American historical plays, reenactments, pageants, festivals, and folkloric presentations. One could also consider contrasts with other ethnically and nationally specific articulations of difference and power found in (white) European American examples. Another version of this line of inquiry would undertake comparisons of U.S.-based forms with other examples found throughout the diaspora—throughout the Americas, in Europe, and in other parts of Asia. We also should not leave out what it would be like to take seriously Kale Fajardo's lead in crafting studies aboard ships—where Filipinos continue to be overrepresented in seafaring labor—because, according to her, "Cockfights at sea are more beautiful than the world cup."[4]

Second, researchers can perform close readings of specific PCN scripts and narratives that are specific to a particular locale or another analytic, such as gender, sexual orientation, or class. Samahang Pilipino at UCLA has established a useful archive of texts that includes scripts, programs, and ephemera. Third, students should also take the opportunity to develop dynamic qualitative research models that place participant observation at the center of their cultural criticism—to experiment not only with how knowledge may be acquired in concert with others, but also to insist that we continue to work in several registers for its dissemination and digestion.

Scholars of cultural studies, Filipino studies, and Filipino American studies can all help to track not only the prospects continually manifested in cultural work, but also its problems. We have being told by leaders, captains of industry, and commentators that our complex modern world can be simplified into a series of primordial battles, Manichean antagonisms, and a circumstance so monumental that only a charging empire can address. What is at stake is a version of history and the contemporary world that is the latest attempt to deny us the intricacy of negotiation and the fullest sense of what liberation could mean: independence from stagnant ideologies of the past, from forms of surveillance that grant more access to our private lives, and to a mythology of the market that lulls us into the late capitalist's false comfort that being a consumer is more important than being a wholly sovereign subject.

There are those whose analysis of the relationship between power and place seems plausible, especially in light of the repositioning of the United States in the post–Cold War world. For example, Samuel Huntington's clash-of-civilization thesis has become part of the indispensable repertoire for our current theater of war. To "stay strong," Huntington wrote in 1993, "the West must exploit differences and conflicts among Confucian and Islamic states . . . [t]o strengthen international institutions that reflect and legitimate [W]estern interests and values, and to promote the involvement of non-Western states in those institutions."[5]

Among those non-Western states is the Philippines—or what Walden Bello has referred to as the "second front" in the war on terror.[6] In the July 2003 issue of the *Atlantic Monthly,* Robert Kaplan gave an indication of how twenty-first-century imperialists no longer disguise their work. His essay's opening lines show how matter of fact the work of empire has become: "It is a cliché these days to observe that the United States now possesses a global empire—different from Britain's and Rome's but an empire nonetheless. . . . [H]ow should we operate on a tactical level to manage an unruly world? What are the rules and what are the tools?"[7]

Kaplan offered ten rules for local commanders stationed throughout the U.S. empire, including "Emulate second century Rome" (rule number two) and the cryptic "Be light and lethal" (rule number five). But what caught my attention was rule number seven: "Remember the Philippines." Here he celebrated the U.S. colonization of the Philippines by clouding it in the euphemism of "consolidated control." Rather than concluding that the Philippine–American War was fought between unmatched opponents and eventually resulted in congressional hearings describing torture,

Kaplan agreed with another author's assessment that the conflict was "one of the most successful counterinsurgencies waged by a western army in modern times."[8] Kaplan heaped praise on U.S. commanders during that time who "were particularly successful in utilizing small, mobile units; developing native intelligence sources; and gaining information by interrogating captured guerrillas. In some parts of the archipelago the United States was able to exploit ethnic divisions; in other parts it was foolish even to try. . . . [I]n areas still not pacified by our troops, it is perfectly appropriate to see more soldiers than aid workers."[9]

Even if President George W. Bush did not read Kaplan's essay, he nevertheless offered his own version of how the Philippine and American administrations are engaged in this permanent war. In October 2003, Bush told the Philippine Congress that Iraq, like the Philippines, could still be transformed into a vibrant democracy: "Some say the culture of the Middle East will not sustain the institutions of democracy. The same doubts were once expressed about the culture of Asia. Those doubts were proven wrong nearly six decades ago."[10] He went on to say that the United States had "liberated the Philippines from colonial rule" but failed to mention that the liberation from one empire meant colonization by another for almost fifty more years.

We should all take a closer look at these comments, because too many decision makers continue to advance the notion that cultures are homogeneous, monolithic, and unchanging. Anyone who has spent time even casually in the Middle East or Asia will realize there is no such thing as a singular "Middle Eastern culture" or a similarly unified "Asian culture." These artificial categories collapse religions, races, ethnicities, and traditions into easy slogans, brands, and, worse yet, styles.

The work of nations is precisely to turn chance and indeterminacy into fate and the seemingly inevitable or natural. With varying degrees of success, the world's majority have made recourse to the nation as a vehicle for performing the precious collective will. But too many of us have also witnessed how nationalism can become a particularly durable style of imagining that benefits elites, emboldens patriarchs, and encourages capitalists. Our task as both critics and actors (on all stages) is to look across historical time periods without falling back onto easy essentialisms, to check ourselves when we assume that what was cherished in another time and place should mean the same for ours. Cultural performances like those I have studied in this book give us an opportunity to be respectfully and critically skeptical about how each generation throws forth its own challenge to be relevant. Rather than establishing clear lines of benefaction from one generation to the next, cultural performances reveal that multiple pasts engage multiple presents. Official modes of conceiving the past, especially those sanctioned by states and their elite surrogates, cannot capture how these performative inheritances actually function. Nor can the crafty art of the state grasp how few of us live inside the categories of academics or policymakers. As fragile as the repertoires have been—fashioned out of bribery, ambition, angst, or mockery—our movements and choreographies continue to be some of the most precious resources for rewriting the past, *as if it were still a part of us, still connected.*

# Epilogue

*Memoria*

PHANTOM PAIN. My interest in this topic began as a dissertation for a doctoral program, while my fascination with performances of all types has a much longer history. My father served twenty-six years in the U.S. Army, retiring in the early 1970s as a staff sergeant. His tours of duty included the Korean and Vietnam wars, with training that took him to Guam, Hawai'i, Georgia, New Jersey, Virginia, and West Germany. His health was never an issue until he retired. He found work years later operating a forklift on an Army base in Central California. One afternoon he drove the machine down a steep grade, lost control, and jumped from the cab before it crashed at the bottom of a ramp. The truck's fork slammed into him, requiring his left arm to be amputated at the shoulder. On the day my mother came with the news about the surgery my dad would need, I asked her whether he could grow the arm back like a starfish. Every month my brother, mother, and I caught an olive-drab bus that headed north from the Monterey Peninsula to San Francisco's Letterman Army Medical Center, where he spent his initial recovery. After six months, he returned home. For years, he would tell us how he could still feel pain "there," not just at the shoulder but also along the length of the amputated arm, down to his wrist. He recalled sensations of the removed limb slowly lifting and lowering as if it were *still a part of him, still connected, still in pain.*

MUSCLE MEMORY. My parents poured their love of music into my brother and me. Some of their vinyl LPs—Tyrone Washington's *Natural Essence,* Ed Thigpen's *Out of the Storm,* a Ramsey Lewis special "goes Latin" session—have become a treasured part of my collection. They would tell me of mambo's heyday in the 1950s, when they visited Tokyo's clubs where patrons danced in kimonos and tuxedoes. And yet just a few years before California's Proposition 13 made it nearly impossible to continue the funding of music education in public schools, I was lucky to get started on free classes.[1] I showed my parents a sheet from school that listed band instruments that I could take home. I received training twice a week from Owen Dunsford, my first music teacher. Mom circled the word "clarinet" on the page. Every Sunday night, she and my father enjoyed the "champagne style" of the Lawrence Welk orchestra that featured reed players such as Pete Fountain, Peanuts Hucko, and Henry Cuesta. I worked my way through woodwind trios and quartets and eventually became a section leader and eventually played from the first chair in junior high and in honor bands until I graduated from high school. But my passion in music found its expression through the piano. A year after I started on the clarinet, my parents sacrificed a lot to purchase a Wurlitzer upright from Abinante's Music on Alvarado Street in Monterey. After the six free lessons that came with the purchase ran out, I recall making a visit to the store with my father, where he picked out from a rack some sheet music that I have long since associated with him: "Tenderly" by Jack Lawrence and Walter Gross. I committed it to memory and have rearranged it dozens of times for weddings (Christian and Jewish), receptions, private parties, banquets, a luau, and one Bat Mitzvah. Around this time, I began to take lessons from Heinrich von Bender, an elegant gentleman who taught out of his gorgeous home in an older section of the peninsula. Just about every room, including the narrow hallway, was crowded with a spinet. "Herr von Bender," as he insisted on being addressed, claimed to be the *last* student of the *last* student of Franz Liszt. For the many years I marched in bands with my clarinet I always had to use a lyre music holder clamped to the lower barrel of the instrument. But when I started playing the piano, I rarely needed the sheet music after reading through it once or twice. "Muscle memory," the maestro barked in his thick, clipped accent. "It's in your hands, your fingers, your wrists now. The music has a shape, and your body recalls it when it's time to play." This came in handy years later when I played with the bassist Farris Smith in the piano trio we formed in San Francisco. "No paper on stage," he would insist.

NEUROSCIENTISTS refer to the term "proprioception" as the sense afforded by a matrix of parts within the body working in concert to inform each other—that is, the body's awareness of itself through sensors located in our inner ear and throughout our joints and muscles. Actors, dancers, musicians, even those working on their golf swing discipline the proprioceptive aspect of their bodies to reach beyond seemingly natural limits and to make what they do appear effortless. Consider the information culled from the proprioceptive as well as the pain communicated to and through phantom limbs. Information understood as pain travels along a complex path—from nerve endings to tissue masses outside the spinal column, then to pain-sensing neurons inside the spinal column, and finally to the brain. When those neurons, whose sole job it is to sense pain, no longer receive messages, they pass along instead nonsense or garbled data, information that is interpreted by the brain as pain. The monitoring continues, allowing amputees to feel something that is no longer there.[2]

Both of these experiences taught me young that our bodies carry vital and sometimes confusing information about who we are. From my experiences in learning music, I continue to think about the various techniques and forms of discipline to which we often subject our bodies to be *in concert* with others or our surroundings. From my father's case, I have wondered about how we continue to feel the presence of unseen things, of things taken away. As much as I wanted to relate, I had no "sense" of what it could mean to experience my father's inexplicable pain. I began to wonder about other kinds of absences, especially when reading a sociologist's account of spectral presences: how family members, friends (and even foes), ancestors, and teachers continue to inform and haunt *as if they were still a part of us, still connected.*[3] What else can our bodies tell us?

# Notes

## Prologue

1. "An Act Making Appropriations for the Support of the Army for the Fiscal Year Ending June Thirtieth, Nineteen Hundred and Two," March 2, 1901, Enrolled Acts and Resolutions of Congress, 1789– , General Records of the U.S. Government, Record Group 11, National Archives, Washington, D.C.

2. "Hope and Memory," *Adbusters* 12, no. 3, 2004, n.p.

3. See Thomas A. Bailey, "Dewey and the Germans at Manila Bay," *American Historical Review* 45, no. 1 (1939): 59–81.

4. Oscar King Davis, "Stories of Admiral Dewey," *McClure's Magazine,* vol. 13, no. 1, 1899, 43–44.

5. Idem, "Dewey's Capture of Manila," *McClure's Magazine,* vol. 13, no. 2, 1899, 172.

6. Ibid., 176.

7. Ibid., 174.

8. Ibid., 180.

9. Bailey, "Dewey and the Germans at Manila Bay," 75.

10. Teodoro A. Agoncillo and Milagros C. Guerrero, *History of the Filipino People* (Quezon City: R. P. Garcia, 1973), 43.

11. Bailey, "Dewey and the Germans at Manila Bay," 78.

12. Agoncillo and Guerrero, *History of the Filipino People,* 44.

13. *New York Herald,* July 29, 1899. Davis, "Dewey's Capture of Manila," 171.

14. The text of the relevant section reads, "Until it has been officially proclaimed that a state of war or insurrection against the authority of the United States no longer exists in the Philippine Islands, it shall be unlawful for any person to advance orally or by writing or printing or like methods, the independence of the Philippine Islands or their separation from the United States whether by peaceable or forcible means,

or to print, publish or circulate any handbill, newspaper or publication, advocating such independence or separation": *Public Laws Annotated*, quoted in Doreen G. Fernandez, *Palabas: Essays on Philippine Theater History* (Honolulu: University of Hawai'i Press, 1997), 82.

15. Michael Cullinane, "Ilustrado Politics: The Response of the Filipino Educated Elite to American Colonial Rule, 1898–1907," Ph.D. diss., University of Michigan, Ann Arbor, 1989, 173.

16. Vicente L. Rafael, "White Love: Surveillance and Nationalist Resistance in the U.S. Colonization of the Philippines," in *Cultures of United States Imperialism*, ed. Amy Kaplan and Donald E. Pease (Durham, N.C.: Duke University Press, 1993), 185–218.

17. Fernandez, *Palabas*, 95–103.

18. Ibid., 98–99.

19. The following two paragraphs draw on Sally B. Woodbridge and John M. Woodbridge, *San Francisco Architecture: The Illustrated Guide to over 1,000 of the Best Buildings, Parks, and Public Artworks in the Bay Area* (San Francisco: Chronicle Books, 1992); James B. Alexander, *San Francisco: Building the Dream City* (San Francisco: Scottwall Associates, 2002); Bernice Scharlach, *Big Alma: San Francisco's Alma Spreckels* (San Francisco: Scottwall Associates, 1990).

20. Kevin Fagan, "A Square Is Born," *San Francisco Chronicle*, July 26, 2002.

21. John King, "A Fresh Look for Union Square," *San Francisco Chronicle*, March 21, 1997.

22. Marita Sturken, *Tangled Memories: The Vietnam War, the AIDS Epidemic, and the Politics of Remembering* (Berkeley: University of California Press, 1997); 47–48.

23. Rodel Rodis, "The Wording of the Plaque," *Philippine News*, May 17, 2005.

24. John King, "Filipinos Want Full Story Told on Dewey Memorial," *San Francisco Chronicle*, March 31, 1997.

25. Ibid.

26. Rodel E. Rodis, e-mail correspondence, January 30, 2009.

## Introduction

1. Svetlana Boym, *The Future of Nostalgia* (New York: Basic Books, 2002).

2. For works that pay similar attention to the relationship between repertoire and cultural identities, see, e.g., Lon Kurashige, *Japanese American Celebration and Conflict: A History of Ethnic Identity and Festival, 1934–1990* (Berkeley: University of California Press, 2002); Rachel Buff, *Immigration and the Political Economy of Home: West Indian Brooklyn and American Indian Minneapolis, 1945–1992* (Berkeley: University of California Press, 2001); April R. Schultz, *Ethnicity on Parade: Inventing the Norwegian American through Celebration* (Amherst: University of Massachusetts Press, 1995); Nhi Lieu, "Private Desires on Public Display: Vietnamese American Identities in Multi-Mediated Leisure and Niche Entertainment," Ph.D. diss., University of Michigan, Ann Arbor, 2004; Robert A. Orsi, *The Madonna of 115th Street: Faith and Community in Italian Harlem, 1880–1950* (New Haven, Conn.: Yale University Press, 1985).

3. See David Reimers, *Still the Golden the Door: The Third World Comes to America,* 2nd ed. (New York: Columbia University Press, 1992), 116. On the Immigration and Nationality Act of 1965, see ibid., chap. 3. Corporate Student System Report CSS170D and CPEC Report DEG704, Office of the President, University of California, Berkeley.

4. Michael A. Fletcher, "Minority Graduate Galas Highlight a Timely Issue," *Washington Post,* May 19, 2003, A1; Ben Gose, "California Regent Questions Paying for Minority Graduation Events," *Chronicle of Higher Education,* July 19, 1996.

5. The poet Joseph Balaz inverts core and periphery when he writes, "Hawai'i is da mainland to me": Joseph P. Balaz, "Da Mainland to Me," in *Asia/Pacific as Space of Cultural Production,* ed. Rob Wilson and Arif Dirlik (Durham, N.C.: Duke University Press, 1995), 176.

6. Diana Taylor, *The Archive and the Repertoire: Performing Cultural Memory in the Americas* (Durham, N.C.: Duke University Press, 2003), 2.

7. I thank the Temple University Press reader who suggested that I make this link more explicit.

8. Joseph Roach, *Cities of the Dead: Circum-Atlantic Performance* (New York: Columbia University Press, 1996), 2; emphasis added.

9. Mikhail Bakhtin, *Rabelais and His World,* trans. Helene Iswolsky (Cambridge, Mass.: M.I.T. Press, 1968); and Derek Walcott, *The Antilles: Fragments of Epic Memory* (New York: Farrar, Straus and Giroux, 1993).

10. Roach, *Cities of the Dead,* 3.

11. Ibid.

12. Roach, *Cities of the Dead,* 28–29.

13. Robert Warshow, "Clifford Odets: Poet of the Jewish Middle Class," in *The Immediate Experience: Movies, Comics, Theatre and Other Aspects of Popular Culture* (New York: Doubleday, 1962), 58.

14. Ibid., 60–61.

15. Ibid., 62.

16. Ibid., 63.

17. Erin Khue Ninh, "Ingratitude: A Cultural Theory of Power in Asian American Women's Literature," Ph.D. diss., University of California, Berkeley, 2005, 82.

18. Ibid., 1.

19. R. Zamora Linmark, personal communication, April 18, 2006. See also Eric Estuar Reyes, "American Developmentalism and Hierarchies of Difference in R. Zamora Linmark's *Rolling the R's,*" *Journal of Asian American Studies* 10, no. 2 (June 2007): 117–140.

20. Bienvenido Santos, *The Day the Dancers Came: Selected Prose Works* (Manila: Bookmark, 1967).

21. Corpus, quoted in Joann Faung Lee, *Asian Americans: Oral Histories of First to Fourth Generation Americans from China, the Philippines, Japan, India the Pacific Islands, Vietnam and Cambodia* (New York: New Press, 1992), 84.

22. Victor Turner, *From Ritual to Theatre: The Human Seriousness of Play* (New York: PAJ Publications, 1982), 13; emphasis added.

23. *Black's Law Dictionary,* 8th ed. (St. Paul, Minn.: Thomson/West, 2004), s.v. "Performance."

24. Michel Foucault, "Nietzsche, Genealogy, History," in idem, *Language, Counter Memory, Practice* (Ithaca, N.Y.: Cornell University Press, 1977), 139.

25. Reynaldo C. Ileto, "Outlines of a Nonlinear Emplotment of Philippine History," in *The Politics of Culture in the Shadow of Capital,* ed. Lisa Lowe and David Lloyd (Durham, N.C.: Duke University Press), 98.

26. Ileto makes clear why the progressive narratives are embraced so fervently by apologists and activists alike. "The reason most educated Filipinos find the linear-development mode a natural one for ordering such phenomena as revolts and the consolidation of state power in the name of nationalism is because this framework puts them at the forefront of the development process. Whether as apologists or activists, they are able to recognize themselves in a comfortable way in the past, and they are assured of a primary role in the fulfillment of the end toward which history moves": ibid., 104–105.

27. Foucault, "Nietzsche, Genealogy, History," 146.

28. Ileto, "Outlines of a Nonlinear Emplotment of Philippine History," 125–126.

29. See the provocative essays that take up the issues of locality, living "abroad," and producing art in Dana Frii-Hansen, Alice G. Guillermo, and Jeff Baysa, *At Home and Abroad: Twenty Contemporary Filipino Artists* (San Francisco: Asian Art Museum, 1998).

30. See David Lloyd and Paul Thomas, *Culture and the State* (New York: Routledge, 1998).

31. Stuart Hall, "Notes on Deconstructing the 'Popular'," in *People's History and Socialist Theory,* ed. Raphael Samuel (London: Routledge, 1981), 239. For example, when considering the meaning of symbols of terror in contemporary Britain, Hall had this to say:

> The streets are full of kids who are not "fascist" because they may wear a swastika on a chain. On the other hand, perhaps they could be.... What this sign means will ultimately depend, in the politics of youth culture, less on the intrinsic cultural symbolism of the thing in itself, and more on the balance of forces between, say, the National Front and the Anti-Nazi League, between White Rock and the Two Tone Sound. (Ibid., 237–238)

32. Scholars of Asian American studies have taken up a variety of cultural forms of several ethnic groups. A common thread is that the premium placed on a traditional notion of assimilation no longer holds and that articulations of ethnicity serve as direct evidence for the irrepressibility of an Asian American subjectivity. Among the most notable works in this vein are Shilpa Davé, LeiLani Nishime, and Tasha G. Oren, eds., *East Main Street: Asian American Popular Culture* (New York: New York University Press, 2005); Jennifer Lee and Min Zhou, *Asian American Youth: Culture, Identity and Ethnicity* (Philadelphia: Temple University Press, 1997), Mimi Thi Nguyen and Thuy Linh Nguyen, eds., *Alien Encounters* (Durham, N.C.: Duke University Press, 2007), which feature chapters on Asian Indian film cultures, textual analyses of Southeast Asian literature, and Filipino American beauty pageants, respectively. Maria P. P. Root, *Filipino Americans: Transformation and Identity* (Thousand Oaks, Calif.: Sage, 1997), and Anthony Tiongson, Ricardo Gutierrez, and Edgardo Gutierrez, eds., *Positively No Filipinos Allowed: Building Communities and*

*Discourse* (Philadelphia: Temple University Press, 2006), focus exclusively on Filipino Americans.

Work that focuses on ethnically specific Asian American expressive forms of culture includes Sunaina Maira, *Desis in the House: Indian American Youth Culture in New York City* (Philadelphia: Temple University Press, 2002); Martin Manalansan, *Global Divas: Filipino Gay Men in the Diaspora* (Durham, N.C.: Duke University Press, 2003); Linda Maram, *Creating Masculinity in Los Angeles's Little Manila: Working-Class Filipinos and Popular Culture in the United States* (New York: Columbia University Press, 2006). Maram's work is a cultural history that focuses on the mid-twentieth century, while Maira and Manalansan examine post-1965 contexts. All three pay close attention to ethnographically informed analyses of youth cultures, relying on interviews and direct participant observation. They also write convincingly about subjects who turn to each other not merely in moments of escape or resignation but also to reclaim and re-energize the very deep tradition of community as an essential aspect of "American" life. I find the work of Doreen G. Fernandez and Eugene Van Erven on Philippine performance and politics indispensable.

33. For example, the professional academic organization Performance Studies International lists more than a dozen replies to the question, "What is Performance Studies?": see the Performance Studies International website at http://psi-web.org/texts/what%20is%20text.htm

34. Susan Leigh Foster, *Corporealities* (London: Routledge, 1995); Marta Savigliano, *Tango and the Political Economy of Passion* (Boulder, Colo.: Westview Press, 1995); Barbara Browning, *Samba: Resistance in Motion* (Bloomington: Indiana University Press, 1995). Three doctoral programs in the United States offer training specifically in this growing area: New York University's Performance Studies Department, Northwestern University's Performance Studies Department (located in the School of Communication), and the World Arts and Culture Department at the University of California, Los Angeles (which originated from a merger of dance scholars with folklorists).

35. Daphne A. Brooks, *Bodies in Dissent: Spectacular Performances of Race and Freedom, 1850–1910* (Durham, N.C.: Duke University Press, 2006); David Román, *Acts of Intervention: Performance, Gay Culture, and AIDS* (Bloomington: Indiana University Press, 1998); idem, *Performance in America: Contemporary U.S. Culture and the Performing Arts* (Durham, N.C.: Duke University Press, 2005); Jose Muñoz, *Disidentifications: Queers of Color and the Performance of Politics* (Minneapolis: University of Minnesota Press, 1999); Ann Cvetkovich, *An Archive of Feelings: Trauma, Sexuality, and Lesbian Public Cultures* (Durham, N.C.: Duke University Press, 2003); Jan Cohen-Cruz, *Local Acts: Community-Based Performance in the United States* (New Brunswick, N.J.: Rutgers University Press, 2003).

36. Dorinne Kondo, *About Face: Performing Race in Fashion and Theater* (London: Routledge, 1997); Josephine Lee, *Performing Asian America: Race and Ethnicity on the Contemporary Stage* (Philadelphia: Temple University Press, 1998); Karen Shimakawa, *National Abjection: The Asian American Body on Stage* (Durham, N.C.: Duke University Press, 2002), James Moy, *Marginal Sights: Staging the Chinese in America* (Iowa City: University of Iowa Press, 1994); Krystyn Moon, *Yellowface: Creating the Chinese in American Popular Music and Performance, 1850s–1920s* (New Brunswick, N.J.: Rutgers University Press, 2005); Yuko Kurahashi, *Asian American Culture on*

*Stage: The History of the East West Players* (New York: Routledge Press, 1999); Deborah Wong, *Speak It Louder: Asian Americans Making Music* (New York: Routledge, 2004); Adelaida Reyes, *Songs of the Caged, Songs of the Free: Music and the Vietnamese Refugee Experience* (Philadelphia: Temple University Press, 1999); Mari Yoshihara, *Musicians from a Different Shore: Asians and Asian Americans in Classical Music* (Philadelphia: Temple University Press, 2007).

37. See "U.S. Joins Another Set of Anti-terrorist Drills with Philippine Troops," Associated Press, January 23, 2002; James S. Robbins, "Freedom Eagle," *National Review*, January 18, 2002.

38. See Yen Le Espiritu, *Home Bound: Filipino American Lives across Cultures, Communities, and Countries* (Berkeley: University of California Press, 2003); Jesse Quinsaat et al., eds., *Letters in Exile: An Introductory Reader on the History of Pilipinos in America* (Los Angeles: Asian American Studies Center, UCLA, 1976).

39. Yvette Collymore, "Rapid Population Growth, Crowded Cities Present Challenges in the Philippines," Population Reference Bureau report, June 2003, Washington, D.C.; "Number of Overseas Filipino Workers with Remittances, Total and Average Remittance in Cash and in Kind by Sex," National Statistics Office report, 1996, 1997–1998, 1999, 2000, 2001, 2002, 2004; "Number of Overseas Filipino Workers with Cash Remittances Sent, Total and Average Cash Remittance, by Mode of Remittance and by Sex," National Statistics Office report, 1996, 1997–1998, 1999, 2000, 2001, 2002, 2004. "Overseas Filipino Workers' Remittances (2002–2005)," Bangko Sentral ng Pilipinas.

40. See Leti Volpp, "American Mestizo: Filipinos and Anti-miscegenation Laws in California," *University of California, Davis, Law Review* 33, no. 4 (2000): 795–835; Mae M. Ngai, *Impossible Subjects: Illegal Aliens and the Making of Modern America* (Princeton, N.J.: Princeton University Press, 2004), 96–126.

41. Catherine Choy, *Empire of Care: Nursing and Migration in Filipino American History* (Durham, N.C.: Duke University Press, 2003); Dorothy Fujita-Rony, *American Workers, Colonial Power: Philippine Seattle and the Transpacific West, 1919–1941* (Berkeley: University of California Press, 2003); Augusto F. Espiritu, *Five Faces of Exile: The Nation and Filipino American Intellectuals* (Stanford, Calif.: Stanford University Press, 2005); Maram, *Creating Masculinity in Los Angeles's Little Manila*.

42. Jonathan Okamura, *Imagining the Filipino American Diaspora: Transnational Relations, Identities, and Communities* (New York: Garland Publishers, 1998); Rhacel Salazar Parreñas, *Servants of Globalization: Women, Migration, and Domestic Work* (Stanford, Calif.: Stanford University Press, 2001); idem, *Children of Global Migration: Transnational Families and Gendered Woes* (Stanford, Calif.: Stanford University Press, 2005); Rhacel Salazar Parreñas and Lok C. D. Siu, eds., *Asian Diasporas: New Formations, New Conceptions* (Stanford, Calif.: Stanford University Press, 2007); Espiritu, *Home Bound*; Emily Ignacio, *Building Diaspora: Filipino Community Formation on the Internet* (New Brunswick, N.J.: Rutgers University Press, 2005); Manalansan, *Global Divas*.

43. Sharon Delmendo, *Star-Entangled Banner: One Hundred Years of America in the Philippines* (New Brunswick, N.J.: Rutgers University Press, 2004); Angel Shaw and Luis Francia, eds., *Vestiges of War: The Philippine–American War and the Aftermath of an Imperial Dream, 1899–1999* (New York: New York University Press, 2002); Allan Isaac, *American Tropics: Articulating Filipino America* (Minneapolis: University

of Minnesota Press, 2006). See also Paul A. Kramer, *The Blood of Government: Race, Empire, the United States, and the Philippines* (Chapel Hill: University of North Carolina Press, 2006); Julian Go and Anne L. Foster, eds., *The American Colonial State in the Philippines: Global Perspectives* (Durham, N.C.: Duke University Press, 2003); Amy Kaplan and Donald E. Pease, eds., *Cultures of United States Imperialism* (Durham, N.C.: Duke University Press, 1993).

44. Renato Constantino, *Neocolonial Identity and Counter-Consciousness: Essays on Cultural Decolonization* (White Plains, N.Y.: M. E. Sharpe, 1979); Howard Zinn, *Declarations of Independence: Cross-Examining American Ideology* (New York: HarperCollins, 1990).

45. Royal F. Morales, *Makibaka: The Pilipino American Struggle* (Los Angeles: Mountainview Publishers, 1974); Frank Chin et al., eds., *Aiiieeeee! An Anthology of Asian-American Writers* (Washington, D.C.: Howard University Press, 1974); E. San Juan Jr., *Carlos Bulosan and the Imagination of the Class Struggle* (Quezon City: University of the Philippines Press, 1972); Quinsaat et al., *Letters in Exile.*

46. Maira, *Desis in the House,* 148, 194–200.

47. Sarita Echavez See, "A Queer Horizon: Paul Pfeiffer's Disintegrating Figure Studies," paper presented at the Philippine Palimpsests: Filipino Studies in the Twenty-first Century conference, University of Illinois, Urbana-Champaign, March 7–8, 2008.

48. Lucy Mae San Pablo Burns, "'Splendid Dancing': Filipino 'Exceptionalism' in Taxi Dancehalls," *Dance Research Journal* 40, no. 2 (Winter 2008): 23–40.

49. Arjun Appadurai, *Fear of Small Numbers: An Essay on the Geography of Anger* (Durham, N.C.: Duke University Press, 2006).

50. As Dylan Rodriguez puts it, Filipino American subjectivity is premised on "a critical labor that must be permanently and productively enabled and provoked by the racial apocalypse to which it is anchored": see Dylan Rodriguez, "'Its Very Familiarity Disguises Its Horror': White Supremacy, Genocide, and the Statecraft of Pacifica Americana," paper presented at the Philippine Palimpsests: Filipino Studies in the Twenty-first Century conference, University of Illinois, Urbana-Champaign, March 7–8, 2008.

51. Robyn M. Rodriguez, "Globalizing Labor," paper presented at the Philippine Palimpsests: Filipino Studies in the Twenty-first Century conference, University of Illinois, Urbana-Champaign, March 7–8, 2008.

## Chapter 1. The Art of the State

*Epigraph:* Ngũgĩ wa Thiong'o, *Penpoints, Gunpoints, and Dreams: Towards a Critical Theory of the Arts and the State in Africa* (Oxford: Oxford University Press, 1998), 53–54, 61.

1. See Arthur F. Wertheim, *Vaudeville Wars: How the Keith-Albee and Orpheum Circuits Controlled the Big-Time and Its Performers* (New York: Palgrave Macmillan, 2006), esp. chaps. 3–4.

2. I thank Jean Vengua and John Rosa for introducing me to the online collection "Traveling Culture: Circuit Chautauqua in the Twentieth Century," available at http://memory.loc.gov/ammem/collections/chautauqua (accessed February 20, 2008). See also Andrew Rieser, *The Chautauqua Moment: Protestants, Progressives,*

*and the Culture of Modern Liberalism* (New York: Columbia University Press, 2003); Richie C. Quirino, *Pinoy Jazz Traditions* (Pasig City: Anvil, 2004), 12–44.

3. Raymundo Bañas y Castillo, *Pilipino Music and Theater* (Quezon City: Manlapaz Publishing, 1969), 184–185.

4. For an example of pre–World War II Filipino musical travels throughout Asia, see Angel M. Peña, *A Man and His Music: An Autobiography* (Quezon City: Ateneo de Manila University Press, 2007).

5. Cultural Center of the Philippines, *Encyclopedia of Philippine Art,* vol. 6 (Manila: Cultural Center of the Philippines, 1994); Bañas y Castillo, *Pilipino Music and Theater,* 185–186.

6. Ernesto Vallejo, in *Philippines Herald* (Manila), August 30, 1929.

7. See James Lincoln Collier, *Jazz: The American Theme Song* (New York: Oxford University Press, 1993); Burton Peretti, *Jazz in American Culture* (Chicago: Ivan R. Dee, 1997); Samuel A. Floyd, *The Power of Black Music: Interpreting Its History from Africa to the United States* (New York: Oxford University Press, 1995).

8. Artemio Agnes, quoted in Quirino, *Pinoy Jazz Traditions,* 13.

9. See Vicente Rafael, ed., *Discrepant Histories: Translocal Essays on Filipino Cultures* (Philadelphia: Temple University Press, 1995); Benito M. Vergara Jr., *Displaying Filipinos: Photography and Colonialism in Early 20th Century Philippines* (Quezon City: University of the Philippines Press, 1995); Warwick Anderson, *Colonial Pathologies: American Tropical Medicine, Race and Hygiene in the Philippines* (Durham, N.C.: Duke University Press, 2006).

10. See Peter W. Stanley, ed., *Reappraising an Empire: New Perspectives on Philippine-American History* (Cambridge, Mass.: Harvard University Press, 1984); Renato Constantino, *The Philippines: A Past Revisited* (Quezon City: Tala Publishing Services, 1975); Renato Constantino and Letizia R. Constantino, *The Philippines: The Continuing Past* (Quezon City: Foundation for Nationalist Studies, 1978); Teodoro A. Agoncillo and Oscar M. Alfonso, *History of the Filipino People,* 2nd ed. (Quezon City: University of the Philippines Press, 1967). See also E. San Juan Jr.'s historiographical survey of American "Filipinology" in "One Hundred Years of Producing and Reproducing the 'Filipino,'" *Amerasia Journal* 24, no. 2 (Summer 1998): 1–33.

11. Reynaldo Alejandro, *Philippine Dance: Mainstream and Crosscurrents* (Quezon City: Vera-Reyes, 1978); Basilio Esteban S. Villaruz, "Sayaw: An Essay on Philippine Dance," in *Tuklas Sining: Essays on Philippine Arts,* ed. Nicanor G. Tiongson (Manila: Sentrong Pangkultura ng Pilipinas, 1991), 230–271.

12. For biographical material on Bocobo, see Celia Bocobo Olivar, *Aristocracy of the Mind: A Precious Heritage, a Biography of Jorge Bocobo* (Quezon City: New Day Publishers, 1981).

13. See Daniel F. Doeppers, *Manila, 1900–1941: Social Change in a Late Colonial Metropolis* (New Haven, Conn.: Southeast Asia Studies, Yale University, 1984).

14. See Constantino, *The Philippines,* 247–383; Onofre D. Corpuz, *An Economic History of the Philippines* (Quezon City: University of the Philippines Press, 1997); Ruby R. Paredes, ed., *Philippine Colonial Democracy* (New Haven, Conn.: Yale University Press, 1988); William J. Pomeroy, *American Neo-colonialism: Its Emergence in the Philippines and Asia* (New York: International Publishers, 1970). For commentary on how economic changes gave rise to Sakdalista challenges, see James S. Allen, "The

Philippine Problem Enters a New Phase," *Pacific Affairs* 11, no. 2 (1938): 159–170; Samuel Weinman, "Behind the Sakdalista Uprising," *The Nation*, vol. 140, no. 3647, May 29, 1935, 625–626; Ifor B. Powell, "The Commonwealth of the Philippines," *Pacific Affairs* 9, no. 1 (1936): 33–43; James S. Allen, "Japan and Philippine Independence," *The Nation*, vol. 145, no. 23, December 4, 1937, 610–612.

15. Geronima T. Pecson and Maria Racelis, eds., *Tales of the American Teachers in the Philippines* (Manila: Carmelo and Bauermann, 1959); Jo Anne Barker Maniago, "The First Peace Corps: The Work of the American Teachers in the Philippines, 1900–1910," M.A. thesis, Boston University, 1974.

16. Arthur MacArthur Jr., quoted in Daniel B. Schirmer and Stephen Rosskamm Shalom, eds., *The Philippines Reader: A History of Colonialism, Necolonialism, Dictatorship, and Resistance* (Boston: South End Press, 1987), 45.

17. Quoted in Constantino, *The Philippines*, 241–242.

18. Ibid., 237–255; Agoncillo and Alfonso, *History of the Filipino People*, 296–297, 378–379.

19. Quoted in Constantino, *The Philippines*, 243, 246.

20. Ibid., 246, 345.

21. Ibid., 327–328.

22. Ibid.

23. Ibid., chap. 7.

24. Ibid.

25. I am borrowing Trimillos's term: see Ricardo D. Trimillos, "The Changing Context of Philippine Dance Performance," *Dance Research Annual* 15 (1985): 107.

26. Mary Racelis and Judy Celine Ick, eds., *Bearers of Benevolence: The Thomasites and Public Education in the Philippines* (Pasig City: Anvil Publishers, 2001); idem, *To Islands Far Away: The Story of the Thomasites and Their Journey to the Philippines* (Manila: Public Affairs Section, U.S. Embassy, 2001).

27. Bocobo Olivar, *Aristocracy of the Mind*, 11.

28. For more on the *pensionado* program, see William Alexander Sutherland, *Not by Might: The Epic of the Philippines* (Las Cruces: Southwest Publishing, 1953).

29. Kimberly A. Alidio, "Between Civilizing Mission and Ethnic Assimilation: Racial Discourse, U.S. Colonial Education and Filipino Ethnicity, 1901–1946," Ph.D. diss., University of Michigan, Ann Arbor, 2001, 96–105.

30. Jose D. Fermin, *1904 World's Fair: The Filipino Experience* (Quezon City: University of the Philippines Press, 2004). See also Robert W. Rydell, "The Trans-Mississippi and International Exposition: 'To Work Out the Problem of Universal Civilization,'" *American Quarterly* 33, no. 5 (1981): 587–607; Eric Breitbart, *A World on Display: Photographs from the 1904 St. Louis World's Fair* (Albuquerque: University of New Mexico Press, 1997), 51–62; Burton Benedict, "International Exhibitions and National Identity," *Anthropology Today* 7, no. 3 (1991): 5–9.

31. Bocobo Olivar, *Aristocracy of the Mind*, 13.

32. Ibid., 30.

33. Ibid.

34. In addition to Bocobo Olivar's biography, see another written by a former student: Juan F. Rivera, *The Father of the First Brown Race Civil Code: The Story of the Civil Code of the Philippines* (Quezon City: Law Center, University of the Philippines, 1978).

35. Jorge G. Bocobo, "Our National Assets," speech broadcast on the KZRM radio station, July 9, 1934. Jorge G. Bocobo Papers, Special Archives and Research Division, University of the Philippines, Quezon City (hereafter, Boboco Papers), box 1, folder 19.

36. Ibid.; emphasis added.

37. Ibid.

38. Ibid.

39. Ibid.

40. Ibid.

41. Ibid.

42. Bocobo Olivar, *Aristocracy of the Mind,* 34.

43. Ibid.; emphasis added.

44. Jorge G. Bocobo, "The Philippine Contribution to World Culture," Bocobo Papers, box 1, folder 30.

45. Idem, "The Education of the Filipino Woman," March 13, 1949, Bocobo Papers, box 1, folder 20.

46. Ibid.; emphasis added.

47. Ibid.

48. Ibid.

49. Ibid.

50. Idem, "Filipino Contact with America," n.d., Bocobo Papers, box 1, folder 24.

51. Idem, "The Philippine Contribution to World Culture," n.p.

52. Ibid.

53. "Rediscovering Native Dances—University of the Philippines Tackles Job Recording Indigenous Dances and Also Melodies," *Graphic* (Manila), August 12, 1937.

54. Ibid., 111–112.

55. Reynaldo G. Alejandro, *Sayaw Silangan: The Dance in the Philippines* (New York: Dancer Perspectives Foundation, 1972), 47.

56. "Rediscovering Native Dances."

57. Salud C. Datoc, *Folk Dance Movement in the Philippines, 1920–Post Liberation Era,* program, Francisca Reyes Aquino Memorial Heritage Foundation, 10.

58. On the American establishment of physical education in the Philippines and the role played by the YMCA, see Bocobo Olivar, *Aristocracy of the Mind,* 37–82.

59. Francisca Reyes Aquino, *Philippine Folk Dances and Games* (New York: Silver, Burdett, 1927), vii.

60. Idem, *Philippine National Dances* (New York: Silver, Burdett, 1946), iii; emphasis added. On the notion that American expressive forms of culture posed threats to other indigenous cultures, including those in Europe, see Richard F. Kuisel, *Seducing the French: The Dilemma of Americanization* (Berkeley: University of California Press, 1993).

61. Aquino, *Philippine National Dances,* 1.

62. Ibid., vi.

63. Datoc, *Folk Dance Movement in the Philippines,* 2.

64. Sally Ann Ness, *Body, Movement, and Culture: Kinesthetic and Visual Communication in a Philippine Community* (Philadelphia: University of Pennsylvania Press, 1989), 186–187.

65. Datoc, *Folk Dance Movement in the Philippines,* 3–4;

66. Ness, *Body, Movement, and Culture,* 187.

67. See Ivy Lily Mendoza, "A Legacy of Philippine Dances," *Philippine Panorama* (Manila), February 24, 1991, 26.

68. Ibid.

69. Ibid., 10.

70. Sucheng Chan, *Asian Americans: An Interpretive History* (Boston: Twayne Publishers, 1991), 3.

71. See Robert H. Weibe, *The Search for Order, 1877–1920* (Westport, Conn.: Greenwood Press, 1980).

72. Linda Tomko, "Women, Artistic Dance Practices, and Social Change in the United States, 1890–1920," Ph.D. diss., University of California, Los Angeles, 1991.

73. See Luther H. Gulick and Harry Smith, "Dancing as a Part of Education: Happy Results of Rhythmic Play by New York School Children," *World's Work,* October 1907, 9445–9452; Linda Tomko, "Fete Accompli: Gender, 'Folk-dance,' and Progressive-Era Political Ideals in New York City," in *Corporealities: Dancing Knowledge, Culture and Power,* ed. Susan Leigh Foster (New York: Routledge, 1996), 155–176.

74. Tomko, "Fete Accompli," 163.

75. See Gregory Kent Stanley, *The Rise and Fall of the Sportswoman: Women's Health, Fitness, and Athletics, 1860–1940* (New York: Peter Lang, 1996); Donald Mrozek, *Sport and American Mentality, 1880–1910* (Knoxville: University of Tennessee Press, 1983); Martha Verbrugge, *Able-Bodied Womanhood, Personal Health and Social Change in Nineteenth Century Boston* (New York: Oxford University Press, 1988); Allen Guttmann, *Women's Sports: A History* (New York: Columbia University Press, 1988); Stephanie L. Twin, *Out of the Bleachers: Writings on Women and Sports* (Old Westbury, N.Y.: Feminist Press, 1979); Ellen Gerber et al., *The American Woman in Sport* (Reading, Mass.: Addison-Wesley, 1974); Frances Cogan, *All American Girl: The Ideal of Real Womanhood in Mid-Nineteenth Century America* (Athens: University of Georgia Press, 1989); Dorothy S. Ainsworth, *The History of Physical Education in Colleges for Women* (New York: A. S. Barnes, 1930).

76. Quoted in Stanley, *The Rise and Fall of the Sportswoman,* 66.

77. See Harry L. Kingman, "Physical Education in China, India, Japan, Latin America and the Philippine Islands," M.A. thesis, International YMCA College, 1916; George Edward Goss, "History of Physical Education in the Philippine Islands," M.A. thesis, YMCA College, 1917; Edward J. Mazurkiewicz, "Contributing Factors in the Development of Physical Education in the Philippines," M.A. thesis, YMCA College, 1916; Serafin Aquino, "Philippine Games and Folk Dances," M.A. thesis, YMCA College, 1922.

78. Quoted in Kingman, "Physical Education in China, India, Japan, Latin America and the Philippine Islands," 6–7.

79. Ibid., 15.

80. Ibid., 20.

81. Mazurkiewicz, "Contributing Factors in the Development of Physical Education in the Philippines," 1.

82. Ibid.., 2.

83. Ibid., 2–3.

84. "The start was slow but just as soon as the natural rivalry between town and provinces was made use of, a deep and general interest in all forms of sport was developed. Cock pits were largely deserted when it was announced that on a 'fiesta' day a track and field meet, or a baseball game, or a basketball contest would take place. All games were fiercely contested and the rooting and cheering just as rabid as in any college or city in the states": ibid., 4.

85. Ibid., 67.

86. Forbes, quoted in Goss, "History of Physical Education in the Philippine Islands," 12.

87. Ibid.

88. Ibid., 34.

89. Aquino, "Philippine Games and Folk Dances," 4.

90. Ibid.

91. Ibid., 6–7; emphasis added.

92. See Regino R. Ylanan and Carmen Wilson Ylanan, *The History and Development of Physical Education and Sports in the Philippines* (Quezon City: University of the Philippines Press, 1974); Bocobo Olivar, *Aristocracy of the Mind.*

93. Ylanan and Ylanan, *The History and Development of Physical Education and Sports in the Philippines,* 9.

94. Ibid., 17, 29.

95. Ibid., 25.

96. Related views of the "nation," and "race" are found in early-twentieth-century documents such as José Vasconcelos, *La Raza Cósmica* (Baltimore: Johns Hopkins University Press, 1997 [1925]), and W.E.B. DuBois, *The Souls of Black Folk: Authoritative Text, Contexts, Criticism, ed. Henry Louis Gates Jr. and Terri Hume Oliver* (New York: W. W. Norton, 1999 [1903]). Vasconcelos, a minister of education in Mexico, was interested in developing iconographic pedagogies for largely non-literate populations. DuBois's works have inspired many angles of research. I am especially drawn to his use of folk songs to open each his volume's essays. He called them the "sorrow songs, . . . some echo of haunting melody from the only American music which welled up from black souls in the dark past."

97. See Benjamin Suchoff, ed., *The Essays of Bela Bartok* (New York: St. Martin's Press, 1976), 340–344.

98. Helen F. Samson, *Contemporary Filipino Composers: Biographical Interviews* (Quezon City: Manlapaz Publishing, 1976), 44.

99. Ibid., 46.

100. Ibid.

101. For an accessible and brief history of some of the nationalist composers of the 1930s, see Antonio C. Hila, "Musika: An Essay on Philippine Music," in Tiongson, *Tuklas Sining,* 102–145; Antonio C. Hila, "Defining the Nationalist Tradition in Philippine Music," in *Music in History, History in Music* (España, Manila: University of Santo Tomas Press, 2004), 57–70.

102. Karl Marx, *The Eighteenth Brumaire of Louis Bonaparte* (New York: International Publishers, 1963 [1852]), 15.

103. See Reynaldo Ileto, *Filipinos and Their Revolution: Event, Discourse, and Historiography* (Manila: Ateneo de Manila University Press, 1998).

## Chapter 2. "Take It from the People"

*Epigraph:* Richard Wright, *The Color Curtain: A Report on the Bandung Conference,* repr. ed. (Jackson: University Press of Mississippi, 1994 [1956]), 128.

1. José Lardizabal et al., eds., *Bayanihan* (Manila: Bayanihan Folk Arts Center, 1987), 82.

2. Ibid.

3. Ibid., 81.

4. Ibid., 139.

5. Ibid., 208.

6. For biographical information on Lucrecia R. Kasilag, see Vilma R. Santiago-Felipe, "A Gem of a Person, a Jewel of an Artist," in *The National Artists of the Philippines* (Manila: Cultural Center of the Philippines, Anvil Press, 1998), 209–217, and her entry in Herminia M. Ancheta and Michaela B. Gonzales, eds., *Filipino Women in Nation Building* (Quezon City: Phoenix Publishing, 1984), 160–162.

7. Renato Constantino and Letizia R. Constantino, *The Philippines: The Continuing Past* (Quezon City: Foundation for Nationalist Studies, 1978), chaps. 8–10; Mariel N. Francisco and Fe Maria C. Arriola, *The History of the Burgis: Which Is All about How the Elite Made It to the Top of the Pile* (Quezon City: GCF Books, 1987), 46–47, 90, and 98.

8. Samuel Gilmore, "Doing Culture Work: Negotiating Tradition and Authentication in Filipino Folk Dance," *Sociological Perspectives* 43, no. 4 (2000): 21–42.

9. See Vijay Prashad, *The Darker Nations: A People's History of the Third World* (New York: New Press, 2007), esp. his chapter on the Bandung Conference; C. R. Hensman, ed., *From Gandhi to Guevara: The Polemics of Revolt* (London: Allen Lane, 1969); Geoffrey Barraclough, *An Introduction to Contemporary History* (New York: C. A. Watts, 1964), esp. chap. 6.

10. Dance and performance are rich sites for telling stories that are not often or well told in the traditional historical record. Works that convincingly call attention to the narrative function that dance can engender are Susan Leigh Foster, *Choreography and Narrative: Ballet's Staging of Story and Desire* (Bloomington: Indiana University Press, 1996); Burt Ramsey, *Alien Bodies: Representations of Modernity, "Race," and Nation in Early Modern Dance* (London: Routledge, 1998); J. Ellen Gainor, ed., *Imperialism and Theatre: Essays on World Theatre, Drama, and Performance* (London: Routledge, 1995); Peggy Phelan and Jill Lane, eds., *The Ends of Performance* (New York: New York University Press, 1998); Della Pollock, ed., *Exceptional Spaces: Essays in Performance and History* (Chapel Hill: University of North Carolina Press, 1998).

11. David Wurfel, *Filipino Politics: Development and Decay,* 2nd ed. (Quezon City: Ateneo de Manila University Press, 1991); Thomas J. McCormick, *America's Half-Century: United States Foreign Policy in the Cold War and After,* 2nd ed. (Baltimore: Johns Hopkins University Press, 1995).

12. Joaquin, quoted in Francisco and Arriola, *The History of the Burgis,* 128.

13. See Walden Bello, *Dark Victory: The United States, Structural Adjustment and Global Poverty* (London: Pluto Press, 1994); Jerry Mander and Edward Goldsmith, eds., *The Case against the Global Economy and a Turn toward the Local* (San Francisco: Sierra Club Books, 1996).

14. Stephen R. Shalom, *The United States and the Philippines: A Study of Neocolonialism* (Quezon City: New Day Publishers, 1986). Valencia is quoted in Francisco and Arriola, *The History of the Burgis*, 137.

15. Quoted in Shalom, *The United States and the Philippines*, 65.

16. See Melvyn P. Leffler, "The American Conception of National Security and the Beginnings of the Cold War, 1945–1948," *American Historical Review* 89, no. 2 (1984): 346–381. "Since attacks against the United States could only emanate from Europe and Asia," Leffler writes, "the Joint Chiefs of Staff concluded as early as November 1943 that the United States must encircle the Western Hemisphere with a defensive ring of outlying bases. In the Pacific this ring had to include the Aleutians, the Philippines, Okinawa, and the former Japanese mandates. . . . The Philippines were the key to southeast Asia, Okinawa to the Yellow Sea, the Sea of Japan, and the industrial heartland of northeast Asia. From these bases on America's 'strategic frontier,' the United States could preserve its access to vital raw materials in Asia, deny these resources to a prospective enemy, help preserve peace and stability in troubled areas, safeguard critical sea lanes, and, if necessary, conduct an air offensive against the industrial infrastructure of any Asiatic power, including the Soviet Union": ibid., 350–351.

17. See also Benedict J. Kerkvliet, *The Huk Rebellion: A Study of Peasant Revolt in the Philippines* (Berkeley: University of California Press, 1977). See also Luis Taruc, *Born of the People* (New York: International Publishers, 1953).

18. The figures are in Shalom, *The United States and the Philippines*, 82. See Patricio N. Abinales, *Making Mindanao: Cotabato and Davao in the Formation of the Philippine Nation-State* (Quezon City: Ateneo de Manila University Press, 2000).

19. Gore Vidal makes this point in *The Decline and Fall of the American Empire* (Berkeley: Odonian Press, 1992).

20. Quoted in McCormick, *America's Half-Century*, 136.

21. Quoted in ibid., 71.

22. Michael Schaller, "Securing the Great Crescent: Occupied Japan and the Origins of Containment in Southeast Asia," *Journal of American History* 69, no. 2 (1982): 392–414.

23. Shalom, *The United States and the Philippines*, 71; emphasis added. See also Anna Kasten Nelson, "President Truman and the Evolution of the National Security Council," *Journal of American History* 72, no. 2 (1985): 360–378.

24. Malcolm McLaren, "Commodity and Delight," San Francisco Museum of Modern Art Design Lecture, Yerba Buena Center for the Arts, San Francisco, April 13, 1998.

25. U. S. Department of State, "A Report to the President by the National Security Council on the Position of the United States with Respect to the Philippines," in *Foreign Relations of the United States, 1950*, November 9, 1950 (Washington, D.C.: Government Printing Office, 1976), 1514–1520. See also Robert H. Johnson, "Exaggerating America's Stakes in Third World Conflicts," *International Security* 10, no. 3 (1985–1986): 32–68.

26. Ibid.

27. Washington's "mixture of internationalism-cum-anticommunism provided the means and the occasion to discipline those parts of the Third World deemed

unreasonable or unruly or unstable into accepting the American rules of the international game. Economic and military assistance in nation building were the rewards offered; covert coups and overt interventions were the penalties": McCormick, *America's Half-Century,* xiv. See also *Naval War College Review* 27 (1975): 51–108.

28. Jose Crisol, "Psychological Warfare in the Philippines," *Philippine Armed Forces Journal* (November 1952): 18–21.

29. Quoted in Shalom, *The United States and the Philippines,* 82.

30. "A Report to the President by the National Security Council on the Position of the United States with Respect to the Philippines," November 9, 1950, in U.S. Department of State, *Foreign Relations of the United States, 1950* (Washington, D.C.: U.S. Government Printing Office, 1976), 1514–1520 (hereafter, NSC 84/2).

31. Wurfel, *Filipino Politics,* 75.

32. NSC 84/2.

33. Howard Taubman, "Cold War on the Cultural Front," *New York Times Magazine,* April 13, 1958, 12–13, 107–108.

34. Ibid., 12. See "Nuclear Clock at Brussels World's Fair," *Science,* vol. 126, no. 3263, 1957, 66; *This Is America: Official United States Guide Book, Brussels World's Fair, 1958* (Washington, D.C.: Office of the U.S. Commissioner General, 1958); Robert H. Haddow, *Pavilions of Plenty: Exhibiting America Abroad in the 1950s* (Washington, D.C.: Smithsonian Institution Press, 1997).

35. Ibid., 12.

36. Christina Klein, *Cold War Orientalism: Asia in the Middlebrow Imagination, 1945–1961* (Berkeley: University of California Press, 2003), 13.

37. Taubman, "Cold War on the Cultural Front," 12.

38. Lardizabal, *Bayanihan,* 140.

39. Benitez quoted in ibid., 202.

40. Gertrudes R. Ang, "The Tinikling as a Literary Symbol of Philippine Culture," *Philippine Quarterly of Culture and Society* 6, no. 4 (1978): 210–217.

41. De Guzman, quoted in Lardizabal, *Bayanihan,* 78.

42. Terry, quoted in ibid., 78

43. Terry, quoted in Isabel A. Santos and Priscilla G. Cabanatan, *Helen, Bayanihan and the Filipino: A Trilogy for Culture* (Manila: Helena Z. Benitez Heritage Foundation, 1994), 42.

44. Dharam, quoted in ibid., 65.

45. Lardizabal, *Bayanihan,* 79.

46. Ibid., 80.

47. Ibid.

48. Ibid., 81; emphasis added.

49. Ibid., 204.

50. Ibid., 83; emphasis added. For biographical information on Urtula, see Guia Albano-Imperial, "The Heart of a Dancer," in *The National Artists of the Philippines,* 337–345, and her entry in Ancheta and Gonzales, *Filipino Women in Nation Building,* 287–288.

51 Lardizabal, *Bayanihan,* 117; emphasis added.

52. Ricardo D. Trimillos, "The Changing Context of Philippine Dance Performance," *Dance Research Annual* 15 (1985): 105–106.

53. Lardizabal, *Bayanihan*, 130; emphasis added.
54. Ibid., 130–131.
55. Ibid., 131.
56. Ibid., 132.
57. Santos and Cabanatan, *Helen, Bayanihan and the Filipino*, 25.
58. Ibid.
59. Benitez, quoted in ibid., 26.
60. Trimillos, "The Changing Context of Philippine Dance Performance," 107.
61. Lardizabal, *Bayanihan*, 25–26.
62. Ibid., 118.
63. Ibid., 207.
64. Ibid., 130.
65. Ibid., 153.
66. Ibid., 125; emphasis added. See also Marian Horosko, *Martha Graham: The Evolution of Her Dance Theory and Training* (Gainesville: University Press of Florida, 2002); Martha Graham, *Blood Memory* (New York: Doubleday, 1991).
67. Details of the following section are reported in Puri K. Katigbak, "The Philippine Folk Dance 'War,'" *Philippine Panorama*, n.d. For biographical information on Benitez, see her entry in Ancheta and Gonzales, *Filipino Women in Nation Building*, 148–151.
68. Santos and Cabanatan, *Helen, Bayanihan and the Filipino*, 16.
69. Katigbak, "The Philippine Folk Dance 'War,'" n.p.
70. Ibid.
71. Ibid.
72. Ang referred to such troupes as "effective goodwill missions" and "dancing diplomats": Ang, "The Tinikling as a Literary Symbol of Philippine Culture," 212.
73. Lardizabal, *Bayanihan*, 68.
74. Ibid., 87–88; emphasis added.
75. Belmonte interview transcript, New York Public Library Dance Collection (hereafter, NYPLDC), file no. 3-665; Nick Joaquin, "Introduction, Heritage: Educated Feet," in Leonor Orosa Goquingco, *The Dances of the Emerald Isles: A Great Philippine Heritage* (Quezon City: Ben-Lor Publishers, 1980), 9; Roces and Tiongson, quoted in Santos and Cabanatan, *Helen, Bayanihan, and the Filipino*, 86–87. See Néstor García Canclini, *Hybrid Cultures: Strategies for Entering and Leaving Modernity* (Minneapolis: University of Minnesota Press, 1995), 4.
76. Rosalia M. Santos interview transcript, NYPLDC, file no. 3-674. Santos is quoted in Reynaldo G. Alejandro, interview by the author, New York, April 6, 2007.
77. Reynaldo Alejandro, *Philippine Dance: Mainstream and Crosscurrents* (Quezon City: Vera-Reyes, 1978), 91; emphasis added.
78. Haunani Kay Trask was referring to the "hotel version" of the hula performed in contemporary Hawai'i: see Mindy Pennybacker, "Decolonizing the Mind," *The Nation*, October 4, 1999, 31–35. Trask and Alejandro would probably be offended by Leonor Goquingco's statement, "Attractively presented, booked well in advance, and properly promoted, here and abroad, these swirling, kaleidoscoping performances of sounds, movement and color could help sell Tours-of-the-Philippines in travel agencies all over the world": see Leonor O. Goquingco, "There's Gold in Ethnicity," *Philippine Panorama* (Manila), May 22, 1977, 37.

79. Cadar H. Usopay, "The Bayanihan: How Authentic Is Its Repertoire?" *Solidarity* 5, no. 12 (December 1970): 47, 51.

80. Stuart Hall, "Cultural Identity and Diaspora," in *Colonial Discourse and Post-Colonial Theory: A Reader,* ed. Patrick Williams and Laura Chrisman (New York: Columbia University Press, 1994), 392–403.

81. Ernest Renan, "What Is a Nation?" (1882), in *Nation and Narration,* ed. Homi K. Bhabha (New York: Routledge, 1990), 8–22.

82. Renato Constantino, "Westernizing Factors in the Philippines," in *Neocolonial Identity and Counter-Consciousness: Essays on Cultural Decolonization,* ed. István Mészáros (London: Merlin Press, 1978), 211–226.

83. Ibid., 225.

84. Regina Bendix, *In Search of Authenticity: The Formation of Folklore Studies* (Madison: University of Wisconsin Press, 1997).

85. See García Canclini, *Hybrid Cultures,* 114–115: "The ultimate purpose of authoritarian celebration seems to go beyond the interests of the hegemonic class that sponsors it. What such diverse groups attempt to do in spiritualizing the production and consumption of culture, in detaching it from the social and the economic, in eliminating all experimentation and reducing the symbolic life of society to the ritualization of a dogmatically affirmed national or cosmic order is, at bottom, to neutralize the instability of the social."

86. Arnold Molina Azurin, *Reinventing the Filipino Sense of Being and Becoming: Critical Analyses of the Orthodox Views in Anthropology, History, Folklore and Letters* (Quezon City: University of the Philippines Press, 1995), 139–140.

87. Marian Pastor Roces, "An Incomplete Listing of Contexts in Which Appeals to Tradition Are Made in the Philippines Presently," in *Contemporary Art in Asia: Traditions/Tensions,* ed. Apinan Poshyananda (New York: Asia Society Galleries, 1996), 85.

88. Ibid., 87.

89. Los del Río, "Macarena," *A Mi Me Gusta* (compact disc, RCA International, 1994).

## Chapter 3. Dancing into Oblivion

*Credits:* Portions of this chapter appeared as "Dancing into Oblivion: The Pilipino Cultural Night and the Narration of Contemporary Filipina/o America," *Kritika Kultura* 6 (November 2005): 42–85. The description of the *Kasaysayan ng Lahi* performance (1983) appears courtesy of Mel Ilomin.

*Epigraph:* Helen Toribio and Abe Ignacio, interview by the author, Santa Clara, Calif., May 8, 1998.

1. The chapter title is a play on the title of the popular CD compilation series *Living in Oblivion: The '80s Greatest Hits* (Capitol, 1993), which features artists such as Kajagoogoo, Re-Flex, and Haysi Fantayzee. Arleen de Vera, "Rizal Day Queen Contests, Filipino Nationalism, and Femininity," in *Asian American Youth: Culture, Identity and Ethnicity,* ed. Jennifer Lee and Min Zhou (New York: Routledge, 2004), 67–81.

2. Reynaldo Alejandro, *Philippine Dance: Mainstream and Crosscurrents* (Quezon City: Vera-Reyes, 1978), 99.

3. Karen Umemoto, "On Strike! San Francisco State College Strike, 1968–69: The Role of Asian American Students," *Amerasia Journal* 15, no. 1 (1989): 3–41; William Wei, *The Asian American Movement* (Philadelphia: Temple University Press, 1993).

4. Jonathan Y. Okamura, e-mail correspondence, December 4, 2007; Dean Alegado, e-mail correspondence, December 6, 2007.

5. Barcenas, quoted in Yen Le Espiritu, *Home Bound: Filipino American Lives across Cultures, Communities, and Countries* (Berkeley: University of California Press, 2003), 193.

6. Ibid., 194.

7. Calderon, quoted in ibid., 197.

8. Ibid., 195. I thank George Lipsitz for pointing out how competing reward systems pushed by student organizations, parents, and the larger campus life can cause college students to feel pulled to be simultaneously more and less Filipino: George Lipsitz, e-mail correspondence, September 17, 2007.

9. As James Lee put it, "Multiculturalism imagines anew how to reorganize the heretofore unequal representation of American life; its more difficult task lies in its capacity or even its willingness to distribute uneven resources in American communities. The fantasy of multiculturalism's practitioners depends on this parallel movement of more equitable representation and resources: to win hearts and minds in the space of our imagined communities, to gain the bread and land for those living in the landscapes of our real neighborhoods": James Kyung-Jin Lee, *Urban Triage: Race and the Fictions of Multiculturalism* (Minneapolis: University of Minnesota Press, 2004), xiv. See also Avery Gordon and Christopher Newfield, eds., *Mapping Multiculturalism* (Minneapolis: University of Minneapolis Press, 1996); David Theo Goldberg, ed., *Multiculturalism: A Critical Reader* (Boston: Blackwell Publishers, 1994).

10. See Joyce Appleby, Lynn Hunt, and Margaret Jacob, *Telling the Truth about History* (New York: W. W. Norton, 1994), 1.

11. Manning Marable, *Race, Reform and Rebellion: The Second Reconstruction in Black America, 1945–1982* (Jackson: University of Mississippi Press, 1984), 193–198.

12. Anna B. Madamba, *Underemployment among Asians in the United States: Asian Indian, Filipino, and Vietnamese Workers* (New York: Garland Publishing, 1998), 45, 124. See also Don Mar, "Asian Americans in the Labor Market: Public Policy Issues," *AAPI Nexus* 3, no. 2 (2005): 39–58.

13. See Joel Krieger, *Reagan, Thatcher and the Politics of Decline* (Oxford: Polity, 1996); Stuart Hall, *The Hard Road to Renewal: Thatcherism and the Crisis of the Left* (London: Verso, 1988); Michael Rogin, *Ronald Reagan, the Movie and Other Episodes in Political Demonology* (Berkeley: University of California Press, 1987).

14. Thomas Byrne Edsall and Mary D. Edsall are on target in their analysis of how the consensus over race, rights and taxes was organized in the late 1970s:

> The tax revolt, in tandem with sustained partisan conflict over racial policies—and over social/moral issues ranging from gun control to school prayer to abortion—catalyzed the mobilization of a conservative presidential majority. California became the testing ground for this new conservatism—California with its soaring property taxes, especially in the Los Ange-

> les area (which already faced a school busing order); with its Democratic legislature and its Democratic governor both unwilling to use revenue surpluses to provide tax relief; and with its easy access to the ballot for almost any group seeking a statewide referendum. . . . The tax revolt was a major turning point in American politics. It provided new muscle and new logic to the formation of a conservative coalition opposed to the liberal welfare state. The division of the electorate along lines of taxpayers versus tax recipients dovetailed with racial divisions: blacks (along with the growing Hispanic population) were disproportionately the beneficiaries of government-led efforts to redistribute rights and status, and the black middle and working classes were far more dependent on government programs and jobs than their white counterparts. Race melded into a conservative-driven agenda that sought to polarize the public against the private sector. The tax revolt provided conservatism with a powerful internal coherence, shaping an anti-government ethic, and firmly establishing new grounds for the disaffection of white working- and middle-class voters from their traditional Democratic roots. (Thomas Byrne Edsall and Mary D. Edsall, *Chain Reaction: The Impact of Race, Rights, and Taxes on American Politics* [New York: W. W. Norton, 1991], 130)

15. "In this case as in many others, guesses about the perceptions and expectations of whites supersede the constitutional rights and empirical realities of blacks and other minorities. It certainly stands in sharp contrast to the 1973 Rodriguez decision, which minimized the importance of education as a federally guaranteed right when the case involved Mexican American children. In Bakke, white expectations and perceptions of being hindered in their pursuit of the educational opportunities they desired were considered worthy of federal protection": George Lipsitz, *The Possessive Investment in Whiteness: How White People Profit from Identity Politics* (Philadelphia: Temple University Press, 1998), 37.

16. Peter Schrag, *Paradise Lost: California's Experience, America's Future* (Berkeley: University of California Press, 1998); Michael Omi and Howard Winant, *Racial Formation in the United States: From the 1960s to the 1990s*, 2nd ed. (New York: Routledge, 1994), 113–136; Michael Goldfield, *The Color of Politics: Race and the Mainsprings of American Politics* (New York: New Press, 1997), 296–317; Barbara Ehrenreich, *Fear of Falling: The Inner Life of the Middle Class* (New York: Pantheon, 1989). See *Regents of the University of California v. Bakke*, 438 U.S. 265 (1978). For an analysis of how the Bakke decision was debated within and around Asian American communities, see Data Y. Takagi, *The Retreat from Race: Asian-American Admissions and Racial Politics* (New Brunswick, N.J.: Rutgers University Press, 1992), 109–139. Derrick Bell's analysis of the Bakke decision is on target. "Working-class and upwardly striving middle-class whites perceive correctly that the share of educational opportunities available to their children are limited. That share, they believe, is threatened by programs designed to help minorities. Their belief is strengthened by the conviction that blacks are not supposed to get ahead of whites, and by the realization that poor whites are powerless to alter the plain advantages in educational opportunity available to the upper classes": Derrick A. Bell, *Race, Racism and American Law*, 2nd ed. (Boston: Little, Brown, 1980), 457.

17. See Michel Crozier, Samuel P. Huntington, and Joji Watanuji, *The Crisis of Democracy: Report on the Governability of Democracies to the Trilateral Commission* (New York: New York University Press, 1975), 6–7.

18. See Eleanor B. Leacock, *The Culture of Poverty: A Critique* (New York: Simon and Schuster, 1971).

19. Edsall and Edsall, *Chain Reaction,* 198–214.

20. See Bernard Weinraub, "Campaign Trail: A Beloved Mug Shot for the Bush Forces," *New York Times,* October 3, 1988, A22: "Governor Dukakis has been portrayed by Mr. Bush as soft on crime. (Mr. Ailes, who has been known to go for the jugular, has said, 'The only question is whether we depict Willie Horton with a knife in his hand or without it.')." On the "Mississippification" of California, see Lipsitz, *The Possessive Investment in Whiteness,* 211–233. Reagan's reference to a "welfare queen" was reported in "'Welfare Queen' Becomes Issue in Reagan Campaign," *New York Times,* February 15, 1976, 51.

21. Marable, *Race, Reform and Rebellion,* 198.

22. Ibid., 199–200. See also idem, *Black Leadership* (New York: Columbia University Press, 1998).

23. Edsel Matthews, "About Koncepts: The Meaning of Multi-Cultural Arts," *Konceptualizations* (October–December 1994); "The San Francisco Asian American Arts Community Needs Assessment Project," report, San Francisco Art Commission, May 8, 1995.

24. Devorah Majors, "Cultural Equity Paper," Nathan Cummings Foundations, May 26, 1994. See also discussions of the state of art making from visual and performance disciplines in Carlos Villa, Worlds in Collision: Dialogues on Multicultural Art Issues (San Francisco: International Scholars, 1994). Villa conceived of a series of dialogues with leading critics, artists, and scholars over the multicultural education in previously elite art institutions, the possibility of art making under shrinking national budgets, and more. On Filipino American immigration in the post-1965 period, see John M. Liu, Paul M. Ong, and Carolyn Rosenstein, "Dual Chain Migration: Post-1965 Filipino Immigration to the United States," *International Migration Review* 25, no. 3 (Fall 1991): 487–514; John M. Liu, "The Contours of Asian Professional, Technical and Kindred Work Immigration," *Sociological Perspectives* 35, no. 4 (Winter 1992): 673–705.

25. See Evelyn Hu-DeHart, "The History, Development, and Future of Ethnic Studies," *Phi Delta Kappan* 75, no. 1 (September 1993): 50–55; Lane R. Hirabayashi and Marilyn C. Alquizola, "Asian American Studies: Reevaluating for the 1990s," in *The State of Asian America: Activism and Resistance in the 1990s,* ed. Karin Aguilar–San Juan (Boston: South End Press, 1994), 351–364; Sucheng Chan, *In Defense of Asian American Studies: The Politics of Teaching and Program Building* (Urbana: University of Illinois Press, 2005).

26. See Alejandro Portes and Ruben G. Rumbaut, *Legacies: The Story of the Immigrant Second Generation* (Berkeley: University of California Press, 2001); Espiritu, *Home Bound.* James Lee wrote, "The politics of representation took center stage over the politics of resource": Lee, Urban Triage, xxviii. Scholars tuned in to the intersection of youth cultures, national identities, and globalization are turning to California as a "fascinating and politically charged regional site in which young people are grappling with the meanings of globalization in response to immigration

from Latin America and Asia, border cultures and linguistic creolization, demographic shifts, and punitive state legislation targeting immigrants and youth": quoted in Sunaina Maira and Elisabeth Soep, eds., *Youthscapes: The Popular, the National, the Global* (Philadelphia: University of Pennsylvania Press, 2004), xxix.

27. Lee, *Urban Triage,* xii.

28. All of the material quoted from the 1983 production is transcribed by the author from the original videocassette recording *Kasaysayan ng Lahi,* November 12, 1983, Samahang Pilipino Archive, University Archives Special Collection, University of California, Los Angeles (hereafter, SPA), record series (RS) 701. The UCLA show had no direct relation to Imelda Marcos's extravaganza of the same name, which coincided with the Miss Universe Pageant held in Manila in 1974. Those interested in Marcos's marriage of cultural and political work should consult Pearlie Baluyut, "Institutions and Icons of Patronage: Arts and Culture in the Philippines during the Marcos Years, 1965–1986," Ph.D. diss., University of California, Los Angeles, 2004.

29. Of the approximately one thousand attendees, the majority of respondents to an evaluation questionnaire heard about the event by word of mouth. The majority of respondents were also students at UCLA or on other campuses, had prior interest in such performances, and were between eighteen and twenty-one: "Evaluation Questionnaire, Pilipino Cultural Night, 12 November 1983," SPA, RS 701, Cultural Folder 1982–1983.

30. "Beginnings are first and important but not always evident, that beginning is basically an activity which ultimately implies return and repetition rather than simple linear accomplishment, that beginning and beginning-again are historical whereas origins are divine, that a beginning not only creates but is its own method because it has intention": Edward W. Said, *Beginnings: Intention and Method* (New York: Basic Books, 1975), xiii.

31. Rosaura Sanchez's work on "macro-textual" commentary analysis avoids interpretive strategies in which specific cultural studies remain locked formalistically onto the objects themselves: see Rosaura Sanchez, *Telling Identities: The Californio Testimonios* (Minneapolis: University of Minnesota Press, 1995). I appreciate the approach to cultural research undertaken by scholars such as José Limon in *Dancing with the Devil: Society and Cultural Poetics in Mexican-American South Texas* (Madison: University of Wisconsin Press, 1994).

32. Wayne Harada, "1951–2006, Entertainer Gary Bautista, 54," *Honolulu Advertiser,* January 31, 2006.

33. See Madge Bello and Vince Reyes, "Filipino Americans and the Marcos Overthrow: The Transformation of Political Consciousness," *Amerasia Journal* 13, no. 1 (1986–1987): 73–83.

34. On "imperso-nation," see Sumita S. Chakravarty, *National Identity in Indian Popular Cinema, 1947–1987* (Austin: University of Texas Press, 1993). Countering the notion that impersonators seek the spotlight, Jeff Chang points out how such performers seek the comfort and anonymity of shadows. "Critics love auteurs, not interpreters. You and the karaoke crowd, as Kraftwerk once coldly called them, are velvet hotel-showroom dummies. Even after the show is done, the shine that mimicry confers on you flows upward. The faceless crowds in the mountain motor lodge or the beachside bar don't want you, they want a faithful facsimile of the original": Jeff Chang, "Karaoke Careers," *San Francisco Bay Guardian,* October 4, 2000, 44. Homi

Bhabha's formulation may be playfully applied as well. "Colonial mimicry is the desire for a reformed, recognizable Other, as a subject of a difference that is almost the same, but not quite. Which is to say, that the discourse of mimicry is constructed around an ambivalence; in order to be effective, mimicry must continually produce its slippage, its excess, its difference": Homi K. Bhabha, *The Location of Culture* (London: Routledge, 1994), 86.

35. A portmanteau of the names Jesus, Mary, and Joseph—often used to express exasperation.

36. Dom and Sachiko Magwili, interview by the author, audio recording, March 2, 1998, Los Angeles.

37. Bienvenido N. Santos, "Immigration Blues," in *The Scent of Apples: A Collection of Stories* (Seattle: University of Washington Press, 1992 [1955]), 3–20.

38. Angela Y. Davis, *Blues Legacies and Black Feminism: Gertrude "Ma" Rainey, Bessie Smith, and Billie Holiday* (New York: Pantheon Books, 1998), 33.

39. See Barbara S. Gaerlan, "In the Court of the Sultan: Orientalism, Nationalism and Modernity in Philippine and Filipino American Dance," *Journal of Asian American Studies* 2, no. 3 (October 1999): 251–287. One of my instructors during my undergraduate days was fond of hyping the risk of traveling to that region: "Mindanao—it's like Dodge City down there!"

40. Dance scholarship helps us make sense out of the narrative nature of dance, especially from artists working in communities that work through the legacies of colonization. The most useful works in this field of study combine a healthy postmodern skepticism toward anthropological authority with a refusal to get bogged down in the tedium of aesthetic formalism. These works take seriously the notion that dance can assume the burden of telling complicated stories and experimenting with challenging identities in hostile times. In addition to Susan Leigh Foster, *Corporealities* (London: Routledge, 1995); idem, *Choreography and Narrative: Ballet's Staging of Story and Desire* (Bloomington: Indiana University Press, 1996); Sally Ann Ness, *Body, Movement, and Culture: Kinesthetic and Visual Communication in a Philippine Community* (Philadelphia: University of Pennsylvania Press, 1989); idem, "Dancing in the Field: Notes from Memory," in *Corporealities: Dancing, Knowledge, Culture, and Power*, ed. Susan Leigh Foster (New York: Routledge, 1996), 133–158; idem, *Where Asia Smiles: An Ethnography of Philippine Tourism* (Philadelphia: University of Pennsylvania Press, 2002); Marta Savigliano, *Tango and the Political Economy of Passion* (Boulder, Colo.: Westview Press, 1995); Barbara Browning, *Samba: Resistance in Motion* (Bloomington: Indiana University Press, 1995), see Celeste F. Delgado and José E. Muñoz, eds., *Everynight Life: Culture and Dance in Latin/o America* (Durham, N.C.: Duke University Press, 1997).

41. See Diana Taylor and Juan Villegas, eds., *Negotiating Performance: Gender, Sexuality, and Theatricality in Latin/o America* (Durham, N.C.: Duke University Press, 1994).

42. *Kasaysayan ng Lahi*, SPA.

43. See Reynaldo C. Ileto, *Pasyon and Revolution: Popular Movements in the Philippines, 1840–1910* (Quezon City: Ateneo de Manila University Press, 1979).

44. This distinction between the epic and the lyrical is drawn from Max Harris, *Dialogical Theatre: Dramatizations of Mexico and the Questions of the Other* (New York: St. Martin's Press, 1993).

45. Featured in Pennee Bender, Joshua Brown, and Andrea Ades Vasquz, dirs., *Savage Acts: Wars, Fairs and Empire* (American Social History Productions, 1995); Peter Davis, dir., *This Bloody Blundering Business* (Cinema Guild, Tricontinental Film, 1975); Paul Jacobs, Saul Landau, and Eve Pell, eds., *To Serve the Devil* (New York: Vintage Books, 1971).

46. Catherine Porter, "Review of America Is in the Heart," *Pacific Affairs* 19, no. 3 (1946): 331–332; Paul F. Cressey, "Review of America Is in the Heart," *Far Eastern Quarterly* 6, no. 2 (1947): 206.

47. E. San Juan Jr., *Carlos Bulosan and the Imagination of the Class Struggle* (Quezon City: University of the Philippines Press, 1972).

48. Carlos Bulosan, *America Is in the Heart: A Personal History* (Seattle: University of Washington Press, 1973); Oscar Peñaranda, Serafin Syquia, and Sam Tagatac, "Introduction to Filipino American Literature," in *Aiiieeeee!!! An Anthology of Asian-American Writers,* ed. Frank Chin et al. (Washington, D.C.: Howard University Press, 1974), 36–54. E. San Juan Jr. noted that in the 1970s, Bulosan's resurrected text became important to young activists, students, and artists in California: E. San Juan Jr., interview by the author, audio recording, Los Angeles, 1997. See also Jovina Navarro, comp., *Lahing Pilipino: A Pilipino American Anthology* (Davis, Calif.: Mga Kapatid, 1977); idem, *Diwang Pilipino: Pilipino Consciousness* (Davis, Calif.: Asian American Studies, UCLA, 1974); Emily Cachapero et al., eds., *Liwanag: Literary and Graphic Expressions by Filipinos in America* (San Francisco: Liwanag Publications, 1975). Michael Denning discusses Bulosan as a Popular Front–era writer testifying through a "migrant narrative" in *The Cultural Front: The Laboring of American Culture in the Twentieth-Century* (London: Verso, 1996), 269–282.

49. Bulosan wrote:

> When you dance for the first time, the world is like a cradle upon the biggest ocean in the universe. There are no other sounds except the beating of your hearts, and when the wild blaring of the trumpet and the savage boom-boom of the drum bring you back to reality, you get scared and begin to misstep and falter. Your hands weaken their hold on the rapturous being near you, and you want to apologize to her but the words are stuck in your throat. Suddenly you become conscious of the staring people around you, appraising you with obscene eyes and lascivious tongues, and slowly you lead the beauteous creature in your arms back to her seat. Then the orchestra becomes a cymbal of crashing noises, meaningless and riotous, and you return to your corner, trembling with cold and sudden fear. You are pushed back to reality, to the world of puny men and women who are circumscribed by fear. Then you, too, are one among them and one of them, prisoned by their fears and the ugliness of their lives. You go to the window and lean far out, savoring the bitter taste on your tongue. (Bulosan, *America Is in the Heart,* 77–78)

50. See Caridad Concepcion Vallangca, *The Second Wave: Pinay and Pinoy, 1945–1960* (San Francisco: Strawberry Hill Press, 1987); Antonio Pido, *The Pilipinos in America: Macro/Micro Dimensions of Immigration and Integration* (New York: Center for Migration Studies, 1986).

51. I thank Alex Fabros Jr. for sharing his knowledge of military history. See Bureau of Naval Personnel, U.S. Navy, "Filipinos in the United States Navy," October

1976, "Filipinos" file, Vertical File Collection, Navy Department Library, Washington, D.C. For accounts of Filipinos in the U.S. Navy, see Jesse Quinsaat et al., eds., *Letters in Exile: An Introductory Reader on the History of Pilipinos in America* (Los Angeles: Asian American Studies Center, UCLA, 1976), 96–111; and Yen Le Espiritu, *Filipino American Lives* (Philadelphia: Temple University Press, 1995), 105–115.

52. See Catherine Choy, *Empire of Care: Nursing and Migration in Filipino American History* (Durham, N.C.: Duke University Press, 2003); E. San Juan Jr., "Interrogating Transmigrancy, Remapping Diaspora: The Globalization of Laboring Filipinos/as," *Discourse* 23, no. 3 (Fall 2001): 52–74; John Mei Liu, "The Contours of Asian Professional, Technical and Kindred Work Immigration," *Sociological Perspectives* 35, no. 4 (Winter 1992): 673–705; John M. Liu, Paul M. Ong, and Carolyn Rosenstein, "Dual Chain Migration: Post-1965 Filipino Immigration to the United States," *International Migration Review* 25, no. 3 (Fall 1991): 487–514. Although focused largely on Southern California, Paul Ong, Edna Bonacich, and Lucie Cheng, eds., *The New Asian Immigration in Los Angeles and Global Restructuring* (Philadelphia: Temple University Press, 1994), updates the theoretical work and historical documentation of Lucie Cheng and Edna Bonacich, *Labor Immigration under Capitalism: Asian Immigrant Workers in the United States before World War II* (Berkeley: University of California Press, 1984). Both works track how Filipinos have been part of the global flow of natural and human resources over the twentieth century.

53. A Filipina opposes affirmative action and affirms the myth of individuated achievement in Yolanda Cruz, "A Twofer's Lament," *New Republic*, vol. 211, no. 16, October 17, 1994, 29. For an example of Filipino Americans celebrating bourgeois liberalism, see Veltisezar Bautista, *The Filipino Americans: From 1763 to the Present—Their History, Culture, and Traditions* (Naperville, Ill.: Bookhaus Publishers, 1998).

54. Interview with Augusto F. Espiritu, Oral History Project, Samahang Pilipino Archive class, October 27, 1997.

55. Francisco and Arriola's description of the burgis (victims as much as they are perpetuators of a "colonial mentality") points to how elites simultaneously look to the future and to the past. "Burgis is . . . having a terribly outdated colonial mentality in the guise of internationalism. It is being able to quote Shakespeare but not caring to know who Amado Hernandez is. It is sitting through a local Broadway play without cringing at the sight and sound of Filipinos aping British and American accents, and justifying it by saying that Filipinos can't write plays worth staging. It is relying on Time and Newsweek's version of world events and Hollywood's definition of the meaning of life. It is boasting that the Filipino is one of the most talented and creative in the world, but believing that the masses are lazy, or cursed by a genetically low IQ": Francisco and Arriola, *The History of the Burgis*, 11.

## Chapter 4. Repetitive Motion

*Credits:* Portions of this chapter appeared as "The Day the Dancers Stayed: On Pilipino Cultural Nights," in *Filipino Americans: Transformation and Identity*, edited by Maria P. P. Root (Thousand Oaks, Calif.: Sage Publications, 1997), pp. 163–182. Reprinted by permission of Sage Publications, Inc.

*Epigraph:* Lan Cao and Himilce Novas, *Everything You Need to Know about Asian-American History* (New York: Plume, 1996), 177. The authors fail to mention that the presence of Asian American studies classes at the University of California, Irvine, has been due largely to the efforts and sacrifice of hundreds of students, faculty, staff, parents, and community members. They, like most folks struggling to make ethnic studies a reality on campuses throughout the country, know that this is easier said than done.

1. Eric Hobsbawm and Terence Ranger, eds., *The Invention of Tradition* (Cambridge: Cambridge University Press, 1983).

2. Benedict Anderson, *Imagined Communities: Reflections on the Origin and Spread of Nationalism* (London: Verso, 1983), 6.

3. On the relationship of cultural patrimony to nationalism in Latin America, see Néstor García Canclini, *Hybrid Cultures: Strategies for Entering and Leaving Modernity* (Minneapolis: University of Minnesota Press, 1995), 58–65, 132–144.

4. My primary sources of analysis include oral histories and interviews with performers and their consultants that I conducted, as well as those collected by others and deposited at several campuses; attendance at shows from 1989 to 1999; and participant observation research. I played one of the lead acting roles in the San Francisco State University Pilipino American Collegiate Endeavor (PACE) production *Muling Pagsilang ng Ating Kasaysayan* (Rebirth of Our History) in 1992. For PACE's *Cultural Evidence* in 1993, I wrote and composed music for a sketch while serving as an elected student leader for the group. For UCI Kababayan's *Street of Dreams* in 1996, I composed, performed, and arranged music with a jazz trio while participating in several other aspects related to the production (music rehearsals, actor auditions, and post-production dialogues).

5. David Reimers, *Still the Golden the Door: The Third World Comes to America*, 2nd ed. (New York: Columbia University Press, 1992), 116.

6. On the Immigration and Nationality Act of 1965, see ibid., chap. 3.

7. Corporate Student System Report CSS170D and CPEC Report DEG704, Office of the President, University of California, Berkeley.

8. R. J. Payomo, interview by the author, audio recording, Santa Clara, Calif., March 22, 1998; Anna Alves, interview by the author, July 26, 1997, Los Angeles.

9. Quinsaat et al., *Letters in Exile,* 158. Reaching even further back, Quinsaat's reader lists a broad range of student and community-based organizations working in the early part of the twentieth century, editing weekly periodicals, holding picnics, sparring with debating teams, and engaging in other activities. See Steve Louie and Glenn K. Omatsu, eds., *Asian Americans: The Movement and the Moment* (Los Angeles: Asian American Studies Center, UCLA, 2001); William Wei, *The Asian American Movement* (Philadelphia: Temple University Press, 1993); Karen Umemoto, "'On Strike!' San Francisco State College Strike, 1968–1969: The Role of Asian American Students," *Amerasia Journal* 15, no. 1 (1989): 3–41; Fred Ho et al., eds., *Legacy to Liberation: Politics and Culture of Revolutionary Asian Pacific America* (San Francisco: AK Press, 2000).

10. Helen Toribio and Abe Ignacio, interview by the author, Santa Clara, Calif., May 8, 1998; Dom and Sachiko Magwili, interview by the author, audio recording, March 2, 1998, Los Angeles.

11. See "Associated Students of the University of California, Senate Meeting Agenda," February 22, 2006, Berkeley, Calif.

12. Jacinto, quoted in Theodore S. Gonzalves, ed., *Stage Presence: Conversations with Filipino American Performing Artists* (San Francisco: Meritage Press, 2007), 44.

13. Jaime Jacinto and Ave Jacinto, oral-history transcript, SPA.

14. Jacinto's comments were delivered at the Asian Pacific American Roundtable, California State University, Los Angeles, April 12, 1996. Jacinto drew on the distinction between participational and presentational modes adumbrated by Ricardo Trimillos.

15. Richard Schechner, *Performance Studies: An Introduction* (London: Routledge, 2002), 57.

16. Ibid., 45; emphasis added.

17. Victor Turner, *The Ritual Process: Structure and Anti-structure* (Chicago: Aldine Publishing, 1969), 95.

18. Schechner, *Performance Studies,* 73.

19. Dom Magwili, interview by the author, Los Angeles, March 2, 1998. García Canclini wrote: "The literature on ritualism is concerned chiefly with rites or entry or of passage: who, and with what requirements, may enter a house or a church; what steps must be fulfilled in order to pass from one civil status to another or to assume an office or an honor": García Canclini, *Hybrid Cultures,* 24.

20. "An Act Prescribing the Code and the National Flag, Anthem, Motto, Coat-of-Arms and Other Heraldic Items and Devices of the Philippines," Philippine Republic Act 8491 (hereafter, RA8491), February 12, 1998.

21. Ibid.

22. See Antonio C. Hila, "Musika: An Essay on Philippine Music," in *Tuklas Sining: Essays on Philippine Arts,* ed. Nicanor G. Tiongson (Manila: Sentrong Pangkultura ng Pilipinas, 1991), 120–121; Ambeth Ocampo, "Displaying the Flag and Playing the Anthem," *Philippine Daily Inquirer,* May 30, 2007.

23. "When the Philippine flag is flown with another flag, the flags, if both are national flags, must be flown on separate staffs of the same height and shall be of equal size. The Philippine flag shall be hoisted first and lowered last" RA8491, sec. 12. Sec. 34 of the same act prohibits the use of the flag "in discotheques, cockpits, night and day clubs, casinos, gambling joints and places of vice or where frivolity prevails."

24. Sharon Delmendo, *Star-Entangled Banner: One Hundred Years of America in the Philippines* (New Brunswick, N.J.: Rutgers University Press, 2004).

25. Richard Alba, John Logan, Amy Lutz, and Brian Stults, "Only English by the Third Generation? Loss and Preservation of the Mother Tongue among the Grandchildren of Contemporary Immigrants," *Demography* 39, no. 3 (2002): 467–484; Hyon B. Shin and Rosalind Bruno, "Language Use and English-Speaking Ability: 2000," Census 2000 Brief, 2003, C2KBR-29, 2, 4.

26. See Raymond Tatalovich, *Nativism Reborn? The Official English Language Movement and the American States* (Lexington: University Press of Kentucky, 1995); Harvey A. Daniels, ed., *Not Only English: Affirming Multilingual Heritage* (Urbana, Ill.: National Council of Teachers of English, 1990); Kathryn A. Woolard and Bambi B. Schieffelin, "Language Ideology," *Annual Review of Anthropology* 23 (1994): 55–82.

27. Augusto F. Espiritu, *Five Faces of Exile: The Nation and Filipino American Intellectuals* (Stanford, Calif.: Stanford University Press, 2005), 109; Leo Reisberg, "As Asian Enrollments Diversify, So Too Do Students' Demands," *Chronicle of Higher Education,* vol. 45, no. 37, 1999, A42; Noe Sauro, "Passion for the Native Tongue," *California Aggie,* November 26, 2003.

28. Samuel Gilmore, "Doing Culture Work: Negotiating Tradition and Authentication in Filipino Folk Dance," *Sociological Perspectives* 43, no.4 (2000), 9.

29. García Canclini discusses how a nationalist patrimony is inculcated in public displays—through parades, murals, museums, and processions:

> The dramatization of the patrimony is the effort to simulate that there is an origin, a founding substance, in relation with which we should act today. This is the basis of authoritarian cultural policies. The world is a stage, but what must be performed is already prescribed. The practices and objects of value are found and catalogued in a fixed repertory. To be cultured implies knowing that repertory of symbolic goods and intervening correctly in the rituals that reproduce it. For that reason the notions of collection and ritual are key to deconstructing the links between culture and power. . . . The historical patrimony that is celebrated consists of founding events, the heroes who played the main roles in them, and the fetishized objects that evoke them. The legitimate rites are those that stage the desire for repetition and perpetuation of order. (García Canclini, *Hybrid Cultures,* 110)

30. Max Harris, *Dialogical Theatre: Dramatizations of the Conquest of Mexico and the Question of the Other* (New York: St. Martin's Press, 1993), 6.

31. Israel Zangwill, *The Melting Pot: Drama in Four Acts* (New York: Macmillan, 1909).

32. Michael Omi and Howard Winant, *Racial Formation in the United States: From the 1960s to the 1990s,* 2nd ed. (New York: Routledge, 1994), 14–23. See also Barbara B. Lal, *The Romance of Culture in an Urban Civilization: Robert E. Park on Race and Ethnic Relations* (London: Routledge, 1990); Rolf Linder, *The Reportage of Urban Culture: Robert Park and the Chicago School* (New York: Cambridge University Press, 1996); Stanford M. Lyman, *Militarism, Imperialism, and Racial Accommodation: An Analysis and Interpretation of the Early Writings of Robert E. Park* (Fayetteville: University of Arkansas Press, 1992). See also Robert Ezra Park, *The Collected Papers of Robert Ezra Park,* ed. Everett Cherrington et al. (Glencoe, Md.: Free Press, 1950–1955).

33. See Shirley Geok-lin Lim and Amy Ling, eds., *Reading the Literatures of Asian America* (Philadelphia: Temple University Press, 1992), 51. On the significance of the quest motif, see Edward Said, *Culture and Imperialism* (New York: Alfred A. Knopf, 1993), 210–211. Said writes:

> In all the great explorers' narratives of the late Renaissance (Daniel Defert has aptly called them the collection of the world—la collecte du monde) and those of the nineteenth-century explorers and ethnographers, not to mention Conrad's voyage up the Congo, there is the topos of the voyage south as Mary Louise Pratt has called it, referring to Gide and Camus, in

> which the motif of control and authority has "sounded uninterruptedly." For the native who begins to see and hear that persisting note, it sounds "the note of crisis, of banishment, banishment from the heart, banishment from home." This is how Stephen Dedalus memorably states it in the Library episode Ulysses, the decolonizing native writer—such as Joyce, the Irish writer colonized by the British—re-experiences the quest-voyage motif from which he had been banished by means of the same trope carried over from the imperial into the new culture and adopted, reused, relived.

34. "Where would we be . . . without a touch of essentialism?" For Stuart Hall, paying attention to the overly determined labor of cultural production means having to admit that there are no pure forms:

> Always these forms are the product of partial synchronization, of engagement across cultural boundaries, of the confluence of more than one cultural tradition, of the negotiations of dominant and subordinate positions, of the subterranean strategies of recoding and transcoding, of critical signification, of signifying. Always these forms are impure, to some degree hybridized from a vernacular base. Thus, they must always be heard, not simply as the recovery of a lost dialogue bearing clues for the production of new musics (because there is never any going back to the old in a simple way), but as what they are—adaptations, molded to the mixed, contradictory, hybrid spaces of popular culture. (Stuart Hall, "What Is This 'Black' in Black Popular Culture?" in *Black Popular Culture: A Project,* ed. Michelle Wallace [Seattle: Bay Press, 1992], 28–29)

Hall redirects my attention concerning how we have had to rely on conceptions of culture that are inadequate for grappling with performance genres such as the PCN. On the postmodern destruction of anthropological authority and the positing of the "cultural" as an autonomous sphere, see Ruth Behar and Deborah A. Gordon, *Women Writing Culture* (Berkeley: University of California Press, 1995); James Clifford, *The Predicament of Culture: Twentieth-Century Ethnography, Literature, and Art* (Cambridge, Mass.: Harvard University Press, 1988); George E. Marcus and Michael M. J. Fischer, *Anthropology as Cultural Critique: An Experimental Moment in the Human Sciences,* 2nd ed. (Chicago: University of Chicago Press, 1999).

35. See Milton Gordon, *Assimilation in American Life: The Role of Race, Religion, and National Origins* (New York: Oxford University Press, 1971); idem, *Human Nature, Class, and Ethnicity* (New York: Oxford University Press, 1978). For critiques and revisions, see Stephen Steinberg, *Turning Back: The Retreat from Racial Justice in American Thought and Policy* (Boston: Beacon Press, 1995).

36. See Catherine Ceniza Choy, "Towards Trans-Pacific Social Justice: Women and Protest in Filipino American History," *Journal of Asian American Studies* 8, no. 3 (2005): 293–307. The San Francisco Bay Area group Philippine Ethnic Art and Culture Exchange (PEACE) solicited the participation of community members for a multimedia installation titled "Voices from the Diaspora Filipina 1898–1998." On the Gabriela Network USA, see http://www.gabnet.org.

37. See Theodore S. Gonzalves, "When the Walls Speak a Nation: Contemporary Murals and the Narration of Filipino America," *Journal of Asian American Studies* 1,

no. 1 (February 1998): 31–63. See Victor Merina, "Visiting the Homeland," in *Asian Americans: Oral Histories of First to Fourth Generation Americans from China, the Philippines, Japan, India, the Pacific Islands, Vietnam and Cambodia,* ed. Joann Lee (New York: New Press, 1991), 45–49.

38. Marivi Soliven Blanco, "Poking Fun at Pinoys," in *Suddenly Stateside: Funny Essays on Pinoy Life in America* (Quezon City: Milflores Press, 2002). See also Katharine W. Jones, "'I've Called 'em Tom-ah-toes All My Life and I'm Not Going to Change!': Maintaining Linguistic Control over English Identity in the U.S.," *Social Forces* 79, no. 3 (2001): 1061–1094; Angela C. Pao, "False Accents: Embodied Dialects and the Characterization of Ethnicity and Nationality," *Theatre Topics* 14, no. 1 (2004): 353–372.

39. Barbara S. Gaerlan, "In the Court of the Sultan: Orientalism, Nationalism and Modernity in Philippine and Filipino American Dance," *Journal of Asian American Studies* 2, no. 3 (October 1999): 275.

40. Interview with Ron Cabarloc, Oral History Project, Samahang Pilipino Archive class, September 23, 1995.

41. Ibid.

42. Ibid.

43. Ted Benito and Meg Malpaya Thornton, "Pilipino Cultural Night," *East Wind,* 1989, 52.

44. Pamela Burdman, "UC Berkeley Minority Admissions Dropping," *San Francisco Chronicle,* June 26, 1997.

45. San Francisco State University Bulletin, 1991–1994. I thank Daniel Phil Gonzales of San Francisco State University's Asian American Studies Department, Lori Chan of the San Francisco State University Registrar's Office, and Meredith Eliassen of the San Francisco State University J. Paul Leonard Special Collections Department for assistance with the data.

46. See Theodore S. Gonzalves, "The Day the Dancers Stayed: On Pilipino Cultural Nights," in *Filipino Americans: Transformation and Identity,* ed. Maria P. P. Root (Thousand Oaks, Calif.: Sage, 1997), 163–182; R. Bong Vergara, "Reevaluating the Pilipino Cultural Night," unpublished paper, SPA.

47. Program, *Cultural Evidence,* San Francisco State University, Pilipino American Collegiate Endeavor, 1993. Some of the evening's works were also presented at the National Asian American and Telecommunication Association's International Film Showcase and at the Asian American Jazz Festival.

48. See Rachel Devitt, "Lost in Translation: Filipino Diaspora(s), Postcolonial Hip Hop, and the Problems of Keeping It Real for the 'Contentless' Black Eyed Peas," *Asian Music* (Winter–Spring 2008): 108–134; Oliver S. Wang, "Spinning Identities: A Social History of Filipino American DJs in the San Francisco Bay Area, 1975–1995," Ph.D. diss., University of California, Berkeley, 2004; Lakandiwa M. de Leon, "Filipinotown and the DJ Scene: Cultural Expression and Identity Affirmation in Filipino American Youth in Los Angeles," in *Asian American Youth: Culture, Identity and Ethnicity,* ed. Jennifer Lee and Min Zhou (New York: Routledge, 2004), 191–206.

49. Gertrudes R. Ang, "The Tinikling as a Literary Symbol of Philippine Culture," *Philippine Quarterly of Culture and Society* 6, no. 4 (1978), 213–214.

50. Ibid., 214.

51. Gaerlan, "In the Court of the Sultan," 260.

## Chapter 5. Making a Mockery of Everything We Hold True and Dear

*Credits:* The description of the *PCN Salute* performance appears courtesy of Allan Manalo. The poem "For My Stylin' Brothers" (1975) is quoted courtesy of Vince Reyes.

*Epigraph:* Dario Fo, *The Tricks of the Trade* (New York: Routledge, 1991), 109.

1. The three citations are quoted from Ron Jenkins, *Dario Fo and Franca Rame: Artful Laughter* (New York: Aperture, 2001), 192, 194.

2. Antonio Scuderi, "Unmasking the Holy Jester Dario Fo," *Theatre Journal* 55 (2003): 276.

3. Quoted in Jenkins, *Dario Fo and Franca Rame,* 50.

4. See Josephine Lee, *Performing Asian America: Race and Ethnicity on the Contemporary Stage* (Philadelphia: Temple University Press, 1997); Karen Shimakawa, *National Abjection: The Asian American Body on Stage* (Durham, N.C.: Duke University Press, 2002); Dorinne Kondo, *About Face: Performing Race in Fashion and Theater* (New York: Routledge, 1997); James Moy, *Marginal Sights: Staging the Chinese in America* (Iowa City: University of Iowa Press, 1993); Robert G. Lee, *Orientals: Asian Americans in Popular Culture* (Philadelphia: Temple University Press, 1999); Krystyn Moon, *Yellowface: Creating the Chinese in American Popular Music and Performance, 1850s–1920s* (New Brunswick, N.J.: Rutgers University Press, 2005); Adelaida Reyes, *Songs of the Caged, Songs of the Free: Music and the Vietnamese Refugee Experience* (Philadelphia: Temple University Press, 1999); Deborah Wong, *Speak It Louder: Asian Americans Making Music* (New York: Routledge, 2004); Sunaina Maira, *Desis in the House: Indian American Youth Culture in New York City* (Philadelphia: Temple University Press, 2002); Shilpa Davé, LeiLani Nishime, and Tasha G. Oren, eds., *East Main Street: Asian American Popular Culture* (New York: New York University Press, 2005); Mimi Thi Nguyen and Thuy Linh Nguyen, eds., *Alien Encounters: Popular Culture in Asian America* (Durham, N.C.: Duke University Press, 2007).

The following dissertations point to exciting directions in Asian American performance studies, especially in the field of dance ethnography and cultural studies: SanSan Kwan, "Choreographing Chineseness: Global Cities and the Performance of Identities," Ph.D. diss., New York University, 2003; Priya Srinivasan, "Performing Indian Dance in America: Interrogating Modernity, Tradition and the Myth of Cultural Purity," Ph.D. diss., Northwestern University, Evanston, Ill., 2003; Yutian Wong, "Choreographing Asian America: Club O'Noodles and Other Mis-Acts," Ph.D. diss., University of California, Riverside, 2001; Sean Metzger, "The Chinese Fetish: Fashioning Asian/American Bodies in Theatre and Film," Ph.D. diss., University of California, Davis, 2005.

5. See Darby Li Po Price, "Mixed Laughter: Mediating Multiracial Identities in American Ethnic Comedy," Ph.D. diss., University of California, Berkeley, 1998.

6. Nerissa S. Balce, "Comedy's Violent Desires: Postcolonial Humor and Transnational Asian American Short Fiction," paper presented at the Philippine Palimpsests: Filipino Studies in the Twenty-first Century conference, University of Illinois, Urbana-Champaign, March 7–8, 2008, 2.

7. Ibid., 8.

8. Price makes use of Leny Strobel's multipart stages experienced by Filipino Americans after 1965: Price, "Mixed Laughter," 227. See also Leny Strobel, "The Cultural Identity of Third-Wave Filipino Americans," *Journal of the American Association for Philippine Psychology* 1, no. 1 (1994): 37–54.

9. Allan S. Manalo, Kevin Camia, and Patty Cachapero, "PCN Salute," *Zyzzyva* 13, no. 3 (1997), 176. I will refer to the published version as well as to live performances of the sketch from 1995 to 2000. From 1998 to 2003, I served as the group's musical director and occasionally performed in sketches as an actor.

10. *In Living Color* (1990–1994) and *Culture Clash* (1993–1996) were broadcast on the Fox television network.

11. See Esther Kim Lee, *A History of Asian American Theater* (Cambridge: Cambridge University Press, 2006); Yuko Kurahashi, *Asian American Culture on Stage: The History of the East West Players* (New York: Garland Publishing, 1999).

12. Kondo, *About Face,* 189.

13. Al Robles, "Jazz of My Youth" and "Fillmore Black Ghetto," in *Rappin' with Ten Thousand Carabaos in the Dark: Poems by Al Robles* (Los Angeles: Asian American Studies Center, UCLA, 1996), 88–89, 90–99. See also Darlene Rodrigues, "Al Robles: Interview," in *Words Matter: Conversations with Asian American Writers,* ed. King Kok Cheung (Honolulu: University of Hawai'i Press, 2000), 154–172.

14. Carlos Villa, *Ritual Performance,* videocassette (The Farm, San Francisco, 1980). See also Moira Roth, "The Art of Multicultural Weaving: Carlos Villa's Ritual," *High Performance* 12, no. 3 (1989): 28–33.

15. "Pearl Ubungen," in *Stage Presence: Conversations with Filipino American Performing Artists,* ed. Theodore S. Gonzalves (San Francisco: Meritage Press, 2007), 11–37. See also Yafonne, "Tagulaylay/The Presidio: Getting at the Core of the Filipino American War," *Asian Week,* October 19, 2000.

16. Theodore S. Gonzalves, "Ermena Marlene Vinluan," in *Asian American Playwrights: A Bio-Bibliographical Critical Sourcebook,* ed. Miles Xian Liu (Westport, Conn.: Greenwood Press, 2002), 340–346.

17. *Jessica Hagedorn and the West Coast Gangster Choir,* videocasette (San Francisco, 1975).

18. "Danongan Kalanduyan," in Gonzalves, *Stage Presence,* 167–180.

19. Mark de la Viña, "Pinoy Pride," *San Jose Mercury News,* July 30, 2002.

20. Benjamin Pimentel, "Filipino Group Finds Its Own Humor," *San Francisco Chronicle,* August 13, 2000.

21. Brad Rosenstein, "Review of Bomba," *San Francisco Bay Guardian,* June 24, 1998, 78.

22. Pimentel, "Filipino Group Finds Its Own Humor."

23. Elizabeth H. Pisares, "Daly City Is My Nation: Race, Imperialism and the Claiming of Pinay/Pinoy Identities in Filipino American Culture," Ph.D. diss., University of California, Berkeley, 1999, 156–157.

24. Manalo et al., "PCN Salute," 171.

25. Marivi Soliven Blanco, "Poking Fun at Pinoys," in *Suddenly Stateside: Funny Essays on Pinoy Life in America* (Quezon City: Milflores Press, 2002). On discrimination based on accents, see Beatrice Bich-Dao Nguyen, "Accent Discrimination and

the Test of Spoken English: A Call for an Objective Assessment of the Comprehensibility of Nonnative Speakers," *California Law Review* 81, no. 5 (1993): 1325–1361; Mari J. Matsuda, "Voices of America: Accent, Anti-discrimination Law, and a Jurisprudence for the Last Reconstruction," *Yale Law Journal* 100 (1991): 1329–1407; *Fragante v. City of Honolulu*, 888 F.2d 591 (9th Cir. 1989).

26. Blanco, "Poking Fun at Pinoys," 2.

27. Lawrence W. Levine, *Black Culture and Black Consciousness: Afro-American Folk Thought from Slavery to Freedom* (Oxford: Oxford University Press, 1977), 322–323.

28. Lewis Herman and Marguerite Shalett Herman, *Foreign Dialects: A Manual for Actors, Directors and Writers* (New York: Routledge, 1997 [1943]), 191; emphasis added. See also George G. Struble, "Bamboo English," *American Speech* 4, no. 4 (1929): 276–285.

29. Manalo et al., "PCN Salute," 172.

30. A video documentary produced by the Filipino American National Historical Society, *Filipino Americans: Discovering Their Past for the Future*, dir. John F. Wehman (Filipino American National Historical Society, 1994), re-creates the accents of first-generation Filipino immigrants to the United States and Hawai'i while reciting text from oral-history collections.

31. Manalo et al., "PCN Salute," 173.

32. Ibid., 174.

33. Culture Clash has also collaborated with Asian American theater artists—for example, the 18 Mighty Mountain Warriors and cast members from Tongue in a Mood and Teatro ng Tanan. "The fact that Columbus celebrations were already being planned for the quincentennial, the bloated and overblown decade of the Hispanic had just fizzled out, and we were still hung-over from the alleged 'feel-good-pick-yourself-up-by-the-bootstraps' attitude of the Reagan–Bush era (which wiped out many of the nation's not-for-profit art collectives) left us downright pissed, confused and full of rage against the fuckin' machine! . . . It was time to face the dragon and make *carne asada* out of him or her. I'm not saying we were responsible for reigniting the entire Chicana/o movement, but we played our small roles, giving birth to a renaissance on college campuses all over *Aztlán* (the Southwest). It reaffirmed for us once again the power of political theatre, that everything is political and that Diego Rivera was probably right in concluding that art and politics were inextricably connected": Richard Montoya, Ric Salinas, and Herbert Siguenza, *Culture Clash: Life, Death and Revolutionary Comedy* (New York: Theatre Communications Group, 1998), 60–61.

34. Ibid., 94.

35. Vince Reyes, "For My Stylin' Brothers," *Liwanag* 1 (1975): 140–141.

36. Manalo et al., "PCN Salute," 174. Rizal's propagandist novels, *Noli Me Tangere* (Touch Me Not; 1887) and *El Filibusterismo* (The Subversive; 1888), were banned in the Philippines for calling out Spanish and Catholic corruption.

37. See Arleen de Vera, "Rizal Day Queen Contests, Filipino Nationalism, and Femininity," in *Asian American Youth: Culture, Identity and Ethnicity*, ed. Jennifer Lee and Min Zhou (New York: Routledge, 2004), for a fascinating discussion of how Filipino Americans have called on a homeland icon to meet diasporic commitments.

38. Manalo et al., "PCN Salute," 174.

39. Ibid., 175.

40. John Manal Castro, dir., *Diary of a Gangsta Sucka* (Bastos Productions, 1993). The short film is included in the DVD version of *The Debut,* whose script was co-written by Castro: Gene Cajayon, dir., *The Debut* (Sony Pictures, 2003).

41. Manalo et al., "PCN Salute," 176.

42. Ibid., 176

43. Rhacel Salazar Parreñas, "'White Trash' Meets the 'Little Brown Monkeys': The Taxi Dance Hall as a Site of Interracial and Gender Alliances between White Working Class Women and Filipino Immigrant Men in the 1920s and 30s," *Amerasia Journal* 24, no. 2 (1998): 115–134; Linda Maram, *Creating Masculinity in Los Angeles's Little Manila: Working-Class Filipinos and Popular Culture in the United States* (New York: Columbia University Press, 2006), chap. 4.

44. Barbara S. Gaerlan, "In the Court of the Sultan: Orientalism, Nationalism and Modernity in Philippine and Filipino American Dance," *Journal of Asian American Studies* 2, no. 3 (October 1999): 256.

45. Ibid.

46. Fredric Jameson, *Postmodernism, or the Cultural Logic of Late Capitalism* (Durham, N.C.: Duke University Press, 1991), 17, 19.

47. Linda Hutcheon, *The Politics of Postmodernism* (New York: Routledge, 1989), 93.

48. Alessandro Portelli, *The Death of Luigi Trastulli, and Other Stories: Form and Meaning in Oral History* (Albany: State University of New York Press, 1991), 170–172.

49. Dario Fo, *Poer nano* (Milan: Ottaviano, 1976), 5–6; emphasis added.

50. Cynthia Enloe, *Bananas, Beaches and Bases: Making Feminist Sense of International Politics,* rev. ed. (Berkeley: University of California Press, 2001), 63.

## Conclusion

*Epigraph:* Christopher Nolan, dir., *Memento* (Newmarket Capital Group, 2000).

1. Sunaina Maira and Elisabeth Soep point to the intersection of emerging youth cultural practices in a location that has increasingly become a "third world state": Sunaina Maira and Elisabeth Soep, eds., *Youthscapes: The Popular, the National, the Global* (Philadelphia: University of Pennsylvania Press, 2004), xxix.

2. Svetlana Boym, *The Future of Nostalgia* (New York: Basic Books, 2002), xv.

3. Ibid., 13.

4. Kale Bantigue Fajardo, "Transportation: Translating Filipino and Filipino American Tomboy Masculinities through Global Migration and Seafaring," *GLQ* 14, nos. 2–3 (2008): 403–424.

5. Samuel P. Huntington, "The Clash of Civilizations?" *Foreign Affairs* (1993): 49.

6. Walden Bello, "A 'Second Front' in the Philippines," *The Nation,* March 18, 2002, 18–22.

7. Robert D. Kaplan, "Supremacy by Stealth," *Atlantic Monthly,* vol. 292, no. 1 (July–August 2003), 66–80.

8. Max Boot, *The Savage Wars of Peace: Small Wars and the Rise of American Power* (New York: Basic Books, 2002), 128.

9. Kaplan, "Supremacy by Stealth," 80.

10. David E. Sanger, "Bush Cites Philippines as Model in Rebuilding Iraq," *New York Times,* October 19, 2003, 1.

## Epilogue

1. Jennifer Sloan McCombs and Stephen J. Carroll, "Ultimate Test: Who Is Accountable for Education if Everybody Fails?" *Rand Review* 29, no. 1 (2005): 10–17. According to Walt Straiton, Proposition 13 "promptly led to the demise of the some of the most outstanding band, orchestra, and choral music education organizations in the nation, along with the decimation of general music for every California student": Walt Straiton, "A Renaissance in American Music Education?" Technology Institute for Music Educators, September 2006, available online at http://www.ti-me.org (accessed May 1, 2009).

2. Frank T. Vertosick Jr., *Why We Hurt: The Natural History of Pain* (New York: Harcourt, 2000), 47–48.

3. Avery F. Gordon, *Ghostly Matters: Haunting and the Sociological Imagination* (Minneapolis: University of Minnesota Press, 1996).

# Bibliography

## Archival Sources and Interviews

### *Jorge G. Bocobo Papers, University Archives and Records Division, University of the Philippines, Diliman, Quezon City, Manila*

Bocobo, Jorge G. "Our National Assets." Speech broadcast over the radio station KZRM, July 9, 1934. Box 1, folder 19.

———. "Speech delivered by Dr. Jorge Bocobo, Fifth President of the University of the Philippines, at his inauguration, Villamor Hall," December 17, 1934. Box 11, folder 3.

———. "New Educational Orientation." Address before the Second Annual Convention of Teachers of Batangas Province, Lipa, February 23, 1935. Box 1, folder 19.

———. "Military Training in the Curriculum." Address at the San Juan de Letran Military Commencement, March 4, 1936. Box 1, folder 19.

———. "Bushido" (Address before the Philippine Association for Oriental Affairs), June 24, 1936. Box 1, folder 13.

———. "Culture and the University." Address at the opening of classes, College of Arts and Sciences, Baguio, University of the Philippines, October 17, 1938. Box 24, folder 5.

———. "Address Delivered by President Jorge Bocobo at the Student Conference of the Young Men's Christian Association, Baguio," December 30, 1938. Box 1, folder 19.

———. "The Education of the Filipino Woman." Speech delivered at the Second Inter-University Debate of Women Law Students, sponsored by the Women Lawyers' Association of the Philippines, March 13, 1949. Box 3, folder 7.

———. "There Is Neither East nor West." Remarks at the World Town Hall seminar, August 23, 1949. Box 1, folder 20.

———. "Afro-Asian Conference, Bandung 1955." Box 11, folder 61.
———. "Our Folk Dances and Songs." *Manila Times*, September 29, 1959. Box 11, folder 7.
———. "Filipino Contact with America," n.d. Box 4, folder 1.
———. "New Trends in Our Educational System," n.d. Box 24, folder 8.
———. "On the Bandung Conference," n.d. Box 11, folder 7.
———. "Philippine Contribution to World Culture." Unpublished ms., n.d. Box 1, folder 30.
———. "The Philippines Fights Communists" (draft). *Manila Times*, n.d. Box 1, folder 30.

### *National Archives and Records Administration, Record Group 350, Records of the Bureau of Insular Affairs; National Archives and Records Administration, College Park, Maryland*

Brown, Elwood S., to Assistant Chief of Bureau; March 27, 1918; Athletic Instructors and Physical Directors.
Edward, Clarence, Bureau of Insular Affairs, to Prof. Jas. T. Young, University of Pennsylvania, April 11, 1903; General, Students.
Fox, Creed F., Chief of Bureau, to Manuel A. Adeva, General Secretary, Filipino Christian Movement in America; October 26, 1934; Filipino Students.
Hughes, R. P., Brig. Gen., Department of the Visayas, Iloilo, Panay, Philippine Islands, to Adjutant General of the U.S. Army, Washington, D.C., October 11, 1900; General, Students.
Marquardt, W. W., Acting Director of Education, to Wm. E. Telzrow, Western Reserve University, Cleveland, Ohio; March 26, 1915; Athletic Instructors and Physical Directors.
Questions to be Submitted to Adult Filipino Students in the United States; doc. 14383.1; General, Students.
Root, Elihu, Secretary of War, to Sen. W. Allison, January 23, 1901; General, Students.
Sullivan, John S., Assistant to the Chief of the Bureau of Insular Affairs, to E. E. Neal, Attorney-at-Law, Pismo Beach, Calif.; July 12, 1928; Filipino Students.
Sullivan, John S., Assistant to the Chief of the Bureau of Insular Affairs, to I. Panlasigui, Mount Vernon, Iowa; June 8, 1926; Filipino Students.
Sutherland, William, Superintendent, to "My Dear Boys"; June 20, 1905; General, Students.
Townshend, Orval P., Assistant to Chief of Bureau, to Walter F. O'Brien, Lawrence, Mass., January 13, 1925; Athletic Instructors and Physical Directors.
Walcutt, Jr., Chas. C., Acting Chief of Bureau, to Emma Ody Pohl, Columbus, Miss., December 2, 1919; Athletic Instructors and Physical Directors.

### *Oral History Archive, Asia Dance Project, New York Public Library for Performing Arts*

Belmonte, Paz Cielo A. Interview by Reynaldo G. Alejandro, January 24, 1977.
Elejar, Eddie. Interview by Reynaldo G. Alejandro, December 14, 1977.

Fajardo, Libertad V. Interviews by Reynaldo G. Alejandro, March 26, 1977.
Merino-Santos, Rosalia. Interview by Reynaldo G. Alejandro, January 17, 1978.
Reyes, Alice. Interview by Reynaldo G. Alejandro, December 12, 1977.
Reyes, Ricardo. Interview by Reynaldo G. Alejandro, October 29, 1977.
Urtula, Lucrecia Reyes. Interview by Reynaldo G. Alejandro, March 26, 1977.
Villarica, Fe Sala. Interview by Reynaldo G. Alejandro, January 21, 1977.

### *Samahang Pilipino Archives, University of California, Los Angeles, Record Series 701*

Alves, Anna. Interview by Barbara Gaerlan, March 1, 1994.
Cabarloc, Ron. Interview by Michelle Sumagaysay, August 20, 1995.
Espiritu, Augusto. Interview by Roger Mationg, August 31, 1995.
Evaluation Questionnaire, Pilipino Cultural Night, Cultural Folder 1982–1983, November 12, 1983.
Jacinto, Joel and Ave. Interview by Genevieve Alcantara, September 25, 1999.
Japor, Ray. Interview by Dennis Feliciano, September 12, 1995.
Masculino, Jennifer Z. Interview by Evangeline Evangelista, August 17, 1995.
Tolentino, Jennifer. Interview by Evangeline Evangelista, n.d.
Vergara, R. Bong. "Reevaluating the Pilipino Cultural Night." Unpublished ms., n.d.

### *Personal Correspondence and Interviews with the Author*

Alegado, Dean. E-mail correspondence, December 6, 2007.
Alejandro, Reynaldo G. Interview, New York, April 6, 2007.
Alves, Anna. Interview, Los Angeles, July 26, 1997.
Aves, Bob. Interview, Quezon City, February 16, 2005.
Cachapero, Patty. E-mail correspondence, September 18, 2001.
Camia, Kevin. E-mail correspondence, November 12, 2002.
Fernandez, Doreen G. Interview, Quezon City, August 24, 1998.
Kalanduyan, Danongan. E-mail correspondence, November 20, 1999.
Linmark, R. Zamora. Personal communication, April 18, 2006.
Lipsitz, George. E-mail correspondence, September 17, 2007.
Magwili, Dom and Sachiko. Interview, Los Angeles, March 2, 1998.
Makechnie, George. Interview, Boston, January 29, 1998.
Manalo, Allan S. E-mail correspondence, November 12, 2002.
Nono, Grace. Interview, Quezon City, February 16, 2005.
Okamura, Jonathan Y. E-mail correspondence, December 4, 2007.
Payomo, R. J. Interview, Santa Clara, Calif., March 22, 1998.
Peña, Angel. Interview, Quezon City, February 2, 2005.
Rafael, Vicente. E-mail correspondence, February 8, 1998.
Rodis, Rodel E. E-mail correspondence, January 30, 2009.
San Juan, E., Jr. Interview, Los Angeles, 1997.
Toribio, Helen, and Abe Ignacio. Interview, Santa Clara, Calif., May 8, 1998.
van Erven, Eugene. E-mail correspondence, May 18, 2002.

## Dissertations and Theses

Alidio, Kimberly A. "Between Civilizing Mission and Ethnic Assimilation: Racial Discourse, U.S. Colonial Education and Filipino Ethnicity, 1901–1946." Ph.D. diss., University of Michigan, Ann Arbor, 2001.

Aquino, Serafin. "Philippine Games and Folk Dances." M.A. thesis, Young Men's Christian Association College, Springfield College, Springfield, Mass., 1922.

Baluyut, Pearlie. "Institutions and Icons of Patronage: Arts and Culture in the Philippines during the Marcos Years, 1965–1986." Ph.D diss., University of California, Los Angeles, 2004.

Buena, Lourdes B. "Interpretive Dances of Bikol Folk Songs for Teaching Physical Education in Elementary Grades." M.A. thesis, Naga College, Naga City, Philippines, 1972.

Cullinane, Michael. "*Ilustrado* Politics: The Response of the Filipino Educated Elite to American Colonial Rule, 1898–1907." Ph.D. diss., University of Michigan, Ann Arbor, 1989, pp. 173.

Dimacali, Pacita. "Philippine Folk Dances: Their Role in the Development of National Identity." M.A. thesis, University of Santo Tomas, Manila, 1975.

Goss, George Edward. "History of Physical Education in the Philippine Islands." M.Ed. thesis, Young Men's Christian Association College, Springfield College, Springfield, Mass., 1917.

Kingman, Harry L. "Physical Education in China, India, Japan, Latin America and the Philippine Islands." M.A. thesis, International Young Men's Christian Association College, Springfield College, Springfield, Mass., 1916.

Kwan, SanSan. "Choreographing Chineseness: Global Cities and the Performance of Identities." Ph.D. diss., New York University, 2003.

Leyco, Zara de Jesus. "Folk Dancing as a Unit of Instruction in Physical Education in the Philippines." M.A. thesis, Adamson University, Manila, 1950.

Lieu, Nhi. "Private Desires on Public Display: Vietnamese American Identities in Multi-Mediated Leisure and Niche Entertainment." Ph.D. diss., University of Michigan, Ann Arbor, 2004.

Maniago, Jo Anne Barker. "The First Peace Corps: The Work of the American Teachers in the Philippines, 1900–1910." M.A. thesis, Boston University, 1974.

Mata, Elena Q. "An Analysis of the Folk Dances of the Mountain Province and the Possibility of Their Inclusion in the Physical Education Program." M.A. thesis, Baguio Colleges, Baguio City, 1952.

Mazurkiewicz, Edward J. "Contributing Factors in the Development of Physical Education in the Philippines." M.A. thesis, Young Men's Christian Association College, Springfield College, Springfield, Mass., 1916.

Metzger, Sean. "The Chinese Fetish: Fashioning Asian/American Bodies in Theatre and Film." Ph.D. diss., University of California, Davis, 2005.

Navea, Carmen. "Physical Education in the Philippines: Its History and Development from 1899 to 1949." M.A. thesis, Arellano University, Manila, 1949.

Ninh, Erin Khue. "Ingratitude: A Cultural Theory of Power in Asian American Women's Literature." Ph.D. diss., University of California, Berkeley, 2005.

Pisares, Elizabeth H. "Daly City Is My Nation: Race, Imperialism and the Claiming of Pinay/Pinoy Identities in Filipino American Culture." Ph.D. diss., University of California, Berkeley, 1999.

Price, Darby Li Po. "Mixed Laughter: Mediating Multiracial Identities in American Ethnic Comedy." Ph.D. diss., University of California, Berkeley, 1998.

Srinivasan, Priya. "Performing Indian Dance in America: Interrogating Modernity, Tradition and the Myth of Cultural Purity." Ph.D. diss., Northwestern University, Evanston, Ill., 2003.

Tirol, Grace Bonje. "Folk Dance Teaching at the University of Bohol, 1973–1974." M.A. thesis, University of Bohol, Tagbilaran City, 1974.

Tomko, Linda. "Women, Artistic Dance Practices, and Social Change in the United States, 1890–1920." Ph.D. diss., University of California, Los Angeles, 1991.

Torralba, Aida Gener. "Preservation and Dissemination of Philippine Folk Dance." M.A. thesis, University of Santo Tomas, Manila, 1974.

Wang, Oliver S. "Spinning Identities: A Social History of Filipino American DJs in the San Francisco Bay Area, 1975–1995." Ph.D. diss., University of California, Berkeley, 2004.

Wong, Yutian. "Choreographing Asian America: Club O'Noodles and Other Mis-Acts." Ph.D. diss., University of California, Riverside, 2001.

## Government Documents

"An Act Making Appropriations for the Support of the Army for the Fiscal Year Ending June Thirtieth, Nineteen Hundred and Two," March 2, 1901. Enrolled Acts and Resolutions of Congress, 1789– , General Records of the U.S. Government, Record Group 11, National Archives, Washington, D.C.

"An Act Prescribing the Code and the National Flag, Anthem, Motto, Coat-of-Arms and Other Heraldic Items and Devices of the Philippines." Philippine Republic Act 8491, February 12, 1998.

*Annual Report of the General Superintendent of Education.* Manila: Bureau of Printing, 1904, 1908, 1910–1913, 1915, 1917–1921, 1923–1924, 1927, 1931, 1934, 1939–1941.

*Fragante v. City of Honolulu,* 888 F.2d 591 (9th Cir. 1989).

Joint Educational Committee of the Philippine Legislature. *Report of the Joint Legislative Committee on Education.* Manila: Bureau of Printing, 1926.

"Number of Overseas Filipino Workers with Cash Remittances Sent, Total and Average Cash Remittance, by Mode of Remittance and by Sex." National Statistics Office report, 1996, 1997–1998, 1999, 2000, 2001, 2002, and 2004.

"Number of Overseas Filipino Workers with Remittances, Total and Average Remittance in Cash and in Kind by Sex." National Statistics Office report, 1996, 1997–1998, 1999, 2000, 2001, 2002, 2004.

*Regents of the University of California v. Bakke,* 438 U.S. 265 (1978.

*Report of Serafin Aquino to Secretary Prudencio Langauon,* March 18, 1951.

"A Report to the President by the National Security Council on the Position of the United States with Respect to the Philippines," November 9, 1950 (NSC 84/2). Pp. 1514–1520 in U.S. Department of State, *Foreign Relations of the United States, 1950.* Washington, D.C.: U.S. Government Printing Office, 1976.

Shin, Hyon B., and Rosalind Bruno. "Language Use and English-Speaking Ability: 2000." *Census 2000 Brief* Report no. C2KBR-29. U.S. Bureau of the Census, Washington, D.C., 2003.

*This Is America: Official United States Guide Book, Brussel's World's Fair, 1958.* Office of the U.S. Commissioner General, Washington, D.C., 1958.

*To Islands Far Away: The Story of the Thomasites and Their Journey to the Philippines.* Public Affairs Section, U.S. Embassy, Manila, 2001.

*U.S. Bureau of Education Circular,* 1911–1948.

U.S. Bureau of Education Memoranda, 1931–1948.

U.S. Navy, Bureau of Naval Personnel. "Filipinos in the United States Navy," October 1976. U.S. Navy Department Library, Washington, D.C., vertical file collection, "Filipinos" file.

## Mass Media

### *Newspaper and Magazine Articles*

Allen, James S. "Japan and Philippine Independence." *The Nation,* vol. 145, no. 23, December 4, 1937, 610–612.

Atabug, Sonia L. "The Big Cultural Boom." *Philippine Panorama,* January 22, 1978.

Bacon, David. "*Tagulaylay.*" *Our Own Voice,* June 2005.

Bello, Walden. "A 'Second Front' in the Philippines." *The Nation,* March 18, 2002.

Burdman, Pamela. "U[niversity] of C[alifornia] Berkeley Minority Admissions Dropping." *San Francisco Chronicle,* June 26, 1997.

Cevallos, F. M. "Let the Folk Dance Be as They Are—Of the Folk." *Sunday Times Variety,* February 25, 1968, 6.

Chang, Jeff. "Karaoke Careers." *San Francisco Bay Guardian,* October 4, 2000, 44.

Craig, Christopher. "Alma Spreckels: The Great-Grandmother of San Francisco." *San Francisco Sentinel,* January 5, 2008.

Cressey, Paul F. "Review of *America is in the Heart.*" *Far Eastern Quarterly,* vol. 6, no. 2, 1947, 206.

Cruz, Yolanda. "A Twofer's Lament." *New Republic,* vol. 211, no. 16, October 17, 1994, 29.

Davis, Oscar King. "Stories of Admiral Dewey." *McClure's Magazine,* vol. 13, no. 1, 1899, 43–44.

———. "Dewey's Capture of Manila." *McClure's Magazine,* vol. 13, no. 2, 1899, 172.

de la Viña, Mark. "Pinoy Pride." *San Jose Mercury News,* July 30, 2002.

de Leon, Felipe P. "Music and You: The Filipino Soul in Music." *Sunday Times Variety,* February 25, 1968, 5.

Fagan, Kevin. "A Square Is Born." *San Francisco Chronicle,* July 26, 2002.

Fletcher, Michael A. "Minority Graduate Galas Highlight a Timely Issue." *Washington Post,* May 19, 2003, A1.

Goquingco, Leonor Orosa. "There's Gold in Ethnicity." *Philippine Panorama* (Manila), May 22, 1977, 37.

Gose, Ben. "California Regent Questions Paying for Minority Graduation Events." *Chronicle of Higher Education,* July 19, 1996.

Gulick, Luther H., and Harry Smith. "Dancing as a Part of Education: Happy Results of Rhythmic Play by New York School Children." *World's Work,* October 1907, 9445–9452.

Harada, Wayne. "1951–2006, Entertainer Gary Bautista, 54." *Honolulu Advertiser,* January 31, 2006.

"Hope and Memory." *Adbusters,* vol. 12, no. 3, 2004.

Kaplan, Robert D. "Supremacy by Stealth." *Atlantic Monthly,* vol. 292, no. 1, July–August 2003, 66–80.

Katigbak, Puri K. "The Philippine Folk Dance 'War.'" *This Week Magazine,* vol. 14, July 14, 1959, 24–25

King, John. "A Fresh Look for Union Square." *San Francisco Chronicle,* March 21, 1997.

———. "Filipinos Want Full Story Told on Dewey Memorial." *San Francisco Chronicle,* March 31, 1997.

Ly, Phuong. "Money Is Not Enough at Christmas: Many Filipino Immigrants Ship Presents Overseas." *Washington Post,* December 24, 2004, B5.

Mendoza, Ivy Lily. "A Legacy of Philippine Dances." *Philippine Panorama* (Manila), February 24, 1991, 26.

Namora-Sietereales, Erlinda. "National Artist: Francisca Reyes Aquino," *Woman's Home Companion,* June 21, 1973, 30–31.

"Nuclear Clock at Brussels World's Fair." *Science,* vol. 126, no. 3263, 1957, 66.

Ocampo, Ambeth. "Displaying the Flag and Playing the Anthem." *Philippine Daily Inquirer,* May 30, 2007.

Pennybacker, Mindy. "Decolonizing the Mind." *The Nation,* October 4, 1999.

Pimentel, Benjamin. "Filipino Group Finds Its Own Humor." *San Francisco Chronicle,* August 13, 2000.

———. "Crossing Borders, Connecting Cultures." *San Francisco Chronicle,* October 8, 2000.

"Rediscovering Native Dances—University of the Philippines Tackles Job Recording Indigenous Dances and Also Melodies." *Graphic* (Manila), August 12, 1937.

Reisberg, Leo. "As Asian Enrollments Diversify, So Too Do Students' Demands." *Chronicle of Higher Education,* vol. 45, no. 37, 1999, A42.

Robbins, James S. "Freedom Eagle." *National Review,* January 18, 2002.

Rodis, Rodel. "The Wording of the Plaque." *Philippine News,* May 17, 2005.

Rondina, Ofelia R. "Colonial Mentality in the Field of Dance?" *Woman's Home Companion,* February 26, 1986, 14.

Rosenstein, Brad. "Review of *Bomba.*" *San Francisco Bay Guardian,* June 24, 1998, 78.

Sanger, David E. "Bush Cites Philippines as Model in Rebuilding Iraq." *New York Times,* October 19, 2003, 1.

Sauro, Noe. "Passion for the Native Tongue." *California Aggie,* November 26, 2003.

"Selling the Philippines." *Philippine Panorama,* vol. 3, September 8, 1974, 14.

Straiton, Walt. "A Renaissance in American Music Education?" Technology Institute for Music Educators, September 2006, available online at http://www.ti-me.org.

Suarez, Domini Torrevillas. "The Filipino Dancers in America." *Philippine Panorama,* January 22, 1978, 13.

Taubman, Howard. "Cold War on the Cultural Front." *New York Times Magazine,* April 13, 1958, 12–13, 107–108.

"Traveling Culture: Circuit Chautauqua in the Twentieth Century." American Memory Collection, Library of Congress, available online at http://memory.loc.gov/ammem/collections/chautauqua.

"U.S. Joins Another Set of Anti-terrorist Drills with Philippine Troops." Associated Press, January 23, 2002.

Villaruz, Basilio Esteban S. "Controversial Bill to Name 'National' Folk Dance Company in Philippines." *Dance Magazine,* vol. 72, no.8, 1998, 32.

Weinman, Samuel. "Behind the Sakdalista Uprising." *The Nation,* vol. 140, no. 3647, May 29, 1935, 625–626.

Weinraub, Bernard. "Campaign Trail: A Beloved Mug Shot for the Bush Forces." *New York Times,* October 3, 1988, A22.

"'Welfare Queen' Becomes Issue in Reagan Campaign." *New York Times,* February 15, 1976, 51.

Yafonne. "*Tagulaylay*/The Presidio: Getting at the Core of the Filipino American War." *AsianWeek,* October 19, 2000.

### *Presentations, Films, and Other Recordings*

Alidio, Kimberly. "Gender, American Empire and Filipino Americans: The Problem of Invisibility for Historical Practice." Presentation at the Philippine Palimpsests: Filipino Studies in the Twenty-first Century conference, University of Illinois, Urbana-Champaign, March 7–8, 2008.

Balce, Nerissa S. "Comedy's Violent Desires: Postcolonial Humor and Transnational Asian American Short Fiction." Presentation at the Philippine Palimpsests: Filipino Studies in the Twenty-first Century conference, University of Illinois, Urbana-Champaign, March 7–8, 2008.

Bender, Pennee et al., dirs. *Savage Acts: Wars, Fairs and Empire.* American Social History Productions, 1995.

Castro, John Manal, dir. *Diary of a Gangsta Sucka.* Bastos Productions, 1993.

Cultural Evidence. Program. Pilipino American Collegiate Endeavor, San Francisco State University, 1993.

Davis, Peter, dir. *This Bloody Blundering Business.* Cinema Guild, Tricontinental Film, 1975.

*Jessica Hagedorn and the West Coast Gangster Choir.* Videocassette. Poetry Center and American Poetry Archives, San Francisco State University, October 30, 1975.

*Kasaysayan ng Lahi.* Videocassette. Pilipino Cultural Night Archives, Samahang Pilipino, University of California, Los Angeles, 1983.

*Living in Oblivion: The '80s Greatest Hits.* Compact disc. Capitol Records, 1993.

Los del Río. *A Mi Me Gusta.* Compact disc. RCA International, 1994.

McLaren, Malcolm. "Commodity and Delight." San Francisco Museum of Modern Art design lecture. Yerba Buena Center for the Arts, San Francisco, April 13, 1998.

Nolan, Christopher, dir., *Memento.* Newmarket Capital Group, 2000.

Rodriguez, Dylan. "'Its Very Familiarity Disguises Its Horror': White Supremacy, Genocide, and the Statecraft of Pacifica Americana." Presentation at the Philippine Palimpsests: Filipino Studies in the Twenty-first Century conference, University of Illinois, Urbana-Champaign, March 7–8, 2008.

Rodriguez, Robyn M. "Globalizing Labor." Presentation at the Philippine Palimpsests: Filipino Studies in the Twenty-first Century conference, University of Illinois, Urbana-Champaign, March 7–8, 2008.

See, Sarita Echavez. "A Queer Horizon: Paul Pfeiffer's Disintegrating Figure Studies." Presentation at the Philippine Palimpsests: Filipino Studies in the Twenty-first Century Conference, University of Illinois, Urbana-Champaign, March 7–8, 2008.

Villa, Carlos, dir. *Ritual Performance.* Videocassette. The Farm, San Francisco, 1980.

Wehman, John F., dir. *Filipino Americans: Discovering Their Past for the Future.* Videocassette. Filipino American National Historical Society, Seattle, 1994.

## Secondary Sources

Abinales, Patricio N. *Making Mindanao: Cotabato and Davao in the Formation of the Philippine Nation-State.* Quezon City: Ateneo de Manila University Press, 2000.

Agoncillo, Teodoro A., and Oscar M. Alfonso. *History of the Filipino People.* Quezon City: University of the Philippines, 1967.

Ainsworth, Dorothy S. *The History of Physical Education in Colleges for Women.* New York: A. S. Barnes, 1930.

Alba, Richard, John Logan, Amy Lutz, and Brian Stults. "Only English by the Third Generation? Loss and Preservation of the Mother Tongue among the Grandchildren of Contemporary Immigrants." *Demography* 39, no. 3 (2002): 467–484.

Albano-Imperial, Guia. "The Heart of a Dancer." Pp. 337–345 in *The National Artists of the Philippines.* Manila: Cultural Center of the Philippines, Anvil Press, 1998.

Alejandro, Reynaldo G. *Sayaw Silangan: The Dance in the Philippines.* New York: Dancer Perspectives Foundation, 1972.

———. *Philippine Dance: Mainstream and Crosscurrents.* Quezon City: Vera-Reyes, 1978.

Alexander, James B. *San Francisco: Building the Dream City.* San Francisco: Scottwall Associates, 2002.

Allen, James S. "The Philippine Problem Enters a New Phase." *Pacific Affairs* 11, no. 2 (1938): 159–170.

Almaguer, Tomas. *Racial Fault Lines: The Historical Origins of White Supremacy in California.* Berkeley: University of California Press, 1994.

Ancheta, Herminia M., and Michaela B. Gonzales, eds. *Filipino Women in Nation Building.* Quezon City: Phoenix Publishing, 1984.

Anderson, Benedict. *Imagined Communities: Reflections on the Origin and Spread of Nationalism.* London: Verso, 1983.

———. *The Spectre of Comparisons: Nationalism, Southeast Asia and the World.* New York: Verso, 1998.

Anderson, Warwick. *Colonial Pathologies: American Tropical Medicine, Race and Hygiene in the Philippines.* Durham, N.C.: Duke University Press, 2006.

Ang, Gertrudes R. "The *Tinikling* as a Literary Symbol of Philippine Culture." *Philippine Quarterly of Culture and Society* 6, no. 4 (1978): 210–217.

Appadurai, Arjun. *Fear of Small Numbers: An Essay on the Geography of Anger.* Durham, N.C.: Duke University Press, 2006.

Appleby, Joyce, Lynn Hunt, and Margaret Jacob. *Telling the Truth about History.* New York: W. W. Norton, 1994.

Aquino, Francisca Reyes. *Philippine Folk Dances and Games.* New York: Silver, Burdett, 1927.

———. *Philippine National Dances.* New York: Silver, Burdett, 1946.

———. *Foreign Folk Dances.* Manila: s.n., 1951.

———. *Rhythmic Activities.* Manila: s.n., 1952.

———. *Fundamental Dance Steps and Music.* Manila: s.n., 1965.

———. *Dances for All Occasions.* Manila: s.n., 1969.

Asuncion, Ninah, "Pilipino Cultural Nights." Unpublished paper, Faculty Mentor Program, University of California, San Diego, June 1998.

Azurin, Arnold Molina. *Reinventing the Filipino Sense of Being and Becoming: Critical Analyses of the Orthodox Views in Anthropology, History, Folklore and Letters.* Quezon City: University of the Philippines Press, 1995.

Bailey, Thomas A. "Dewey and the Germans at Manila Bay." *American Historical Review* 45, no. 1 (1939): 59–81.

———. *A Diplomatic History of the American People.* Englewood Cliffs, N.J.: Prentice-Hall, 1980.

Bakhtin, Mikhail. *Rabelais and His World,* trans. Helene Iswolsky. Cambridge, Mass.: MIT Press, 1968.

Balaz, Joseph P. "Da Mainland to Me." Pp. 175–176 in *Asia/Pacific as Space of Cultural Production,* ed. Rob Wilson and Arif Dirlik. Durham, N.C.: Duke University Press, 1995.

Bañas y Castillo, Raymundo. *Pilipino Music and Theater.* Quezon City: Manlapaz Publishing, 1969.

Barraclough, Geoffrey. *An Introduction to Contemporary History.* New York: C. A. Watts, 1964.

Bautista, Veltisezar. *The Filipino Americans: From 1763 to the Present—Their History, Culture, and Traditions.* Naperville, Ill.: Bookhaus Publishers, 1998.

Behar, Ruth, and Deborah A. Gordon. *Women Writing Culture.* Berkeley: University of California Press, 1995.

Bell, Derrick A. *Race, Racism and American Law,* 2nd ed. Boston: Little, Brown, 1980.

Bello, Madge, and Vince Reyes. "Filipino Americans and the Marcos Overthrow: The Transformation of Political Consciousness." *Amerasia Journal* 13, no. 1 (1986–1987): 73–83.

Bello, Walden. *Dark Victory: The United States, Structural Adjustment and Global Poverty.* London: Pluto Press, 1994.

Bendix, Regina. *In Search of Authenticity: The Formation of Folklore Studies.* Madison: University of Wisconsin Press, 1997.

Benedict, Burton. "International Exhibitions and National Identity." *Anthropology Today* 7, no. 3 (1991): 5–9.

Benito, Ted, and Meg Malpaya Thornton. "Pilipino Cultural Night." *East Wind* (1989): 52.

Bhabha, Homi K. *The Location of Culture.* London: Routledge, 1994.

Blanco, Marivi Soliven. "Poking Fun at Pinoys." Pp. 44–48 in *Suddenly Stateside: Funny Essays on Pinoy Life in America.* Quezon City: Milflores Press, 2002.

Bocobo Olivar, Celia. *Aristocracy of the Mind: A Precious Heritage, a Biography of Jorge Bocobo.* Quezon City: New Day Publishers, 1981.

Boot, Max. *The Savage Wars of Peace: Small Wars and the Rise of American Power.* New York: Basic Books, 2002.

Boym, Svetlana. *The Future of Nostalgia.* New York: Basic Books, 2002.

Breitbart, Eric. *A World on Display: Photographs from the 1904 St. Louis World's Fair.* Albuquerque: University of New Mexico Press, 1997.

Brooks, Daphne A. *Bodies in Dissent: Spectacular Performances of Race and Freedom, 1850–1910.* Durham, N.C.: Duke University Press, 2006.

Browning, Barbara. *Samba: Resistance in Motion.* Bloomington: Indiana University Press, 1995.

Broyles-Gonzalez, Yolanda. *El Teatro Campesino: Theater in the Chicano Movement.* Austin: University of Texas Press, 1992.

Bruchac, Joseph, ed. *Breaking Silence: An Anthology of Contemporary Asian American Poets.* Greenfield Center, New York: Greenfield Review Press, 1983.

Buaken, Manual. *I Have Lived with the American People.* Caldwell, Idaho: Caxton, 1948.

Buff, Rachel. *Immigration and the Political Economy of Home: West Indian Brooklyn and American Indian Minneapolis, 1945–1992.* Berkeley: University of California Press, 2001.

Bulosan, Carlos. *America Is in the Heart: A Personal History.* New York: Harcourt, Brace, 1946.

Burns, Lucy Mae San Pablo. "'Splendid Dancing': Filipino 'Exceptionalism' in Taxi Dancehalls." In *Dance Research Journal* 40, no. 2 (Winter 2008): 23–40.

Cachapero, Emily, et al., eds. *Liwanag: Literary and Graphic Expressions by Filipinos in America.* San Francisco: Liwanag Publications, 1975.

Campomanes, Oscar V. "Filipinos and Their Literature of Exile." Pp. 49–78 in *Reading the Literatures of Asian America,* ed. Shirley Geok-lin Lim and Amy Ling. Philadelphia: Temple University Press, 1992.

———. "The New Empire's Forgetful and Forgotten Citizens: Unrepresentability and Unassimilability in Filipino-American Postcolonialities." *Critical Mass* 2, no. 2 (Spring 1995): 145–200.

Canillo, Alex, et al., eds. *Voices: A Filipino American Oral History.* Stockton, Calif.: Filipino Oral History Project, 1984.

Cao, Lan, and Himilce Novas. *Everything You Need to Know about Asian-American History.* New York: Plume, 1996.

Chakravarty, Sumita S. *National Identity in Indian Popular Cinema, 1947–1987.* Austin: University of Texas Press, 1993.

Chan, Sucheng, *Asian Americans: An Interpretive History.* Boston: Twayne Publishers, 1991.

———. *In Defense of Asian American Studies: The Politics of Teaching and Program Building.* Urbana: University of Illinois Press, 2005.

Cheng, Lucie, and Edna Bonacich, eds. *Labor Immigration under Capitalism: Asian Workers in the United States before World War II.* Berkeley: University of California Press, 1984.

Chin, Frank, et al., eds., *Aiiieeeee! An Anthology of Asian-American Writers.* Washington, D.C.: Howard University Press, 1974.

Choy, Catherine Ceniza. *Empire of Care: Nursing and Migration in Filipino American History.* Durham, N.C.: Duke University Press, 2003.

———. "Towards Trans-Pacific Social Justice: Women and Protest in Filipino American History." *Journal of Asian American Studies* 8, no. 3 (2005): 293–307.

Choy, Philip. *The Coming Man: 19th Century Perceptions of the Chinese.* Hong Kong: Joint Publishing, 1994.

Clifford, James. *The Predicament of Culture: Twentieth-Century Ethnography, Literature, and Art.* Cambridge, Mass.: Harvard University Press, 1988.

Coats, Stephen D. *Gathering at the Golden Gate: Mobilizing for War in the Philippines, 1898.* Fort Leavenworth, Kans.: Combat Studies Institute Press, 2006.

Cogan, Frances. *All American Girl: The Ideal of Real Womanhood in Mid-Nineteenth Century America.* Athens: University of Georgia Press, 1989.

Cohen-Cruz, Jan. *Local Acts: Community-based Performance in the United States.* New Brunswick, N.J.: Rutgers University Press, 2003.

Collier, James Lincoln. *Jazz: The American Theme Song.* New York: Oxford University Press, 1993.

Collymore, Yvette. "Rapid Population Growth, Crowded Cities Present Challenges in the Philippines/Population Reference Bureau (June 2003), available online at http://www.prb.org/Articles/2003/RapidPopulationGrowthCrowdedCities PresentChallengesinthePhilippines.aspx.

Constantino, Renato. *The Philippines: A Past Revisited.* Quezon City: Tala Publishing Services, 1975.

———. "Westernizing Factors in the Philippines." Pp. 211–226 in *Neocolonial Identity and Counter-Consciousness: Essays on Cultural Decolonization,* ed. István Mészáros. London: Merlin Press, 1978.

———. *Neocolonial Identity and Counter-Consciousness: Essays on Cultural Decolonization.* White Plains, N.Y.: M. E. Sharpe, 1979.

Constantino, Renato, and Letizia R. Constantino. *The Philippines: The Continuing Past.* Quezon City: Foundation for Nationalist Studies, 1978.

Cordova, Fred. *Filipinos: Forgotten Asian Americans: A Pictorial Essay, 1763–circa 1963.* Dubuque, Iowa: Kendall Hunt, 1983.

Corpuz, Onofre D. *An Economic History of the Philippines.* Quezon City: University of the Philippines Press, 1997.

Crisol, Jose. "Psychological Warfare in the Philippines." *Philippine Armed Forces Journal* (November 1952): 18–21.

Crozier, Michel, Samuel P. Huntington, and Joji Watanuji. The *Crisis of Democracy: Report on the Governability of Democracies to the Trilateral Commission.* New York: New York University Press, 1975.

Cultural Center of the Philippines. *Encyclopedia of Philippine Art.* Manila: Cultural Center of the Philippines, 1994.

Cvetkovich, Ann. *An Archive of Feelings: Trauma, Sexuality, and Lesbian Public Cultures.* Durham, N.C.: Duke University Press, 2003.

Daniels, Harvey A., ed. *Not Only English: Affirming Multilingual Heritage.* Urbana: National Council of Teachers of English, 1990.

Datoc, Salud C. *Folk Dance Movement in the Philippines, 1920–Post Liberation Era.* Francisca Reyes Aquino Memorial Heritage Foundation, 2.

Davé, Shilpa, LeiLani Nishime, and Tasha G. Oren, eds. *East Main Street: Asian American Popular Culture.* New York: New York University Press, 2005.

Davis, Angela Y. *Blues Legacies and Black Feminism: Gertrude "Ma" Rainey, Bessie Smith, and Billie Holiday.* New York: Pantheon Books, 1998.

de Leon, Lakandiwa M. "Filipinotown and the DJ Scene: Cultural Expression and Identity Affirmation in Filipino American Youth in Los Angeles." Pp. 191–206 in *Asian American Youth: Culture, Identity and Ethnicity,* ed. Jennifer Lee and Min Zhou. New York: Routledge, 2004.

Delgado, Celeste F., and José E. Muñoz, eds. *Everynight Life: Culture and Dance in Latin/o America.* Durham, N.C.: Duke University Press, 1997.

Delmendo, Sharon. *Star-Entangled Banner: One Hundred Years of America in the Philippines.* New Brunswick, N.J.: Rutgers University Press, 2004.

Denning, Michael. *The Cultural Front: The Laboring of American Culture in the Twentieth-Century.* London: Verso, 1996.

de Vera, Arleen. "Rizal Day Queen Contests, Filipino Nationalism, and Femininity." Pp. 67–81 in *Asian American Youth: Culture, Identity and Ethnicity,* ed. Jennifer Lee and Min Zhou. New York: Routledge, 2004.

Devitt, Rachel. "Lost in Translation: Filipino Diaspora(s), Postcolonial Hip Hop, and the Problems of Keeping It Real for the 'Contentless' Black Eyed Peas." *Asian Music* (Winter–Spring 2008): 108–134.

Doeppers, Daniel F. *Manila, 1900–1941: Social Change in a Late Colonial Metropolis.* New Haven, Conn.: Southeast Asia Studies, Yale University, 1984.

DuBois, W.E.B. *Souls of Black Folk: Authoritative Text, Contexts, Criticism,* ed. Henry Louis Gates Jr. and Terri Hume Oliver. New York: W. W. Norton, 1999.

Edelman, Charles. *Brawl Ridiculous: Swordfighting in Shakespeare's Plays.* Manchester: Manchester University Press, 1992.

Edsall, Thomas Byrne, and Mary D. Edsall. *Chain Reaction: The Impact of Race, Rights, and Taxes on American Politics.* New York: W. W. Norton, 1991.

Ehrenreich, Barbara. *Fear of Falling: The Inner Life of the Middle Class.* New York: Pantheon, 1989.

Elphinstone, Mountstuart. *The History of India.* London: J. Murray, 1841.

Enloe, Cynthia. *Bananas, Beaches and Bases: Making Feminist Sense of International Politics,* rev. ed. Berkeley: University of California Press, 2001.

Espiritu, Augusto F. *Five Faces of Exile: The Nation and Filipino American Intellectuals.* Stanford, Calif.: Stanford University Press, 2005.

Espiritu, Yen Le, ed. *Filipino American Lives.* Philadelphia: Temple University Press, 1995.

———. *Home Bound: Filipino American Lives across Cultures, Communities, and Countries.* Berkeley: University of California Press, 2003.

Fajardo, Kale Bantigue. "Transportation: Translating Filipino and Filipino American Tomboy Masculinities through Global Migration and Seafaring." *GLQ* 14, nos. 2–3 (2008): 403–424.

Fermin, Jose D. *1904 World's Fair: The Filipino Experience.* Quezon City: University of the Philippines Press, 2004.

Fernandez, Doreen G. *Palabas: Essays on Philippine Theater History.* Honolulu: University of Hawai'i Press, 1997.

Floyd, Samuel A. *The Power of Black Music: Interpreting Its History from Africa to the United States.* New York: Oxford University Press, 1995.

Fo, Dario. *Poer nano.* Milan: Ottaviano, 1976.

———. *The Tricks of the Trade.* New York: Routledge, 1991.

———. "Contra Jogulatores Obloquentes (Against Jesters Who Defame and Insult)." Pp. 123–143 in *Nobel Lectures: From the Literature Laureates, 1986 to 2006.* New York: New Press, 2006.

Foster, Susan Leigh. *Choreographing History.* Bloomington: Indiana University Press, 1995.

———. *Choreography and Narrative: Ballet's Staging of Story and Desire.* Bloomington: Indiana University Press, 1996.

———, ed. *Corporealities: Dancing Knowledge, Culture and Power.* London: Routledge, 1996.

Foucault, Michel. *Language, Counter Memory, Practice.* Ithaca, N.Y.: Cornell University Press, 1977.

Francisco, Mariel N., and Fe Maria C. Arriola. *The History of the Burgis, Which Is All about How the Elite Made It to the Top of the Pile.* Quezon City: GCF Books, 1987.

Frii-Hansen, Dana, Alice G. Guillermo, and Jeff Baysa. *At Home and Abroad: Twenty Contemporary Filipino Artists.* San Francisco: Asian Art Museum, 1998.

Fujita-Rony, Dorothy. *American Workers, Colonial Power: Philippine Seattle and the Transpacific West, 1919–1941.* Berkeley: University of California Press, 2003.

Gaerlan, Barbara S. "In the Court of the Sultan: Orientalism, Nationalism and Modernity in Philippine and Filipino American Dance." *Journal of Asian American Studies* 2, no. 3 (October 1999): 251–287.

Gainor, J. Ellen, ed. *Imperialism and Theatre: Essays on World Theatre, Drama, and Performance.* London: Routledge, 1995.

García Canclini, Néstor. *Hybrid Cultures: Strategies for Entering and Leaving Modernity.* Minneapolis: University of Minnesota Press, 1995.

Gerber, Ellen, et al. *The American Woman in Sport.* Reading, Mass.: Addison-Wesley, 1974.

Gilmore, Samuel. "Doing Culture Work: Negotiating Tradition and Authentication in Filipino Folk Dance." *Sociological Perspectives* 43, no. 4 (2000): 21–42.

Go, Julian, and Anne L. Foster, eds. *The American Colonial State in the Philippines: Global Perspectives.* Durham, N.C.: Duke University Press, 2003.

Goldberg, David Theo, ed. *Multiculturalism: A Critical Reader.* Boston: Blackwell Publishers, 1994.

Goldfield, Michael. *The Color of Politics: Race and the Mainsprings of American Politics.* New York: New Press, 1997.

Gonzalves, Theodore S. "The Day the Dancers Stayed: On Pilipino Cultural Nights." Pp. 163–182 in *Filipino Americans: Transformation and Identity,* ed. Maria P. P. Root. Thousand Oaks, Calif.: Sage, 1997.

———. "When the Walls Speak a Nation: Contemporary Murals and the Narration of Filipino America." *Journal of Asian American Studies* 1, no. 1 (February 1998): 31–63.

———. "Ermena Marlene Vinluan." Pp. 340–346 in *Asian American Playwrights: A Bio-Bibliographical Critical Sourcebook,* ed. Miles Xian Liu. Westport, Conn.: Greenwood Press, 2002.

———, ed. *Stage Presence: Conversations with Filipino American Performing Artists.* San Francisco: Meritage Press, 2007.

Goquingco, Leonor Orosa. *The Dances of the Emerald Isles: A Great Philippine Heritage.* Quezon City: Ben-Lor Publishers, 1980.

Gordon, Avery F. *Ghostly Matters: Haunting and the Sociological Imagination.* Minneapolis: University of Minnesota Press, 1996.

Gordon, Avery, and Christopher Newfield, eds. *Mapping Multiculturalism.* Minneapolis: University of Minneapolis Press, 1996.

Gordon, Gilbert. *Stage Fights: A Simple Handbook of Techniques.* New York: Theatre Arts Books, 1973.

Gordon, Milton. *Assimilation in American Life: The Role of Race, Religion, and National Origins.* New York: Oxford University Press, 1971.

———. *Human Nature, Class, and Ethnicity.* New York: Oxford University Press, 1978.

Graham, Martha. *Blood Memory.* New York: Doubleday, 1991.

Gramsci, Antonio. *Selections from Cultural Writings,* repr. ed., ed. Geoffrey Nowell-Smith. Cambridge, Mass.: Harvard University Press, 1991.

Guttmann, Allen. *Women's Sports, a History.* New York: Columbia University Press, 1988.

Haddow, Robert H. *Pavilions of Plenty: Exhibiting America Abroad in the 1950s.* Washington, D.C.: Smithsonian Institution Press, 1997.

Hagedorn, Jessica, ed. *Charlie Chan Is Dead: An Anthology of Asian American Fiction.* New York: Penguin, 1993.

Hall, Stuart. "Notes on Deconstructing the 'Popular.'" Pp. 227–240 in *People's History and Socialist Theory,* ed. Raphael Samuel. London: Routledge, 1981.

———. *The Hard Road to Renewal: Thatcherism and the Crisis of the Left.* London: Verso, 1988.

———. "What Is This 'Black' in Black Popular Culture?" Pp. 28–29 in *Black Popular Culture: A Project,* ed. Michelle Wallace. Seattle: Bay Press, 1992.

———. "Cultural Identity and Diaspora." Pp. 392–403 in *Colonial Discourse and Post-Colonial Theory: A Reader,* ed. Patrick Williams and Laura Chrisman. New York: Columbia University Press, 1994.

Harris, Max. *The Dialogical Theatre: Dramatizations of the Conquest of Mexico and the Question of the Other.* New York: St. Martin's Press, 1993.

Hensman, C. R., ed. *From Gandhi to Guevara: The Polemics of Revolt.* London: Allen Lane, 1969.

Herman, Lewis, and Marguerite Shalett Herman. *Foreign Dialects: A Manual for Actors, Directors and Writers.* New York: Routledge, 1997 (1943).

Hila, Antonio C. "Musika: An Essay on Philippine Music." Pp. 102–145 in *Tuklas Sining: Essays on the Philippine Arts,* ed. Nicanor G. Tiongson. Manila: Sentrong Pangkultura ng Pilipinas, 1991.

———. "Defining the Nationalist Tradition in Philippine Music." Pp. 57–70 in *Music in History, History in Music.* España, Manila: University of Santo Tomas Press, 2004.

Hirabayashi, Lane R., and Marilyn C. Alquizola. "Asian American Studies: Reevaluating for the 1990s." Pp. 351–365 in *The State of Asian America: Activism and Resistance in the 1990s*, ed. Karin Aguilar–San Juan. Boston: South End Press, 1994.

Ho, Fred, et al., eds. *Legacy to Liberation: Politics and Culture of Revolutionary Asian Pacific America.* San Francisco: AK Press, 2000.

Hobbs, William. *Techniques of the Stage Fight: Swords, Firearms, Fisticuffs and Slapstick.* London: Studio Vista, 1967.

Hobsbawm, Eric, and Terence Ranger, eds. *The Invention of Tradition.* New York: Cambridge University Press, 1983.

Holborn, Hajo. *A History of Modern Germany.* New York: Alfred A. Knopf, 1967.

Hongo, Garrett, ed. *The Open Boat: Poems from Asian America.* New York: Anchor Books Doubleday, 1993.

Horosko, Marian. *Martha Graham: The Evolution of Her Dance Theory and Training.* Gainesville: University Press of Florida, 2002.

Hu-DeHart, Evelyn. "The History, Development, and Future of Ethnic Studies." *Phi Delta Kappan* 75, no. 1 (September 1993): 50–55.

Huerta, Jorge A. *Chicano Theater: Themes and Forms.* Ypsilanti, Mich.: Bilingual Press/Editorial Bilingue, 1982.

Huntington, Samuel P. "The Clash of Civilizations?" *Foreign Affairs* 72, no. 3 (Summer 1993): 22–49.

Hutcheon, Linda. *The Politics of Postmodernism.* New York: Routledge, 1989.

Ignacio, Abe, et al., eds. *The Forbidden Book: The Philippine–American War in Political Cartoons.* San Francisco: T'Boli Books, 2004.

Ignacio, Emily. *Building Diaspora: Filipino Community Formation on the Internet.* New Brunswick, N.J.: Rutgers University Press, 2005.

Ileto, Reynaldo C. *Pasyon and Revolution: Popular Movements in the Philippines, 1840–1910.* Quezon City: Ateneo de Manila University Press, 1979.

———. "Outlines of a Nonlinear Emplotment of Philippine History." Pp. 98–131 in *The Politics of Culture in the Shadow of Capital*, ed. Lisa Lowe and David Lloyd. Durham, N.C.: Duke University Press, 1997.

———. *Filipinos and Their Revolution: Event, Discourse, and Historiography.* Manila: Ateneo de Manila University Press, 1998.

———. "Philippine Wars and the Politics of Memory." *Positions* 13 (2005): 215–234.

Isaac, Allan. *American Tropics: Articulating Filipino America.* Minneapolis: University of Minnesota Press, 2006.

Jacobs, Paul, Saul Landau, and Eve Pell, eds. *To Serve the Devil.* New York: Vintage Books, 1971.

Jameson, Fredric. *Postmodernism, or the Cultural Logic of Late Capitalism.* Durham, N.C.: Duke University Press, 1991.

Jenkins, Ron. *Dario Fo and Franca Rame: Artful Laughter.* New York: Aperture, 2001.

Joaquin, Nick. "Introduction, Heritage: Educated Feet." Pp. 8–9 in Leonor Orosa Goquingco, *The Dances of the Emerald Isles: A Great Philippine Heritage.* Quezon City: Ben-Lor Publishers, 1980.

Johnson, Robert H. "Exaggerating America's Stakes in Third World Conflicts." *International Security* 10, no. 3 (1985–1986): 32–68.

Jones, Katharine W. "'I've Called 'em Tom-ah-toes All My Life and I'm Not Going to Change!': Maintaining Linguistic Control over English Identity in the U.S." *Social Forces* 79, no. 3 (2001): 1061–1094.

Kerkvliet, Benedict J. *The Huk Rebellion: A Study of Peasant Revolt in the Philippines.* Berkeley: University of California Press, 1977.

Klein, Christina. *Cold War Orientalism: Asia in the Middlebrow Imagination, 1945–1961.* Berkeley: University of California Press, 2003.

Kondo, Dorinne. *About Face: Performing Race in Fashion and Theater.* New York: Routledge, 1997.

Kramer, Paul A. *The Blood of Government: Race, Empire, The United States and the Philippines.* Chapel Hill: University of North Carolina Press, 2006.

Krieger, Joel. *Reagan, Thatcher and the Politics of Decline.* Oxford: Polity, 1996.

Kuisel, Richard F. *Seducing the French: The Dilemma of Americanization.* Berkeley: University of California Press, 1993.

Kurahashi, Yuko. *Asian American Culture on Stage: The History of the East West Players.* New York: Garland Press, 1999.

Kurashige, Lon. *Japanese American Celebration and Conflict: A History of Ethnic Identity and Festival, 1934–1990.* Berkeley: University of California Press, 2002.

Lal, Barbara B. *The Romance of Culture in an Urban Civilization: Robert E. Park on Race and Ethnic Relations.* London: Routledge, 1990.

Lardizabal, José, et al., eds. *Bayanihan.* Manila: Bayanihan Folk Arts Center, 1987.

Lasker, Bruno. *Filipino Immigration to the Continental United States and to Hawai'i.* New York: Arno Press, 1931.

Leacock, Eleanor B. *The Culture of Poverty: A Critique.* New York: Simon and Schuster, 1971.

Lee, Esther Kim. *A History of Asian American Theater.* Cambridge: Cambridge University Press, 2006.

Lee, James Kyung-Jin. *Urban Triage: Race and the Fictions of Multiculturalism.* Minneapolis: University of Minnesota Press, 2004.

Lee, Jennifer, and Min Zhou. *Asian American Youth: Culture, Identity and Ethnicity.* London: Routledge, 2004.

Lee, Joann Faung. *Asian Americans: Oral Histories of First to Fourth Generation Americans from China, the Philippines, Japan, India the Pacific Islands, Vietnam and Cambodia.* New York: New Press, 1992.

Lee, Josephine. *Performing Asian America: Race and Ethnicity on the Contemporary Stage.* Philadelphia: Temple University Press, 1997.

Lee, Robert G. "The Hidden World of Asian Immigrant Radicalism." Pp. 256–288 in *The Immigrant Left in the United States,* ed. Paul Buhle and Dan Georgakas. Albany: State University of New York Press, 1996.

———. *Orientals: Asian Americans in Popular Culture.* Philadelphia: Temple University Press, 1999.

Leffler, Melvyn P. "The American Conception of National Security and the Beginnings of the Cold War, 1945–1948." *American Historical Review* 89, no. 2 (1984): 346–381.

Levine, Lawrence W. *Black Culture and Black Consciousness: Afro-American Folk Thought from Slavery to Freedom.* Oxford: Oxford University Press, 1977.

Limon, José. *Dancing with the Devil: Society and Cultural Poetics in Mexican-American South Texas.* Madison: University of Wisconsin Press, 1994.

Linder, Rolf. *The Reportage of Urban Culture: Robert Park and the Chicago School.* New York: Cambridge University Press, 1996.

Lipsitz, George. *Time Passages: Collective Memory and American Popular Culture.* Minneapolis: University of Minnesota Press, 1990.

———. *The Possessive Investment in Whiteness: How White People Profit from Identity Politics.* Philadelphia: Temple University Press, 1998.

Liu, John M. "The Contours of Asian Professional, Technical and Kindred Work Immigration." *Sociological Perspectives* 35, no. 4 (Winter 1992): 673–705.

Liu, John M., Paul M. Ong, and Carolyn Rosenstein. "Dual Chain Migration: Post-1965 Filipino Immigration to the United States." *International Migration Review* 25, no. 3 (Fall 1991): 487–514.

Lloyd, David, and Paul Thomas. *Culture and the State.* New York: Routledge, 1998.

Louie, Steve, and Glenn K. Omatsu, eds. *Asian Americans: The Movement and the Moment.* Los Angeles: Asian American Studies Center, UCLA, 2001

Lowe, Lisa. *Immigrant Acts: On Asian American Cultural Politics.* Durham, N.C.: Duke University Press, 1996.

Lustre, Napoleon, "Conditions (an Unrestricted List)." *Amerasia Journal* 24, no. 2 (1998): 111–114.

Lyman, Stanford M. *Militarism, Imperialism, and Racial Accommodation: An Analysis and Interpretation of the Early Writings of Robert E. Park.* Fayetteville: University of Arkansas Press, 1992.

Macapagal, Crisanta B. *Folk Dancing in the School Curriculum as Perceived by Junior High School Students of the University of Assumption, Pampanga.* Manila: Philippine Normal College, 1986.

Madamba, Anna B. *Underemployment among Asians in the United States: Asian Indian, Filipino, and Vietnamese Workers.* New York: Garland Publishing, 1998.

Maira, Sunaina. *Desis in the House: Indian American Youth Culture in New York City.* Philadelphia: Temple University Press, 2002.

Maira, Sunaina, and Elisabeth Soep, eds. *Youthscapes: The Popular, the National, the Global.* Philadelphia: University of Pennsylvania Press, 2004.

Manalansan, Martin. *Global Divas: Filipino Gay Men in the Diaspora.* Durham, N.C.: Duke University Press, 2003.

Manalo, Allan S., Kevin Camia, and Patty Cachapero. "PCN Salute." *Zyzzyva* 13, no. 3 (1997): 171–176.

Mander, Jerry, and Edward Goldsmith, eds. *The Case against the Global Economy and a Turn toward the Local.* San Francisco: Sierra Club Books, 1996.

Mar, Don. "Asian Americans in the Labor Market: Public Policy Issues." *AAPI Nexus* 3, no. 2 (2005): 39–58.

Marable, Manning. *Race, Reform and Rebellion: The Second Reconstruction in Black America, 1945–1982.* Jackson: University of Mississippi Press, 1984.

———. *Black Leadership.* New York: Columbia University Press, 1998.

Maram, Linda. *Creating Masculinity in Los Angeles's Little Manila: Working-Class Filipinos and Popular Culture in the United States.* New York: Columbia University Press, 2006.

Marcus, George E., and Michael M. J. Fischer. *Anthropology as Cultural Critique: An Experimental Moment in the Human Sciences*, 2nd ed. Chicago: University of Chicago Press, 1999.

Martinez, J. D. *Combat Mime: A Non-Violent Approach to Stage Combat*. Chicago: Nelson-Hall, 1982.

Marx, Karl. *The Eighteenth Brumaire of Louis Bonaparte*. New York: International Publishers, 1963 (1852).

Matsuda, Mari J. "Voices of America: Accent, Anti-discrimination Law, and a Jurisprudence for the Last Reconstruction." *Yale Law Journal* 100 (1991): 1329–1407.

Matthews, Edsel. "About Koncepts: The Meaning of Multi-Cultural Arts." *Konceptualizations* (October–December 1994).

McCombs, Jennifer Sloan, and Stephen J. Carroll. "Ultimate Test: Who Is Accountable for Education If Everybody Fails?" *Rand Review* 29, no. 1 (2005): 10–17.

McCormick, Thomas J. *America's Half-Century: United States Foreign Policy in the Cold War and After*, 2nd ed. Baltimore: Johns Hopkins University Press, 1995.

Mirikitani, Janice, et al., eds. *Time to Greez! Incantations from the Third World*. San Francisco: Glide Publications, 1975.

Montoya, Richard, Ric Salinas, and Herbert Siguenza. *Culture Clash: Life, Death and Revolutionary Comedy*. New York: Theatre Communications Group, 1998.

Moon, Krystyn. *Yellowface: Creating the Chinese in American Popular Music and Performance*, 1850s–1920s. New Brunswick, N.J.: Rutgers University Press, 2005.

Morales, Royal F. *Makibaka: The Pilipino American Struggle*. Los Angeles: Mountainview Publishers, 1974.

Moy, James. *Marginal Sights: Staging the Chinese in America*. Iowa City: University of Iowa Press, 1993.

Mrozek, Donald. *Sport and American Mentality, 1880–1910*. Knoxville: University of Tennessee Press, 1983.

Muñoz, Jose. *Disidentifications: Queers of Color and the Performance of Politics*. Minneapolis: University of Minnesota Press, 1999.

Navarro, Jovina, ed. *Diwang Pilipino: Pilipino Consciousness*. Davis, Calif.: Asian American Studies, University of California, Davis, 1974.

———, comp. *Lahing Pilipino: A Pilipino American Anthology*. Davis, Calif.: Mga Kapatid, 1977.

Nelson, Anna Kasten. "President Truman and the Evolution of the National Security Council." *Journal of American History* 72, no. 2 (1985): 360–378.

Ness, Sally Ann. *Body, Movement, and Culture: Kinesthetic and Visual Communication in a Philippine Community*. Philadelphia: University of Pennsylvania Press, 1989.

———. "Dancing in the Field: Notes from Memory." Pp. 133–158 in *Corporealities: Dancing, Knowledge, Culture, and Power*, ed. Susan Leigh Foster. New York: Routledge, 1996.

———. *Where Asia Smiles: An Ethnography of Philippine Tourism*. Philadelphia: University of Pennsylvania Press, 2002.

Ngai, Mae M., *Impossible Subjects: Illegal Aliens and the Making of Modern America*. Princeton, N.J.: Princeton University Press, 2004.

Ngũgĩ wa Thiong'o. *Penpoints, Gunpoints, and Dreams: Toward a Critical Theory of the Arts and the State in Africa*. Oxford: Oxford University Press, 1998.

Nguyen, Beatrice Bich-Dao. "Accent Discrimination and the Test of Spoken English: A Call for an Objective Assessment of the Comprehensibility of Nonnative Speakers." *California Law Review* 81, no. 5 (1993): 1325–1361.

Nguyen, Mimi Thi, and Thuy Linh Nguyen, eds. *Alien Encounters: Popular Culture in Asian America.* Durham, N.C.: Duke University Press, 2007.

Okamura, Jonathan. *Imagining the Filipino American Diaspora: Transnational Relations, Identities, and Communities.* New York: Garland Publishers, 1998.

Okihiro, Gary Y. *Teaching Asian American History.* Washington, D.C.: American Historical Association, 1997.

Omi, Michael, and Howard Winant. *Racial Formation in the United States: From the 1960s to the 1990s,* 2nd ed. New York: Routledge, 1994.

Ong, Paul, Edna Bonacich, and Lucie Cheng, eds. *The New Asian Immigration in Los Angeles and Global Restructuring.* Philadelphia: Temple University Press, 1994.

Orenstein, Claudia. *Festive Revolutions: The Politics of Popular Theater and the San Francisco Mime Troupe.* Jackson: University Press of Mississippi, 1998.

Orsi, Robert A. *The Madonna of 115th Street: Faith and Community in Italian Harlem, 1880–1950.* New Haven, Conn.: Yale University Press, 1985.

Pao, Angela C. "False Accents: Embodied Dialects and the Characterization of Ethnicity and Nationality." *Theatre Topics* 14, no. 1 (2004): 353–372.

Paredes, Ruby R., ed. *Philippine Colonial Democracy.* New Haven, Conn.: Yale University Press, 1988.

Park, Robert Ezra. *The Collected Papers of Robert Ezra Park,* ed. Everett Cherrington et al. Glencoe, Md.: Free Press, 1950–1955.

Parreñas, Rhacel Salazar. "'White Trash' Meets the 'Little Brown Monkeys': The Taxi Dance Hall as a Site of Interracial and Gender Alliances between White Working Class Women and Filipino Immigrant Men in the 1920s and 30s." *Amerasia Journal* 24, no. 2 (1998): 115–134.

———. *Servants of Globalization: Women, Migration, and Domestic Work.* Stanford, Calif.: Stanford University Press, 2001.

———. *Children of Global Migration: Transnational Families and Gendered Woes.* Stanford, Calif.: Stanford University Press, 2005.

Parreñas, Rhacel Salazar, and Lok C. D. Siu, eds. *Asian Diasporas: New Formations, New Conceptions.* Stanford, Calif.: Stanford University Press, 2007.

Payomo, R. J., Jr. "Filipino Americans: A Paper on the Filipino-American View of the World." Unpublished ms., Santa Clara University, October 17, 1997.

Pecson, Geronima T., and Maria Racelis, eds. *Tales of the American Teachers in the Philippines.* Manila: Carmelo and Bauermann, 1959.

Peña, Angel M. *A Man and His Music: An Autobiography.* Quezon City: Ateneo de Manila University Press, 2007.

Peñaranda, Oscar, Serafin Syquia, and Sam Tagatac. "Introduction to Filipino American Literature." Pp. 36–54 in *Aiiieeeee!!! An Anthology of Asian-American Writers,* eds. Frank Chin et al. Washington, D.C.: Howard University Press, 1974.

Peretti, Burton. *Jazz in American Culture.* Chicago: Ivan R. Dee, 1997.

Phelan, Peggy, and Jill Lane, eds. *The Ends of Performance.* New York: New York University Press, 1998.

Pido, Antonio. *The Pilipinos in America: Macro/Micro Dimensions of Immigration and Integration.* New York: Center for Migration Studies, 1986.

Pollock, Della, ed. *Exceptional Spaces: Essays in Performance and History.* Chapel Hill: University of North Carolina Press, 1998.

Pomeroy, William J. *American Neo-colonialism: Its Emergence in the Philippines and Asia.* New York: International Publishers, 1970.

Portelli, Alessandro. *The Death of Luigi Trastulli, and Other Stories: Form and Meaning in Oral History.* Albany: State University of New York Press, 1991.

Porter, Catherine. "Review of *America Is in the Heart,*" Pacific Affairs 19, no. 3 (1946): 331–332.

Portes, Alejandro, and Ruben G. Rumbaut. *Legacies: The Story of the Immigrant Second Generation.* Berkeley: University of California Press, 2001.

Powell, Ifor B. "The Commonwealth of the Philippines." *Pacific Affairs* 9, no. 1 (1936): 33–43.

Prashad, Vijay. *The Darker Nations: A People's History of the Third World.* New York: New Press, 2007.

Quinsaat, Jesse et al., eds. *Letters in Exile: An Introductory Reader on the History of Pilipinos in America.* Los Angeles: Asian American Studies Center, UCLA, 1976.

Quirino, Ricardo. *Pinoy Jazz Traditions.* Manila: Anvil Publishing, 2004.

Racelis, Mary, and Judy Celine Ick, eds. *Bearers of Benevolence: The Thomasites and Public Education in the Philippines.* Pasig City: Anvil Publishers, 2001.

Rafael, Vicente L. "White Love: Surveillance and Nationalist Resistance in the U.S. Colonization of the Philippines." Pp. 185–218 in *Cultures of United States Imperialism,* eds. Amy Kaplan and Donald E. Pease. Durham, N.C.: Duke University Press, 1993.

———, ed. *Discrepant Histories: Translocal Essays on Filipino Cultures.* Philadelphia: Temple University Press, 1995.

Ramsey, Burt. *Alien Bodies: Representations of Modernity, "Race," and Nation in Early Modern Dance.* London: Routledge, 1998.

Reimers, David. *Still the Golden the Door: The Third World Comes to America,* 2nd ed. New York: Columbia University Press, 1992.

Renan, Ernest. "What Is a Nation?" Pp. 8–22 in *Nation and Narration,* ed. Homi K. Bhabha. New York: Routledge, 1990 (1882).

Reyes, Adelaida. *Songs of the Caged, Songs of the Free: Music and the Vietnamese Refugee Experience.* Philadelphia: Temple University Press, 1999.

Reyes, Eric Estuar. "American Developmentalism and Hierarchies of Difference in R. Zamora Linmark's *Rolling the R's.*" *Journal of Asian American Studies* 10, no. 2 (June 2007): 117–140.

Reyes, Vince. "For My Stylin' Brothers," *Liwanag* 1 (1975): 140–141.

Rieser, Andrew. *The Chautauqua Moment: Protestants, Progressives, and the Culture of Modern Liberalism.* New York: Columbia University Press, 2003.

Rivera, Juan F. *The Father of the First Brown Race Civil Code: The Story of the Civil Code of the Philippines.* Quezon City: University of the Philippines Law Center, 1978.

Roach, Joseph. *Cities of the Dead: Circum-Atlantic Performance.* New York: Columbia University Press, 1996.

Robles, Al. "Jazz of My Youth" and "Fillmore Black Ghetto." Pp. 88–89 and 90–99 in *Rappin' with Ten Thousand Carabaos in the Dark: Poems by Al Robles.* Los Angeles: Asian American Studies Center, UCLA, 1996.

Roces, Marian Pastor. "An Incomplete Listing of Contexts in Which Appeals to Tradition Are Made in the Philippines Presently." P. 85 in *Contemporary Art in Asia: Traditions/Tensions*, ed. Apinan Poshyananda. New York: Asia Society Galleries, 1996.

Rodrigues, Darlene. "Al Robles: Interview." Pp. 154–172 in *Words Matter: Conversations with Asian American Writers*, ed. King Kok Cheung. Honolulu: University of Hawai'i Press, 2000.

Rogin, Michael. *Ronald Reagan, the Movie and Other Episodes in Political Demonology.* Berkeley: University of California Press, 1987.

Román, David. *Acts of Intervention: Performance, Gay Culture, and AIDS.* Bloomington: Indiana University Press, 1998.

———. *Performance in America: Contemporary U.S. Culture and the Performing Arts.* Durham, N.C.: Duke University Press, 2005.

Root, Maria P. P. *Filipino Americans: Transformation and Identity.* Thousand Oaks, Calif.: Sage, 1997.

Roth, Moira. "The Art of Multicultural Weaving: Carlos Villa's *Ritual.*" *High Performance* 12, no. 3 (1989): 28–33.

Rydell, Robert W. "The Trans-Mississippi and International Exposition: 'To Work Out the Problem of Universal Civilization.'" *American Quarterly* 33, no. 5 (1981): 587–607.

Said, Edward W. *Beginnings: Intention and Method.* New York: Basic Books, 1975.

———. *Culture and Imperialism.* New York: Alfred A. Knopf, 1993.

Samson, Helen F. *Contemporary Filipino Composers: Biographical Interviews.* Quezon City: Manlapaz Publishing, 1976.

Sanchez, Rosaura. *Telling Identities: The Californio Testimonios.* Minneapolis: University of Minnesota, 1995.

San Juan, E., Jr. *Carlos Bulosan and the Imagination of the Class Struggle.* Quezon City: University of the Philippines Press, 1972.

———. *From People to Nation: Essays on Cultural Politics.* Manila: Asian Social Institute, 1990.

———. "One Hundred Years of Producing and Reproducing the 'Filipino.'" *Amerasia Journal* 24, no. 2 (Summer 1998): 1–33.

———. "Interrogating Transmigrancy, Remapping Diaspora: The Globalization of Laboring Filipinos/as." *Discourse* 23, no. 3 (Fall 2001): 52–74.

Santiago-Felipe, Vilma R. "A Gem of a Person, a Jewel of an Artist." Pp. 209–217 in *The National Artists of the Philippines.* Manila: Cultural Center of the Philippines, Anvil Press, 1998.

Santos, Bienvenido. *The Day the Dancers Came: Selected Prose Works.* Manila: Bookmark, 1967.

———. *The Scent of Apples: A Collection of Stories.* Seattle: University of Washington Press, 1992 (1955).

Santos, Isabel A., and Priscilla G. Cabanatan, eds. *Helen, Bayanihan and the Filipino: A Trilogy for Culture.* Manila: Helena Z. Benitez Heritage Foundation, 1994.

Savigliano, Marta. *Tango and the Political Economy of Passion.* Boulder, Colo.: Westview Press, 1995.

Schaller, Michael. "Securing the Great Crescent: Occupied Japan and the Origins of Containment in Southeast Asia." *Journal of American History* 69, no. 2 (1982): 392–414.

Scharlach, Bernice. *Big Alma: San Francisco's Alma Spreckels.* San Francisco: Scottwall Associates, 1990.

Scharlin, Craig. *Philip Vera Cruz: A Personal History of Filipino Immigrants and the Farmworkers Movement,* ed. Glenn Omatsu and Augusto Espiritu. Los Angeles: Institute of Industrial Relations, UCLA Labor Center, and Asian American Studies Center, UCLA, 1994.

Schirmer, Daniel B., and Stephen Rosskamm Shalom, eds. *The Philippines Reader: A History of Colonialism, Necolonialism, Dictatorship, and Resistance.* Boston: South End Press, 1987.

Schrag, Peter. *Paradise Lost: California's Experience, America's Future.* Berkeley: University of California Press, 1998.

Schultz, April R. Ethnicity *on Parade: Inventing the Norwegian American through Celebration.* Amherst: University of Massachusetts Press, 1995.

Scuderi, Antonio. "Unmasking the Holy Jester Dario Fo." *Theatre Journal* 55 (2003): 276.

Shalom, Stephen R. *The United States and the Philippines: A Study of Neocolonialism.* Quezon City: New Day Publishers, 1986.

Shaw, Angel, and Luis Francia, eds. *Vestiges of War: The Philippine–American War and the Aftermath of an Imperial Dream, 1899–1999.* New York: New York University Press, 2002.

Shimakawa, Karen. *National Abjection: The Asian American Body on Stage.* Durham, N.C.: Duke University Press, 2002.

Silbey, David J. *A War of Frontier and Empire: The Philippine–American War, 1899–1902.* New York: Hill and Wang, 2007.

Stanley, Gregory Kent. *The Rise and Fall of the Sportswoman: Women's Health, Fitness, and Athletics, 1860–1940.* New York: Peter Lang, 1996.

Stanley, Peter W. "The Forgotten Philippines, 1790–1946." Pp. 291–316 in *American–East Asian Relations: A Survey,* ed. E. May and J. Thompson Jr. Cambridge, Mass.: Harvard University Press, 1972.

———, ed. *Reappraising an Empire: New Perspectives on Philippine-American History.* Cambridge, Mass.: Harvard University Press, 1984.

Steinberg, Stephen. *Turning Back: The Retreat from Racial Justice in American Thought and Policy.* Boston: Beacon Press, 1995.

Strobel, Leny. "The Cultural Identity of Third-Wave Filipino Americans." *Journal of the American Association for Philippine Psychology* 1, no. 1 (1994): 37–54.

Struble, George G. "Bamboo English." *American Speech* 4, no. 4 (1929): 276–285.

Sturken, Marita. *Tangled Memories: The Vietnam War, the AIDS Epidemic, and the Politics of Remembering.* Berkeley: University of California Press, 1997.

Suchoff, Benjamin, ed. *The Essays of Bela Bartok.* New York: St. Martin's Press, 1976.

Sutherland, William Alexander. *Not by Might: The Epic of the Philippines.* Las Cruces: Southwest Publishing, 1953.

Tabios, Eileen, ed. *Black Lightning: Poetry-in-Progress.* Philadelphia: Temple University Press, 1998.

Tagudin, Catherine. "My Experience with Immigration/Assimilation in America." Pp. 193–197 in *Becoming American, Becoming Ethnic: College Students Explore Their Roots,* ed. Thomas Dublin. Philadelphia: Temple University Press, 1996.

Takagi, Data Y. *The Retreat from Race: Asian-American Admissions and Racial Politics.* New Brunswick, N.J.: Rutgers University Press, 1992.

Takaki, Ronald. *Strangers from a Different Shore.* Boston: Little, Brown, 1989.

Taruc, Luis. *Born of the People.* New York: International Publishers, 1953.

Tatalovich, Raymond. *Nativism Reborn? The Official English Language Movement and the American States.* Lexington: University Press of Kentucky, 1995.

Taylor, Diana. *The Archive and the Repertoire: Performing Cultural Memory in the Americas.* Durham, N.C.: Duke University Press, 2003.

Taylor, Diana, and Juan Villegas, eds. *Negotiating Performance: Gender, Sexuality, and Theatricality in Latin/o America.* Durham, N.C.: Duke University Press, 1994.

*Third World Women.* San Francisco: Third World Communications, 1972.

Tiongson, Anthony, Ricardo Gutierrez, and Edgardo Gutierrez, eds. *Positively No Filipinos Allowed: Building Communities and Discourse.* Philadelphia: Temple University Press, 2006.

Tomko, Linda. "Fete Accompli: Gender, 'Folk-Dance,' and Progressive-Era Political Ideals in New York City," in *Corporealities: Dancing Knowledge, Culture and Power,* ed. Susan Leigh Foster (New York: Routledge, 1996), 155–176.

Trimillos, Ricardo D. "The Changing Context of Philippine Dance Performance." *Dance Research Annual* 15 (1985): 102–110.

———. "Music and Ethnic Identity: Strategies among Overseas Filipino Youth." *Yearbook for Traditional Music* 8 (1986): 9–20.

———. "Music as Marker of Filipino Identity in the U.S." Paper presented at the Filipino American National Historical Society, New York, June 27, 1996.

———. "Histories, Resistances, and Reconciliations in a Decolonizable Space: The Philippine Delegation to the 1998 Smithsonian Folklife Festival." *Journal of American Folklore* 120, no. 479 (Fall 2008): 60–79.

Turner, Victor. *From Ritual to Theatre: The Human Seriousness of Play.* New York: PAJ Publications, 1982.

Twin, Stephanie L. *Out of the Bleachers: Writings on Women and Sports.* Old Westbury, N.Y.: Feminist Press, 1979.

Umemoto, Karen. "On Strike! San Francisco State College Strike, 1968–69: The Role of Asian American Students." *Amerasia Journal* 15, no. 1 (1989): 3–41.

Usopay, Cadar H. "The Bayanihan: How Authentic Is Its Repertoire?" *Solidarity* 5, no. 12 (December 1970): 45–51.

Vallangca, Caridad Concepcion. *The Second Wave: Pinay and Pinoy, 1945–1960.* San Francisco: Strawberry Hill Press, 1987.

van Erven, Eugene. *Radical People's Theatre.* Bloomington: Indiana University Press, 1988.

———. *The Playful Revolution: Theatre and Liberation in Asia.* Bloomington: Indiana University Press, 1992.

Verbrugge, Martha. *Able-Bodied Womanhood, Personal Health and Social Change in Nineteenth Century Boston.* New York: Oxford University Press, 1988.

Vergara, Benito M., Jr. *Displaying Filipinos: Photography and Colonialism in Early 20th Century Philippines.* Quezon City: University of the Philippines Press, 1995.

Vertosick, Frank T., Jr. *Why We Hurt: The Natural History of Pain.* New York: Harcourt Brace, 2000).

Vidal, Gore. *The Decline and Fall of the American Empire.* Berkeley, Calif.: Odonian Press, 1992.

Villa, Carlos, ed. *Worlds in Collision: Dialogues on Multicultural Art Issues.* San Francisco: International Scholars, 1994.

Villaruz, Basilio Esteban S. "Sayaw: An Essay on Philippine Dance." Pp. 230–271 in *Tuklas Sining: Essays on Philippine Arts,* ed. Nicanor G. Tiongson. Manila: Sentrong Pangkultura ng Pilipinas, 1991.

———. *Treading Through: Forty-five Years of Philippine Dance.* Quezon City: University of the Philippines Press, 2006.

Volpp, Leti. "American Mestizo: Filipinos and Antimiscegenation Laws in California." *Universitiy of California, Davis, Law Review* 33, no. 4 (2000): 795–835.

Walcott, Derek. *The Antilles: Fragments of Epic Memory.* New York: Farrar, Straus and Giroux, 1993.

Warshow, Robert. *The Immediate Experience: Movies, Comics, Theatre and Other Aspects of Popular Culture.* New York: Doubleday, 1962.

Wei, William. *The Asian American Movement.* Philadelphia: Temple University Press, 1993.

Weibe, Robert H. *The Search for Order, 1877–1920.* Westport, Conn.: Greenwood Press, 1980.

Wertheim, Arthur F. *Vaudeville Wars: How the Keith-Albee and Orpheum Circuits Controlled the Big-Time and Its Performers.* New York: Palgrave Macmillan, 2006.

Whitney, Philip B. "Forgotten Minority: Filipinos in the United States." *Bulletin of Bibliography and Magazine Notes* 29, no. 3 (July–September 1972): 73–83.

Wong, Deborah. *Speak It Louder: Asian Americans Making Music.* New York: Routledge, 2004.

Woodbridge, Sally B., and John M. Woodbridge. *San Francisco Architecture: The Illustrated Guide to over 1,000 of the Best Buildings, Parks, and Public Artworks in the Bay Area.* San Francisco: Chronicle Books, 1992.

Woolard, Kathryn A., and Bambi B. Schieffelin. "Language Ideology." *Annual Review of Anthropology* 23 (1994): 55–82.

Wright, Richard. *The Color Curtain: A Report on the Bandung Conference.* Jackson: University Press of Mississippi, 1994 (1956).

Wurfel, David. *Filipino Politics: Development and Decay,* 2nd ed. Quezon City: Ateneo de Manila University Press, 1991.

Ylanan, Regino R., and Carmen Wilson Ylanan. *The History and Development of Physical Education and Sports in the Philippines.* Quezon City: University of the Philippines Press, 1974.

Zangwill, Israel. *The Melting Pot: Drama in Four Acts.* New York: Macmillan, 1909.

Zinn, Howard. *Declarations of Independence: Cross-Examining American Ideology.* New York: HarperCollins, 1990.

# Index

THEODORE S. GONZALVES is Associate Professor of American Studies at the University of Hawai'i at Mānoa.